for EMB
and
for RIB on his 80th birthday

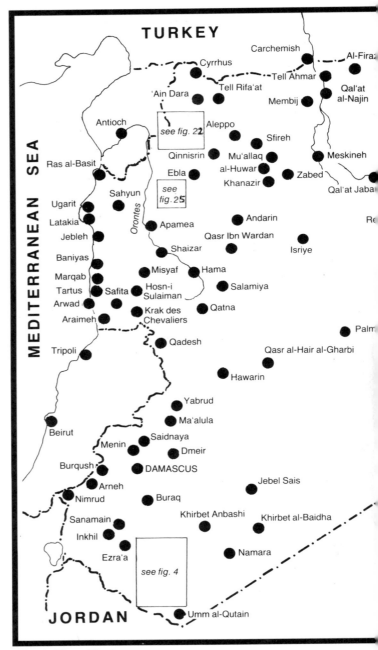

Fig. 1 Map of Syria

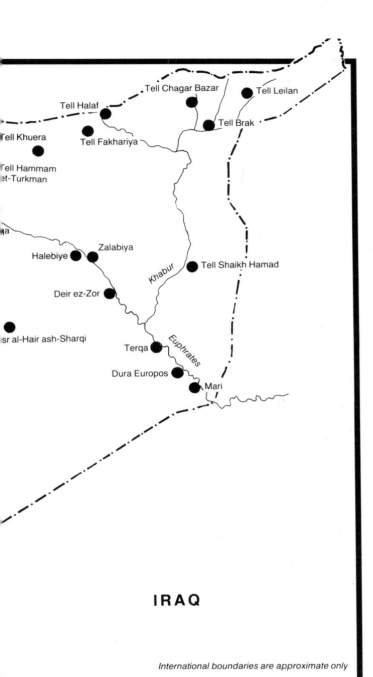

Tell Chagar Bazar

Tell Leilan

Tell Halaf

Tell Khuera

Tell Fakhariya

Tell Brak

Tell Hammam
et-Turkman

Zalabiya

Halebiye

Khabur

Tell Shaikh Hamad

Deir ez-Zor

sr al-Hair ash-Sharqi

Terqa

Euphrates

Dura Europos

Mari

IRAQ

International boundaries are approximate only

Acknowledgements

This book is a result of many visits to Syria over the past twenty years. I am indebted to Paradise Library of Paris, who generously financed my visit in 1991 when researching this book. All arrangements for this trip were made by Jasmin Tours in Britain and Ananaias Travel in Syria, and I am grateful to Jim Smith of Jasmin and Daoud Aslan and Yasser Mahassen of Ananaias for their help in greatly facilitating this trip. Whilst in Syria I was accompanied by Rafeek Kamha, whom I would like to thank for his unfailing practical help and invariable good company.

Wendy Ball, Michael Roaf and Leonard Harrow read through drafts of this book, spotted the many mistakes and made many valuable suggestions. I would like to thank them for their careful scrutiny – and apologise for those suggestions that were ignored, for the mistakes that remained, and for those that crept in afterwards! Most of all, I owe a particular debt to Leonard Harrow of Scorpion whose idea this book originally was. His continual encouragement at all stages has made it all possible.

Note: The spelling of names and place-names in particular is not systematic and reflects likely usage rather than any scientific system.

Contents

Map of Syria

Chapter 1
Introduction   1

Chapter 2
Historical Background   9

Chapter 3
Architectural Background   35

Chapter 4
Damascus and Environs   52

Chapter 5
The Hauran and Southern Syria   69

Chapter 6
The Orontes Valley and Central Syria   90

Chapter 7
The Coast   108

Chapter 8
Aleppo and Environs   125

Chapter 9
The Dead Cities of the North   141

Chapter 10
The Euphrates and the Jazira   159

Chapter 11
Palmyra and the Desert   180

Appendix   197

Time Chart   204

Suggested Reading   205

Glossary of Architectural Terms   208

Index   211

CHAPTER 1

Introduction

Syria is the Middle East's best kept secret. With a wealth of historical splendours matched by few other countries in the region, Syria has remained almost undiscovered. As a result, little has been spoilt, much is unknown, and there is much to discover.

Syria is a land of immense antiquity, boasting cities and archaeological remains that are amongst the oldest in the world. It lay at the western end of the great Silk Road that crossed Asia from China to the Mediterranean, and its caravan cities of Damascus and Aleppo still retain much of the flavour of the Silk Road to this day. Its unique position has also made Syria of high strategic importance, as the world's warring armies from earliest history fought to establish a bridgehead there as a key to further conquests: Hittites, Hurrians and Hebrews, Aramaeans, Assyrians and Arabs, Egyptians, Babylonians, Canaanites, Persians, Greeks, Romans, Crusaders, Turks, Mongols and French. All have come, either staying and settling down or moving on, leaving behind them some of the most spectacular monuments that can be seen anywhere. Today, entire deserted cities, immense castles, and a bewildering array of palaces, mosques, temples, theatres and other ruins are strewn across the country providing the richest and most diverse heritage in the region. More than any other country in the East, Syria is truly the gateway to Asia.

Background

The name 'Syria' was originally Greek deriving from Ashur (Assyria), from the Semitic root *Shryn* in Ugaritic, *Siryon* in Hebrew and *Su-Ri* in Babylonian. The Arabic name for the country, used by the first Muslim conquerors, is *Bilad ash-Sham* or simply *Sham*, meaning 'Country to the Left' [of Arabia] (as opposed to *al-Yaman*, which means 'the right'). Until the 20th century, the name was only loosely defined, referring broadly to a 'Greater Syria' that included Lebanon, Palestine, Jordan and parts of southern Turkey, as well as all of modern Syria which has only existed in its present form since 1939. Any discussion of Syria therefore must of necessity be partly a discussion of the region as a whole as well.

The great caravan routes of antiquity spanned Asia like a gigantic bridge, defining much of the human geography of the regions they crossed for thousands of years. The trade of much of the ancient world depended upon them, and they contributed largely to the spread of ideas, peoples and wealth between Europe and Asia. Syria, at the western end of this 'bridge', was shaped more than most by the routes that crossed it. The Levantine seaports (Alexandretta, Antioch, Latakiya, Tortosa, Tripoli, Beirut, Tyre) facing the west define one facet of the historical geography of Syria, but the cities of the eastern side, Aleppo, Homs, Hama and Damascus, are ports of another kind: 'desert ports'. The western ports linked Syria with the Mediterranean world and Europe the eastern 'ports' linked it with Mesopotamia, the Gulf, Persia and ultimately Central Asia, India and China. Syria acted as a north-south crossroads as well: Egypt, Arabia, the Red Sea and ultimately Africa were linked via Syria to Anatolia and finally Europe. Without pronounced physical features to predetermine the boundaries, it was Syria's location as a meeting place of trade routes that defined its history, and its role in history. On Syria converged all routes. Syria's definition is, as it were, a 'caravan country'.

Syria's two main cities, Aleppo and Damascus, were the keys to these trade routes. Aleppo's position, close to Anatolia and halfway between the Mediterranean and the Euphrates, was the meeting place of routes from Anatolia, Europe, the Mediterranean, Persia, Central Asia and China. Damascus further south received the trade from Arabia, the Red Sea, Africa, India, and Egypt.

As well as trade, ideas were the other great commodity that met in the Syrian melting-pot. They would develop and mix with native Syrian traditions, before being trans-shipped to the rest of the world. Thus, whilst writing was invented in Mesopotamia, it was in Syria that this writing was adapted to the first alphabet, upon which all alphabetic systems, both of the east and west, are ultimately based – possibly Syria's greatest contribution to world civilization. An equally revolutionary idea, Christianity, was born in Palestine – then a part of Syria – and developed in the Syrian cities of Damascus and Antioch before travelling the world. Islam too owes much to its formative years in the Umayyad court of Damascus.

One must approach Syria therefore, with two views in mind. For the traveller, the diversity has made it very much the Middle East's best kept secret, with an undiscovered wealth of sights that have all but disappeared elsewhere in the Middle East. But for the student of history, Syria is above all the gateway to Asia. For anybody drawn to Asia, for someone in search of the allure of the East, there is no better country in which to start.

Geography

The area of 'Greater Syria' never had the pronounced physical cohesiveness that makes other countries in the Middle East geographically so well-defined. The Nile, for example, defines Egypt both geographically and culturally, as the Tigris and Euphrates do Iraq or the mountainous plateau does Turkey. Hence, the greater historical diversity of Syria, and its fragmentation today, divided between five countries. Of course, this modern fragmentation is partly the result of the cynical carving up of the Middle East by the British and French after the First World War, but the lack of well-defined physical and demographic boundaries at least made the task easier for them.

Syria lies at the northern end of one of the world's greatest physical features: the Afro-Asian rift valley system. The Orontes Valley in Syria marks the northern extremity of this great rift and the Rift Valley of Tanzania marks the southernmost, with the Jordan River and Dead Sea marking the lowest point. This makes the geography of Syria essentially longitudinal, dividing the western half into long narrow 'strips'. These 'strips' or geographical zones are: the coastal plain, the western ranges, the central rift valley, and the eastern ranges. The longitudinal division of Syria also fundamentally affects its climate. To the west of the rift, the climate is influenced by the Mediterranean; to the east it is more a continental climate.

The coastal plain bordering the Mediterranean, though very fertile, is nowhere more than a few miles wide. Whilst it contains famous harbours of great antiquity, it is a very straight coastline with no natural shelters. Its vegetation is common to the rest of the Mediterranean littoral, olives, cereals, market vegetables, etc., as it tends to be wetter and more humid than inland Syria, modifying the extremes of temperature between summer and winter.

The western ranges (known as the Amanus in the north, the Nusairi in the centre and the Lebanon in the south) are mainly limestone, with occasional basalt inclusions. They are very rocky, rising to some

1600 metres in Syria, though the highest part of the range is in Lebanon, where it rises to over 3000 metres. Whilst never high or impenetrable enough to form any real barrier to the movement of peoples and ideas, its valleys nonetheless sheltered numerous minorities and semi-isolated communities. It is in these mountains that most of the massive fortresses – Arab, Crusader and Assassin – for which Syria is famous are found. Now very much eroded, these mountains were far more forested in the past, growing various conifers such as pine and cedars, as well as scrub oaks, pistachio and other mountainous trees (plates 37, 42).

The central rift valley, known as the Ghab, comprises mainly the river valley of the Orontes, with Lebanon's Beqa'a Valley forming its southern reaches. It is Syria's most fertile area, with rich agricultural land for most of its length and, along with the coastal area, is the most densely settled part of Syria.

The eastern ranges (known as the Anti-Lebanon in the south where they are highest) rise to 2800 metres at Mt Hermon. In the north they are little more than low hills, in no place more than 1000 metres high. It is on the slopes of these hills facing eastwards that Syria's 'desert ports' are situated: Aleppo, Hama, Homs and Damascus. In contrast to the coastal and western mountainous areas, this inland strip is drier, with greater differences between temperatures, and open to the dust-laden winds from the desert – average annual rainfall in Damascus is only about 250mm, compared to over double that on the coast.

Further east, the divisions are no longer longitudinal. The other main factor which influences Syria's geography is the east-west mountainous barrier of the Anatolian highlands to the north. This creates a wide belt of moister climate across the north, which receives over 200mm annual rainfall, creating the fertile rain-fed grasslands and grain-growing areas known as the Jazira. Thus, the eastern half of Syria comprises roughly three zones: the Jazira Plain to the northeast, the Syrian Desert to the east and south, and the Euphrates Valley dividing the two. A subdivision of the Syrian Desert comprises a possible fourth zone: the Hauran to the southwest.

The Jazira Plain is the vast, level expanse of grassland and semi-desert (plate 84) that lies between the upper arms of the Euphrates and Tigris Rivers (*jazira* means 'island' in Arabic). It is watered by the Balikh and Khabur Rivers, both tributaries of the Euphrates, and with its good rainfall forms Syria's granary. The Euphrates Valley itself is in part a cultural extension of Mesopotamia, and has formed a route since earliest antiquity between Anatolia and Mesopotamia.

Whereas the Euphrates unites Syria with Iraq, the Syrian Desert has always formed a natural barrier with the East. It is a vast expanse of virtually empty desert and semi-desert, but it has always been crossed by nomad tribes and is watered by occasional oases, the most famous of which is Palmyra. Until over-hunting in the 20th century decimated most of the wildlife, the desert areas of Syria abounded in a wide variety of fauna. Hyaena, fox, jackal, gazelle, oryx, ostrich, leopard and even lion were abundant until relatively recently; most have now almost died out or are completely extinct. The further east into the desert the drier and hotter it becomes (though even here winters can be surprisingly harsh – Gertrude Bell's accounts of the Syrian desert in the 19th century seem dominated by descriptions of snow and freezing temperatures). Whilst much of the desert consists of flat plains and even dunes in places, in the central part are a series of spectacular ranges rising some 1400 metres.

Separated from these ranges at the southern edge of the desert on the Jordanian border, the Hauran stands in complete isolation. This is a strange region of barren, black volcanic lava flows interspersed with surprisingly fertile plains which have always supported a high level of population and agricultural activity (plates 9, 10), with the Hauran being as important a granary in history as the Jazira. The strange black rock architecture to which the landscape has given birth can be seen in the large numbers of ruined towns and villages that are scattered throughout the Hauran.

People

The great diversity of the Syrian landscape – hills, valleys, steppe and deserts – have always sheltered an equally diverse variety of peoples of different religions and languages. There are Arabs, Kurds, Circassians, Jews and Armenians, practising Sunni, Sh'ia, 'Alawi, Druze, Maronite, Orthodox, Catholic, Armenian, Jewish and other faiths and sects, speaking the Arabic, Kurdish, Aramaic, Turkish and Armenian languages, not to mention various dialects. This diversity is as much a product of its physical makeup and history as a reflection of it. For the visitor, it is at least a graphic rebuttal of the prevailing image that the West has of the of Middle East: of being almost exclusively Arab, Arabic-speaking, and Muslim. An easy trap to fall into perhaps in these days of Arab nationalism and Islamic fundamentalism, but a far from accurate image nonetheless.

The Arabs

The Arabs make up the overwhelming bulk of the Syrian population (plate 45), though there are substantial minorities as well as the widely differing religions practised amongst the Arabs themselves. History has an image of the Arabs springing unannounced into the Middle Eastern stage from the deserts of Arabia in the 7th century, to submerge the previously Hellenized East under a sea of Arabism and Islam almost overnight. Such an image could not be further from the truth, as the Arabs had a long history in Syria and other countries well before that. The Palmyrene and Ghassanid kingdoms of pre-Islamic Syria – not to mention the Nabateans of Jordan – were essentially Arab cultures, and there were even several Roman emperors who were Arab. Their history goes back even further. There are various mentions of the Arabs in the Assyrian annals of the 1st millennium BC, as tribes of nomads who inhabited the area of the Syrian desert. This is the same area, it is important to remember, where other major Semitic nations such as the Assyrians themselves and even the Akkadians, several thousands of years before, are believed to have come from. Whilst it would be inaccurate to call the ancient Semitic peoples of Syria – Amorites, Canaanites, Phoenicians or Aramaeans – 'Arab', the Arabs can at least be described as their descendants.

Amongst Arabs themselves, particularly in Syria, the term 'Arab' is often used specifically for the Beduin rather than the town or village dweller (plate 79). The Beduin are a greatly romanticized part of Middle Eastern society who, in the West, have always received an excess of attention. But it as much a fallacy to refer to the Beduin as the only 'true' Arabs as it would be to ignore the bulk of settled Arabs who make up Middle Eastern populations and have produced its civilization. This Western myth of the Beduin has even led to such misconceptions as describing Islam as being 'a religion of the desert', and the Beduin as being the source of Arab civilization. The reality is quite different: Islam was born of a merchant class in urbanized Mecca, not of the nomads of central Arabia, and Arab civilization came from the ancient urban centres of Damascus, Baghdad and Cairo, not from the tents. In fact a constant theme throughout much of Middle Eastern history has been the conflict between urban centres of civilization and the nomads of the desert. Indeed, the extreme poverty of 19th century Syria was due as much to continual Beduin depredations on the cultivated and settled lands as the repressiveness of the Ottoman government.

Their language is, of course, Arabic, a language belonging to the Semitic group. Indeed nowadays it is the Arabic language that defines the Arabs, from Morocco to Oman, rather than particular racial affinities. The language spoken in Syria is overwhelmingly Arabic, but there is one minor exception: Aramaic. This was the main language of the Near East for over a thousand years after about 500 BC from which Arabic is ultimately derived. It is still spoken in some Christian communities surprisingly close to Damascus: in Ma'alula and nearby villages, just to the west of the road to Homs – an extraordinary survival indeed, as if Latin were still spoken in villages near Rome. In addition, French was widely spoken as a second language after the incorporation of Syria into the French Mandate, but English is now more common.

The main religion is Islam. Muslims are divided into two main groups, Sunni and Shi'a, the former believing in an elected succession of leaders after the Prophet Muhammad, the latter in an hereditary succession through the line of 'Ali, the Prophet Muhammad's cousin and son-in-law. The Shi'a in addition comprise several important sub-sects in Syria. The main branch believe in a succession of twelve Imams since Muhammad, but the Isma'ilis believe that there were only seven (the seventh being Isma'il, rather than Musa whom the main branch of the Shi'a revere). An extreme offshoot of the Isma'ilis is the Assassin sect (sometimes called the neo-Isma'ilis), who were important in 12th and 13th century Syria but now only survive in a few isolated pockets. A more esoteric offshoot of the Shi'a are the Nusayris, now more commonly known as the 'Alawis, about whom very little is known apart from their extreme veneration of 'Ali, the first Imam (from which their name of 'Alawis derive). Another is the Druze, a similarly secretive offshoot from Shi'ism, who believe in a gradual ascent to unity with God through a series of reincarnations.

The predominance of Islam often leads us to forget the important non-Islamic elements practised by the Arabs. Chief of these are the Christians. They too are divided into different sects, though there is such a multiplicity of them dating back to the early days of Christianity, that the foreigner is often baffled. The main Christian groups in Syria are the Syrian Orthodox (the old West Syrian Church, also known as the Monophysites or Jacobites), the Syrian Catholics (a recent branch of the Syrian Orthodox who look to Rome, sometimes mistakenly known as the Melkites), the Maronites (a Byzantine attempt to compromise between the main schisms), and the Greek Orthodox (previously known as the Melkites). Other Christian sects with smaller minorities in Syria include the Assyrians (the old East Syrian Church, also known as Chaldeans or Nestorians), the Copts, and the Baptists (modern converts from other Christian sects).

Non-Arabs

The largest of the Non-Arab minorities are the Kurds of the far northeast, a smaller part of a people found mainly in neighbouring Iraq, Turkey and Iran. They speak an Indo-European language that is related to Persian, and are predominantly Sunni Muslims. Another non-Arab element is the Circassians, originally Sunni Muslim refugees from late 19th century Russian incursions into the Caucasus. They are European in appearance, and were originally settled in the underpopulated parts of Syria by the Ottoman government in the 19th century. A similar group of Caucasian refugees are the Armenians. They are Christians, speaking an Indo-European tongue, survivors of an ancient Christian kingdom, who escaped into Syria from Turkish repression after the First World War (although they were also a substantial community before). Smaller minorities in Syria include the Jews, though most of these have emigrated, and some Turks and Greeks.

CHAPTER 2

Historical Background

The first settlements

The prehistory of any country normally holds very little of interest for the traveller: there are no great monuments to see, there are few great works of art, and the minutiae of domesticated and wild wheat varieties, mud hut building techniques, and flint technologies that so fascinate the archaeologist, generally make fairly tedious reading to all but the most dedicated.

But in Syria – or elsewhere in the ancient Near East – one cannot write off prehistory so easily. For the Near East is where it all happened, and happened first: it is where the world as we know it first took shape. Domesticating wild varieties of grain and taming wild goats may sound fairly irrelevant to our own highly technological, sophisticated times. But man's first tentative experiments in these directions – planting crops instead of merely gathering them, raising herds instead of hunting them, forming settled communities instead of wandering from place to place – set in place a chain of events that culminated in the greatest revolution of all times: civilization. The effects of these very first events in the Levant and the Anatolian foothills in and around Syria some ten or twelve thousand years ago will never leave mankind. To understand them is to understand ourselves.

It is perhaps sobering to reflect, therefore, when first stepping foot inside Syria, that in many ways the most impressive sights the traveller might see are not necessarily the great marvels of Palmyra or Krak des Chevaliers, but the dusty, tiny little mounds of stone and mud of Syria's prehistory: Mureybit, Bouqras, Ugarit, Abu Hurayra, to name but a few. Such mounds often still have the detritus of everyday life scattered around them: the broken tools they used, the pots and pans they cooked with, the bones of the animals they ate, all so impossibly old that to give their age, rounded off to the nearest thousand years or so, sounds almost as incomprehensible as the noughts added to defence budgets. A far cry, it is true, from the stunning works of art of the later periods that confront one in the Damascus Museum, but at the same time, perhaps the most important works of man that one can see anywhere.

The actual events can be summarized fairly quickly. The beginnings of agriculture started round about 12,000 years ago with the Natufian culture in Syria and Palestine: permanent settlements, such as Abu Hurayra on the Euphrates, grew up where water and grain were plentiful, with temporary campsites elsewhere for hunting. These settlements were occasionally caves or rock shelters, but more usually were mud-built huts in the open. These first tentative experiments in controlling the environment culminated in the Neolithic period, a period which perhaps saw the most profound changes in man's way of life until the Industrial Revolution. Increased experimentation with growing crops and herding sheep and goats led to a mastery over nature that is still with us: plants and animals were domesticated for dependable food supplies; the more permanent settlements required by these agricultural breakthroughs became the world's first true villages; the construction techniques required to build those villages led to major new technological breakthroughs and the first real architecture; the need to store the food led to the invention of pottery; such new techniques created the need for specialisations that developed into the first social structures; the subsequent dependence of the new technology (such as flint tools) on raw materials created trade; the trade led to the interchange of ideas across vast areas, and so forth. In other words, it was incipient civilization.

The most famous of these Neolithic settlements in the Near East is Jericho in the Jordan Valley, but contemporary villages have been excavated by archaeologists throughout Syria: Ra's Shamra (Ugarit) on the coast, and Mureybit, Abu Hurayra, Bouqras and Tell Halaf on the great plains of inland Syria to the east. Even the great cities of later Syrian civilization, such as Aleppo and Damascus, probably have their origins in the Neolithic period. Survivals from this period can still be seen in Syria today: the Beduin of the Syrian desert probably follow much the same lifestyle as the herdsmen of the Neolithic and earlier periods, and the beehive-domed villages of northern Syria have their exact counterpart in the round houses of the later Neolithic in the same area (plate 84).

The first cities

With civilization came cities. The invention of agriculture and the developments of the first settlements gave the Near East a lead in all subsequent cultural developments that was to last many thousands of years. It comes as no surprise, therefore, that the world's first cities occurred in the ancient Near East some five to six thousand years ago. With cities came – in due course – organized society, writing, political systems, finance, organized religion, armies, kings, queens, dates, and so forth.

The first cities developed in the lower Tigris-Euphrates plains in southern Iraq, but the idea soon spread elsewhere throughout the Middle East. Just what we define as a true 'city' (as opposed to merely a large town or even a large collection of buildings) and just how they spread elsewhere remains a much argued point amongst archaeologists. Leaving such definitions aside, urbanization as a concept had arrived by about 3000 BC, and we find the first sites in Syria that had already developed – or were soon to develop – into great cities: Ugarit, Ebla, Qatna, Qadesh, Mari, Habuba Kabira, Hammam et-Turkman, Tell Brak.

It is with the development of these cities that we see the first glimmerings of a distinctive 'Syrian culture'. They correspond roughly with that called by archaeologists the Early Bronze Age (between about 4000 and 2000 BC) in the manner of naming a period after its main artifacts, but for the non-specialist it might provide a clearer picture to call it an Age of Cities. The first of these urban agglomerations may have been colonies from the 4th millennium BC Uruk culture of southern Iraq, graphically demonstrated by the excavations at Habuba Kabira on the Middle Euphrates. Whether such colonies were a part of an 'Uruk – or at least Mesopotamian – Empire' is a hotly debated subject. Such cultural links with Mesopotamia have been well known from the discoveries at the 3rd millennium Sumerian city of Mari. But other discoveries in eastern Syria provide equally important evidence of a strong indigenous culture existing alongside that from Mesopotamia: Tell Brak and Tell Leilan are just two of the many excavations in recent years that are documenting this process.

In western Syria we find developments more independent of Mesopotamia, with large fortified cities, probably forming city-states, such as Ebla, Hama and Ugarit. These often exerted considerable local power and even formed relations with countries as far away as Egypt, Cyprus and Mesopotamia. The most interesting one to come to light in recent years is Ebla (Tell Mardikh), to the southwest of Aleppo, where archaeologists have been uncovering a hitherto unsuspected civilization that flourished in the 3rd millennium BC (figure 21). Ebla then was the greatest military and commercial power in northern Syria that exerted an influence far beyond its boundaries. The discovery of the royal archives numbering many thousands of cuneiform tablets was one of the greatest discoveries in Near Eastern archaeology since the Second World War that has shed dramatic new light on the civilization of the Near East, questioning many long-held views on the origins of biblical history, on the spread of Semitic languages, and the dissemination of ideas throughout the Near East generally.

Ebla's military power probably extended to raiding the Mesopotamian city of Mari on the Euphrates, and it is to Mesopotamia that we must look once more for the events that changed the city-states of Syria and the Levant forever. For out of Mesopotamia came the world's first empire maker: Sargon of Akkad.

The first empires

Towards the end of the 3rd millennium in southern Mesopotamia, the Sumerians were overthrown by a new people, the Akkadians. These belonged to the same broad group as the Eblaites, a group that the world was to hear much more of for thousands of years to come: the Semites. The founder of the Akkadian dynasty was Sargon, king of Sumer and Akkad. Sargon embarked upon a campaign of military conquests that took him as far west as the Mediterranean coast, campaigns that may have been prompted by Eblaite incursions into traditional areas of Mesopotamian influence. Whether his military campaigns were nothing more than raids, as some think, or whether they were the world's first true empire is not important here. What is significant is that they created one of the most important precedents so far in history, a precedent that once set would change world history forever: for Sargon demonstrated in no uncertain terms that foreign lands – if one had the necessary force – were there for the grabbing. The era of empires had arrived and the world would never be quite the same. The rich lands of the Middle East thereafter became an arena, a battleground for conquerors to carve up, that passed back and forth between empires of the north, south, east and west. Syria's position, at the hub of this arena, saw them all come and go.

The period corresponds to Middle Bronze Age, eventually giving way to the Late Bronze then the Iron Age. More recently, these terms have been supplanted by the Old, Middle and New Syrian Periods respectively, but such names still mean little to all but the specialist. Although there would occasionally be a return to the city-states of an earlier epoch (most notably the Phoenician ones on the coast and the

Aramaean ones inland), it was an age of great empires. The names of these first empires thunder through history: Mitannians, Egyptians, Hittites, Assyrians, Persians. The names of the conquerors are equally familiar: Tuthmosis, Sennacherib, Cyrus.

But before embarking on these great names, it is perhaps worth digressing to briefly examine the people who figure so prominently in this period: the Semites. One gets the impression of various 'waves' of Semitic invasions, usually coming out of some ill-defined desert region, to inundate the more settled communities of the Fertile Crescent from the earliest times to the Muslim Arab invasions of the 7th century. Such a 'wave theory', however, gives a rather distorted picture of the true situation. The Semites probably made up the indigenous, settled population of Syria – indeed, we have already encountered them at Ebla, which provides virtually the earliest written records for Syria, long before the traditionally supposed 'first Semitic invasion' by the Amorites round about 2000 BC. The 'invasions' were often little more than raids by particular Semitic tribes, or even gradual peaceful penetration, who provided perhaps the upper echelons of the ruling classes, but were otherwise completely absorbed by their fellow Semites of the towns and the cities they encountered.

Be that as it may, in the wake of Sargon's campaigns came the Amorites, one of the earliest of the Semitic peoples we read about. The first centre of Amorite culture was at Mari, and from there Amorite control spread over much of the Middle Euphrates region and the rest of Syria. Other Amorite centres were established at Yamhad (Aleppo), Byblos, Qatna (near Homs), Harran (near Urfa in Turkey), and Babylon (where eventually the most famous of all Amorite rulers, Hammurabi, emerged) – all places that remained powerful commercial and cultural centres for many centuries.

The Canaanites were another early Semitic peoples associated with Syria soon after 2000 BC, but like the Amorites before them, were probably closely related to the earlier indigenous inhabitants. The Canaanites settled on the coastal strip. It was the Canaanites who, through their Semitic successors the Phoenicians, bequeathed to the world the alphabet: the Canaanite language was probably the first to be written using a system of individual letters rather than words or syllables.

Into this Syrian melting-pot of Amorite and Canaanite cultures erupted a rapid succession of empires that used Syria as their battleground. Following various Egyptian 'probes' (both military and commercial) into Syria as far back as the Twelfth Dynasty and earlier, Tuthmosis I of the New Kingdom 18th Dynasty invaded Syria in about 1500 BC, reaching as far as the Euphrates. The area of Palestine and southern Syria then remained an Egyptian sphere of influence for another century, but northern Syria came under a new empire: the Mitannian. The Mitannians were rather mysterious newcomers to the Middle Eastern scene, based in the area of northeastern Syria. They belonged to a non-Semitic group of people known as the Hurrians, and though they were not Indo-Europeans, they included such familiar Indo-European gods as Mithra, Varuna and Indra in their pantheon. The Mitannians were in turn overthrown by a new empire, the Hittite, an Indo-European group based in Anatolia. They overran most of Syria clashing frequently with the Egyptians, culminating in the very bloody Battle of Qadesh near Homs in 1285 BC between the Pharaoh Rameses II and the Hittite King Mutawallis II. Although the battle itself was indecisive, it saw a permanent end to Egyptian control north of Palestine, leaving much of Syria Hittite until the advent of the most terrible power the ancient world had yet seen: the Assyrians.

The Assyrians were the newest 'wave' of Semites. The power of the Assyrians can be traced back to the beginnings of the 2nd millennium under the Old Assyrian Empire centred on the Middle Tigris region. But it was the Middle Assyrian Empire, mainly under Shalmaneser I and Tukulti-Ninurta I between about 1350 and 1200 BC, that eastern Syria and northern Mesopotamia were brought under the one rule, controlled from their capital at Ashur.

Assyrian rule was re-affirmed in the 9th century BC with the resurgence of Assyrian power in the New Assyrian Empire, but before that there was another major arrival into Syria of Semitic peoples: the Aramaeans. These were another people originating in or around the Syrian desert, whose advent once again was probably a largely peaceful and gradual penetration into Syria over several hundred years rather than any single invasion. The Aramaeans occupied the vacuum left behind by the decline of Hittite and Middle Assyrian power, establishing a number of states that existed side by side with various Neo-Hittite states of northern Syria such as Hama and Carchemish. The most significant of these Aramaean states was Damascus, established in the 11th century and remaining the centre of Syria until the present day. The language of the Aramaeans eventually became the *lingua franca* of the Near East, and the Aramaic script spread as far as Central Asia and India.

The Aramaic states of Syria, however, were extinguished by the resurgent New Assyrian Empire after 900 BC, and this time conquest was more terrible than anything the Middle East had ever experienced. Under the reigns of Ashurnasirpal II, Shalmaneser III and Tiglath-pileser III, the borders of the Empire were extended to incorporate most of the Near East as far as the Mediterranean coast. Resistance met with massive retribution: cities were razed and entire populations – or those that survived – taken off into captivity. Destruction on such a scale would not ravage the Near East again until the Mongol invasions some 2000 years later.

But despite the barbaric image bequeathed to us by Biblical accounts, the Assyrians were great civilizers as well. Under them a very vibrant, very vital civilization flourished. Moreover, they were brilliant organizers, who developed new methods of imperial administration that were continued by subsequent rulers. Through the Assyrians the ancient civilization of Mesopotamia was passed to subsequent generations and disseminated throughout the known world, much of it eventually to influence the fledgeling cultures of Greece and Rome.

It was also against the background of Assyrian domination that another Semitic people were to emerge who were to play such a significant role in Mediterranean history: the Phoenicians. The Phoenicians appeared on the Levantine coast of Syria in the 1st millennium BC, centred on the port cities of Arvad, Amrit, Byblos, Sidon, Tyre and others. Inheriting the commercial talents of their Canaanite forebears, the Phoenicians created a commercial network that encircled the Mediterranean, only to be eventually eclipsed by Rome, though the commercial talents of the coastal people of Lebanon and the Levant survive to this day.

Assyrian power was finally brought to a spectacular end in 612 BC when an allied army of Babylonians and Medes from Persia captured and sacked the Assyrian capital of Nineveh. Never again did Assyria revive, and their rule in Syria was replaced by the Babylonian victors. But the alliance required to destroy their might had brought a new people into the Near Eastern arena, the Persians. Soon the Babylonians themselves were to go the same way as the Assyrians, as the Persians returned, led by Cyrus the Great of the Achaemenian dynasty, in about 540 BC.

The Persians were Indo-Europeans, and though a foreign people to the Semitic inhabitants of Syria, their rule was marked to a large extent by the continuation of Babylonian and Assyrian cultural forms. Indeed, the Achaemenian rulers themselves adopted the cuneiform and Aramaic scripts of the Semites and even took up residence in the ancient seat of Mesopotamian civilization at Babylon.

The eventual collapse of the Persian Empire marked a major turning point in Near Eastern history. Up until then the Near East had been ruled by cultures that were indigenous to the Near East: the great line of conquerors who strode so prominently across the pages of Near Eastern history from Sargon of Akkad to Darius III had all been Near Eastern ones. But Darius III, the Achaemenian, was to be the last, after him Syria would be ruled from the West as foreign territory for the next thousand years, until a renaissance of Near Eastern civilization under the Arabs.

The Graeco-Roman period

In the year 248 AD one of the greatest triumphs in Roman history was held in the city of Rome. It celebrated the millennium of the traditional foundation of Rome by Romulus and Remus. A thousand years from the birth of a small village to the centre of the greatest empire the world had seen. Rome and the Caesars could well be doubly triumphant, and games, feasts and gifts were disbursed by the Emperor on a lavish scale. But ironically, the Emperor who presided over this greatest of all Roman triumphs was not a Roman himself. He was a Syrian: Emperor Philip the Arab.

To see how somebody from a subject people could rise to become Emperor of Rome itself, we must go back to Alexander the Great. Alexander's campaign across Asia was one of the most spectacular military exploits in history. It was relatively brief: it started in 334 BC and finished only 11 years later with Alexander's death in Babylon at the age of 33 – little more than a raid when compared to the ceaseless, lifelong campaigns of earlier conquerors in the Middle East. Yet its effect was to fundamentally change the countries of Asia that he passed through for many centuries to come. Nowhere was this more pronounced than Syria.

Up until the time of Alexander, Syria had been an essentially eastward-looking country. Apart from the Canaanite and subsequent Phoenician fringe on the coast (the influence of which rarely penetrated inland), Syrian civilization remained firmly rooted in Middle Eastern cultural traditions that were already thousands of years old when Alexander arrived. Very few of these traditions came from the West. The Greek conquest changed all of that. Whilst Syrian civilization still remained rooted in eastern traditions, Alexander's conquest opened it to the world of Mediterranean cultures. It gave Syria an increasingly western outlook, an outlook which remains to this day. Conversely – and more importantly – it opened up the Mediterranean world, and ultimately Europe, to the ancient civilizations of the East. For it was from this background of Hellenized Syria that Europe received a revolutionary new idea that would change the course of its history: Christianity. Alexander's conquest is often called 'the end of the ancient Near East', but surely it was a new beginning: for Near Eastern civilization became a world civilization.

The world of Graeco-Roman Syria was an exciting one. It lay at the western end of the great caravan routes across Asia that supplied an insatiable market in the Mediterranean with an inexhaustible supply of luxuries from the East. Syria became enriched, not only with wealth but also with ideas, coming from both east and west to meet in Syria in an immense intellectual foment. Out of it emerged Christianity, a syncretic religion born out of Judaism in Palestine and Greek philosophical ideas in the Hellenized climate of Damascus and Antioch. Antioch itself became one of the richest cities of the Mediterranean, rivalling for a time even Rome itself. The arts and architecture flourished, and Syrian society became one of the most cosmopolitan and outward-looking in the ancient world.

Following the death of Alexander, his empire was divided between his generals, with Seleucus Nicator emerging as ruler of most of Alexander's Asiatic conquests. Antioch, named after Seleucus' father, was founded as the capital of Syria. Over the ensuing centuries, the Seleucid Empire slowly declined with the eastern parts being lost to the Parthians, whilst in Syria itself local Semitic dynasties began to reassert themselves: the Jews under Judas Maccabeus in Judaea in 168 BC, Arab dynasties in Edessa (modern Urfa in Turkey) and Emesa (modern Homs) in about 130 BC, various Phoenician city-states on the coast, and the Nabateans in the south. Of these, the Nabateans became the strongest. An Arab tribe, they took over the ancient kingdom of Edom and, based at Petra, built up a wealthy kingdom controlling the trade routes from the south that, by 83 BC, controlled all of southern Syria up to and including Damascus.

Syria's fragmentation and the political vacuum resulting from the collapse of the Seleucids invited conquest by a new world power, the Romans. Using the excuse provided by rival claims to the throne between the last of the Seleucid rulers, Pompey invaded Syria and, meeting little resistance, annexed it in 64 BC. The Seleucids, though foreigners, had at least ruled Syria from Antioch. Henceforward, it would be ruled from Rome, represented by a Roman proconsul.

With Syria passing to the Romans, control of the western terminus of the trade routes provided Rome with massive new wealth. But it also provided Rome with a massive new front: Syria brought Rome into direct confrontation with Parthia, the new Persian Empire in the East. The subsequent three centuries or so saw almost continual conflict with Parthia, out of which neither side ever emerged as undisputed victor. The first conflict occurred only eight years after the incorporation of Syria into the Roman Empire, when a Roman army under Crassus, the Proconsul of Syria, was annihilated at the Battle of Carrhae (Harran, now just across the Syrian border in Turkey), with Crassus himself slain. Future conflicts would see the borders of Rome at times extend as far as the head of the Persian Gulf, and at other times the Parthians on the shores of the Mediterranean, but on the whole Syria remained firmly a part of the Pax Romana.

The influence of Roman civilization on Syria was immense, but so too was the impact of Syrian civilization on Rome. The spread of Christianity from its first organized centre in Antioch to every corner of the Roman world has already been remarked upon, but before that, eastern religious ideas held a fascination for the Romans. The cults of the Egyptian Isis, the Persian Mithras, the Syrian Baal, and various eastern gnostic and mystery cults achieved great popularity throughout the Roman world. Mithraism in particular for a while looked as though it might anticipate Christianity as the main religion of the West. Though in origins a Persian religion, Mithraism entered the West through the Roman army in Syria absorbing many Syrian philosophical ideas on the way. This melting pot of religious and philosophical ideas in Graeco-Roman Syria continued well into the Byzantine period, as we shall see.

Syrian influence at Rome had already been gaining in prominence, prompting Juvenal's famous remark 'the Syrian Orontes has long since poured its water into the Tiber', when in 187 AD there occurred a marriage between a Libyan general in the Roman army and a high-priest's daughter from Emesa in Syria: Septimus Severus and Julia Domna. A few years later, this general was to become one of Rome's most active emperors, and after his death Syrian influence at Rome became paramount when Julia Domna became the effective ruler of the Empire behind her son, Caracalla. There followed a number of Syrian emperors of Rome: Caracalla, Elagabalus (a Syrian name), and Alexander Severus. Though not related to this family, the emperor Philip the Arab, a Syrian from Shahba in southern Syria, reaffirmed the Syrian connection in the middle of the 3rd century. Indeed, under Elagabalus, himself the head priest of the Temple of Baal of Emesa, the cult of Emesene Baal was proclaimed supreme in the Roman world to the horror of the conservative Roman establishment. Of course the cult of Baal did not catch on in Rome, but another 'Syrian cult' was soon to become triumphant.

Such Syrian influence at the heart of the Roman world helped change European history in two very fundamental ways. Though not Christians themselves, such Syrian emperors – and their promotion of Syrian cults – nonetheless made the spread of Christianity, another eastern religion, more acceptable throughout the Roman world. Moreover, from the time of the Syrian emperors Rome increasingly turned its back upon Europe and looked more and more towards the East, a movement that culminated in Constantine's move of the capital to Byzantium in 330 AD, ensuring the continuity of Roman civilization in the East for another thousand years at the cost of ditching Europe to the barbarians.

But the foundation of the Byzantine Empire lies ahead. Before that, Syria saw the spectacular rise of a new Arab state, a state that combined both Roman and Syrian cultural elements to produce a magnificent new civilization in the heart of the Syrian desert, the remains of which continue to astonish visitors to this day: Palmyra (plate 85). The foundation of Palmyra lay in the vacuum left by the decline of Seleucid power when many small, semi-independent Arab principalities sprang up all over Syria. But with the collapse of the Nabatean control of the trade routes at the end of the 1st century AD, Palmyra's unique geographical position gave it its first major break. Situated in the desert midway between the Euphrates and Damascus, it was able to take charge of the trade routes coming from Persia and the Gulf to the Mediterranean. In particular, it became the middleman between Parthia and Rome, a situation the Palmyrenes exploited to the fullest. It was made a Roman protectorate in the 1st century AD, but it was not a Roman province in the same way that the rest of Syria was. The Romans instead were satisfied with merely installing a garrison there to prevent Parthian influence, which left the Palmyrenes free to concentrate on what they did best: trade and making money. Palmyra amassed immense wealth, which was used to embellish the city of Palmyra to an extent that rivalled Antioch. Though not extending their territories much outside the Syrian desert, the Palmyrenes established a commercial empire that reached throughout the known world, and today Palmyrene monumental remains can be found as far apart as Kharg Island halfway down the Persian Gulf and Newcastle-upon-Tyne in England.

Inevitably, such wealth and influence led to political ambitions. In the political uncertainty between the collapse of the Parthians and the rise of their successors, the Sasanians, the Palmyrenes increasingly relied on themselves for defence. With the capture of large parts of Syria by the Sasanian Persians in 260 AD, the ruler of Palmyra, Odaynath, built up an army that inflicted a crushing defeat upon the Sasanians. In gratitude, the Roman Emperor Galienus, who still held nominal suzerainty over Palmyra, awarded Odaynath the title 'Corrector of all the East', a title previously reserved only for emperors. Accordingly, Odaynath responded by declaring himself 'King of Kings' (an ancient title used by the Persians), but he was murdered in 267 AD, perhaps at the instigation of one of the most interesting conquerors yet to emerge from the East: his wife Queen Zenobia.

Whether or not Zenobia was endowed with the great beauty that tradition ascribes to her, she was certainly endowed with great ambition – and great talent to match. Her military conquests were the most spectacular the Near East had seen since Alexander the Great. She installed her son Wahab-Allath on the throne to succeed Odaynath, but since Wahab-Allath was a minor, real control remained with Zenobia. She defeated the Roman general Heraclianus and gained control of all of Syria in 269. The following year she invaded

Egypt, establishing a governor at Alexandria, and even occupied Anatolia as far as Ankara, where she installed a garrison. In 271, Zenobia proclaimed her son Augustus.

If the seizure of Rome's eastern provinces was not enough, this proclamation of Rome's own highest title was the ultimate insult to Roman prestige. Indeed, Zenobia's conquests were probably the most serious threat to Rome since Hannibal. Rome could no longer stand aside and under Emperor Aurelian retaliated, capturing Palmyra in 272 and taking Zenobia off to Rome – supposedly in chains of gold – where she was pensioned off in Tivoli. Palmyra itself was spared, but the following year it revolted against its Roman garrison, so Aurelian returned and Palmyra was sacked. It never recovered its former glory.

The world of the Near East was in any case changing. In the East, the Sasanians were proclaiming their rediscovered Persian past and the revival of ancient Achaemenian might. In the West on the other hand, the Romans were tiring of the immense weight of their own pagan past as they turned more to Christianity, as well as the unwieldy weight of their increasingly ramshackle empire as they turned more to the East. The foundation of the New Rome at Byzantium, therefore, marks a turning point in the Middle East.

The Byzantine period

At first sight, the Byzantine period in Syria appears to be a continuation of the Roman: it is not marked by any new invasions, revolutions, arrivals of new peoples or even major changes in administration, but was still in fact officially known as the 'Roman Empire'. Even though it was ruled from Constantinople rather than Rome, both were distant capitals for Syria, and the real power continued to emanate from Antioch. The *Pax Romana* was replaced by the *Pax Byzantica*, and Roman Syria merely continued: the same cities continued to flourish comfortably in the same places, albeit a little more shabbily, a little more hedonistically. Roman architectural forms merge imperceptibly into Byzantine, and Syrian society remained the same, cosmopolitan, westward-looking one that it was under Roman rule.

There were fundamental differences, however. To begin with, the Byzantine period was above all an ecclesiastical age: Christianity had all the arrogance and self confidence, not only of a newfound religion, but also of the world's first universal religion. A religion furthermore, adopted as the official state religion of the world's foremost power of the time, the Romans.

This new confidence and continuity applied equally all over the Roman/Byzantine world, but for Syria there was an added dimension.

For Syria saw the origin of Christianity, both in terms of its birthplace in Palestine (then a part of Syria) and its formative growth in Damascus and Antioch. After the initial 'Romanization' of Syria in the first centuries of Roman rule, the adoption of a Syrian religion by the greatest world power of antiquity was therefore a 'Syrianization' of Rome. A newfound world religion and a Syrian one at that – Syrian civilization was with good reason doubly self confident, and stated it in no uncertain terms in an explosion of Christian building all over Syria that still predominates today over all other historic buildings.

The traditional Syrian delight in experimentation with religious and philosophical ideas was given full rein, and Syrian civilization began to remould Christianity. Christianity, on coming of age with its official acceptance in the Roman Empire, had returned home as it were. Hence, Byzantine Syria nurtured some of the earliest Christian fathers, such as John Chrysostom, Eusebius, Arius, Apollinarius and Nestorius; monasticism became established as one of the foundations of the Christian way of life, and important new sects of Christianity were founded, flourished and travelled the world. The Syrians retained too their talent for trade, and much of both Asia and the former Roman world remained in the hands of Syrian merchants, enabling Syrian religious and intellectual ideas to travel in their wake – we even hear of Syrian merchants in China in the 3rd century, anticipating Marco Polo by a thousand years.

The intellectual world of Byzantine Syria was to affect Europe in another very important way. With the final extinction of the Roman Empire in the West, Europe entered a dark age as the barbarian invasions completely overran the former centres of Roman learning. Such was the extinction of civilization by these invasions that classical civilization only just managed to be preserved in the remote monasteries on the very fringes of western Europe. But classical learning was kept alive by the skin of its teeth in another, less well known quarter as well: in the university towns of northern Syria. These universities were established in Edessa, Harran, and Nisibis essentially as centres of theological learning by the Nestorian Christians, but they were a repository of the classical learning of Greece and Rome as well. These works were preserved to be passed on to the first Muslims, who were able to eventually pass them on via Spain and Sicily to a Europe re-awakening from its dark ages on the eve of the Renaissance – a roundabout route indeed, but without it, much of European learning would have been lost forever.

The religious foment of Byzantine Syria had other far-reaching consequences as well. It was an age of hairsplitting theological discussion out of which grew new Christian schisms, many condemned as heresies by the orthodox court in Constantinople. Arianism was rigidly suppressed and eventually disappeared, as was Apollinarianism. But Nestorianism, and to a lesser extent Monophysitism, though suppressed by the Byzantines, took to the immense Syrian trading network of the East and flourished as far away as Central Asia and southern India. At one point, Nestorian Christianity was almost declared the official church of Sasanian Persia.

The Syrian religious foment was not only Christian: different religions entered the scene as well. Resurgent – at times militant – Zoroastrianism under the Sasanians made its influence felt in Syria, and aspects of it survive in the Druze and Yazidi religions today, as did a new syncretic Persian religion that combined various elements of Zoroastrianism, Christianity, Buddhism and Neo-Platonism: Manichaeism. Although Manichaeism was also suppressed by the orthodox Byzantine church, many of its ideas spread westwards to influence later European religious communities such as the Cathars of France. It survived far off in Chinese Turkestan as a pocket of Syrian civilization still writing in Aramaic down to the 13th century. Into the Syrian religious melting-pot came also elements of Buddhism, Gnosticism and even survivals of pre-Christian Syrian cults; out of it, the religious foment eventually filtered down the Syrian trading networks to southern Arabia to inspire the foundation of the last and one of the greatest religious movements to emanate from the Near East: Islam.

Islam, however, belongs to the next part of Syrian history. For the moment, we have an immensely ecclesiastical and intellectual age flourishing under the protection of the Byzantine Empire. Although these movements still largely belonged to the Graeco-Roman intellectual traditions, we see also a resurgence of native Semitic traditions making themselves felt, a resurgence that in many ways anticipated Islam – it certainly made it easier for Islam to take root when it did come. There was a revival of the Aramaic language, which became the liturgical language of the Syrian church. It flourished particularly in the university town of Edessa, which became the centre of an Aramaic renaissance. The Arabs had already made themselves a major factor in Syria with the establishment of the Nabatean and Palmyrene kingdoms in earlier ages, and in the early 6th century in the Hauran the arrival of a new Arab tribe, the Banu Ghassan, heralded the foundation of the latest in this line of Arab states before Islam: the Ghassanid. Other Arab states were established in Iraq as well, so clearly the Arabs were becoming more and more prominent on the Near Eastern scene. The Ghassanid court flourished as a meeting place of Byzantine Greek and Semitic Arab cultures, and remained the main centre of Syrian civilization until the Islamic conquest.

In 527 a man ascended the Roman throne in Constantinople who for a brief while was able to reinstate the ancient glory – as well as much of the borders – or Rome itself: Justinian. Whilst a devout Christian, Justinian was the last of the great Roman Emperors, in the tradition of Hadrian, Trajan and Constantine. He embarked upon a campaign of reconquest both east and west, pushing back the barbarians and instigating one of the most massive campaigns of building and refortification that the empire had ever seen. The capital at Constantinople was embellished on an almost unprecedented scale and in Syria, frontier posts such as Qasr Ibn Wardan (plate 31) and formidable fortifications such as Halebiye (figure 29) were built. Administration was shaken up and the army re-organized. A new era, a renaissance, of Roman glory it seemed, was dawning.

But in the end it was a twilight, not a dawn. In the middle of the 6th century, Syria suffered its first major invasion for many centuries, with the arrival of a Persian army of 30,000 under Chosroes I Anushirvan the Sasanian. Aleppo and Antioch were sacked, and much of the rest of Syria devastated. It seemed that the days of Byzantine Syria were over. The Emperor Heraclius managed to negotiate a truce with the Persians and win back control of much of Syria, only to see it devastated again a few years later by Chosroes II. Once again Heraclius was able to reinstate Byzantine rule in Syria. But its days were numbered in any case, though in the end it was not Persia that dealt the death blow, but an entirely new power from a completely unexpected source. In the year 622 a little known-man entered the remote town of Yathrib in Arabia, on the fringes of the civilized Near East, with a very small band of followers. This event was one of the most important in the history of the world: the man was called Muhammad, the town's name was changed to Medina, and his followers, who called themselves Muslims, less than a century later, ruled an empire stretching from the Atlantic to the borders of China.

The first Islamic empires

Syria was among the Muslims' first conquests. After several preliminary raids, when even Damascus was briefly occupied, the Byzantine and Arab forces came together at the Battle of Yarmouk near the present Jordanian-Syrian border in 636, and the Byzantine forces were routed. All of Syria fell to the Arabs, ending nearly a thousand years of rule by Romans and Greeks virtually overnight. It was the defeated Byzantine emperor himself, Heraclius, who pronounced its epitaph: 'Farewell, O Syria, and what an excellent country this is for the enemy!'

An 'excellent country' indeed the Arabs found it. The centre of

Muslim rule moved from Arabia to Syria. Damascus, the ancient Aramaean centre, became the natural capital of the first Islamic empire. The conquest was a comparatively simple one. The wars earlier that century between the Byzantines and Sasanians had torn the place apart, and the centuries of religious schisms and rivalry before that made a receptive ground for Islam, seen at first as yet another religious schism. More importantly, the previous centuries had seen Arabs and Arab culture in Syria more and more in the ascendant, with the traditional pre-Hellenistic Semitic cultures of Syria re-asserting themselves as we have seen. The Muslims were, therefore, largely welcomed as fellow-countrymen, liberating them from the alien Greeks; the new, simple religion that they espoused, stripped as it was of all inessential trappings with a clear straightforward message, appeared as a refreshing change after the centuries of hair-splitting, increasingly abstruse dogmatism of the Byzantine clergy. Soon, Sasanian Persia too crumbled as easily as the Byzantine empire, and the Arabs with their new message to the world appeared irresistible.

The ancient civilizations of the Near East, dormant for so long, were re-awoken. The seemingly invincible civilizations of the West had all but been inundated under waves of barbarian invasions, the might of the Byzantine army in the Near East evaporated virtually overnight, and whilst a – much reduced – Byzantine Empire was to hang on for a further 850 years, its vital force had been sapped and it became increasingly meaningless. Syria therefore became the centre of a new world order and the leading torchbearer of civilization, with Damascus as its capital under the Umayyad dynasty of caliphs.

But a thousand years of Greek and Roman culture in Syria did not evaporate quite so easily; Syria's Semitic past was re-awoken, it is true, but the overlay of Mediterranean culture had changed it almost beyond recognition. For Syria under the Umayyads retained much of its Byzantine character: it remained westward looking, the society remained cosmopolitan and, despite the puritanical constraints of the new religion, it retained much of its hedonism and free and easy ways. Much of the population remained Christian, and even many in the new Muslim ruling class quickly discovered the pleasures available to them in Syria.

The world saw the most rapid series of military conquests since the days of Alexander. By the beginning of the 8th century, Umayyad rule extended far into Central Asia almost to the borders of China, and included all of what is now Afghanistan, Pakistan and parts of the west coast of India. To the West, all of North Africa and most of Spain were conquered, with even parts of southern France as far as Tours seeing Umayyad armies in the 8th century. Such an empire was far greater than even Rome had been at its greatest; Rome's own power base, the

Mediterranean became an Islamic lake, imposing a north-south division which remains to this day. European princes from Europe were brought in chains to pay homage to the caliph in Damascus, and the power of Islam appeared invincible to the believers. This phenomenal success of Islam in its very first years was in direct contrast to the first years of Christianity, characterized as it was by martyrdom and repression, and endowed Islam with a vitality and a boundless confidence without the self-doubts characterizing Christianity, that it still retains.

But at the same time, Islam was characterized as much by internal conflict as by external conquest, a characteristic that continues to plague it. Since its earliest days it was riven by internal dissensions, divisions that were to have disastrous consequences for Syria. These were revealed as early as 661, less than 30 years after the death of the Prophet Muhammad, when Muhammad's cousin and son-in-law, 'Ali, died by the hand of a fellow-Muslim in Iraq. Unlike Christianity and all of its divisions, however, the differences in Islam were rarely theological (though they might be given a theological expression), but usually political, and Islam even today still remains very much a political religion. In the case of 'Ali's assassination, the issue was the succession of the leadership of Islam – the caliphate – from the Prophet Muhammad. One party, the Sunni, favoured an essentially elected succession whilst the other, the Shi'a, favoured an hereditary succession of leaders through the descendants of 'Ali. The conflicts between the two parties became more and more bitter, finally coming to a head in the mid-8th century when a coalition of Shi'ites and other disaffected elements in Islam, mainly from the eastern parts of the empire, gathered under the leadership of Abu 'l-'Abbas, a rival claimant to the caliphate. The Umayyads of Syria were overthrown and members of the Umayyad family ruthlessly exterminated. A new caliphate was proclaimed under the 'Abbasid family, with its capital first at Kufa in Iraq and subsequently at Baghdad.

The overthrow of the Umayyads and the move of the capital of Islam away from Damascus to Iraq was to have far-reaching consequences, both within Islam and for the world at large. The 'Abbasids of Iraq reduced Syria to provincial status: from being the centre of the civilized world Syria was made merely a backwater. It was a blow, a slap in the face, from which urbane Syria never recovered. The outward-going, cosmopolitan Syrians with centuries of civilization behind them never forgave the Iraqis for this, and a deep bitterness between the two countries still dominates Middle Eastern politics to this day.

More importantly, however, the 'Abbasid triumph turned Islam eastwards. Islam under the Umayyads had been westward-oriented: the Syrians still retained much of their Hellenism, and much of the thrust of the Umayyads was towards the west, with the ultimate goal of overthrowing Constantinople and becoming the new Roman Empire. Indeed, it is significant that the only member of the Umayyad house to survive the 'Abbasid massacre escaped to Spain to found a neo-Umayyad caliphate in Europe. 'Abbasid Iraq changed all that. Although there were still campaigns in the west, it looked increasingly eastwards as its natural areas of expansion, a thrust reinforced with the gradual domination of the 'Abbasid court by powerful Persian vizirial families. Syria and the West became backwaters to the 'Abbasids: Egypt, followed by other North African possessions were the first to break away from direct 'Abbasid rule. Islam turned its back on the West. The 'Abbasid 'revolution' turned Islam (initially no more an eastern religion than Christianity) into a more eastern religion, which it still remains.

The middle Islamic period

With the caliphate turned away from Syria, the region was at least able to develop along its own lines, and a number of local dynasties exerted some degree of independence from 'Abbasid rule. But they never regained the brilliance that Syria enjoyed under the Umayyads. The first of these were the Hamdanids, a dynasty based at Aleppo in the 10th century who soon controlled most of northern Syria, extending their rule eastwards as far as Mosul. The founder of the dynasty, Saif ad-Daula, was even the first Muslim since the Umayyads to seriously threaten the Byzantines.

But the civilization of both the Arabs and the Byzantines were to receive an immense shock with the arrival on scene of a new people who were to change the face of the Middle East once again: the Turks. These were a people from Central Asia, speaking a language totally different from either Arabic or Persian. They were initially brought into the Middle East by the Muslims as slaves. So prized were Turkish slaves, particularly for their fighting qualities, that they were often made into personal bodyguards and even into whole mercenary units in the Muslim armies. But the slaves were too good: they soon became the masters.

The Turks were one of the most warlike people Asia produced, and in the following five centuries changed the face of Asia with several waves of invasions. But the Turks were also great civilizers: the Turkic dynasties founded all over Asia – the empires of the Eastern and the Western Turks in Central Asia, the Ghaznavids in Afghanistan, Seljuks, Timurids, Safavids, Ottomans, and Moguls – were amongst the most brilliant civilizations Asia had seen. They overran the world of

Islam, but embracing Islam themselves, they also revitalized it.

The first wave of Turkish invaders into the Near East were the Seljuks in the middle of the 11th century. They rapidly conquered most of the lands of the 'Abbasid caliphate, reducing the caliphs in Baghdad to mere puppet status while the Seljuk leaders assumed the title sultan, or supreme temporal Islamic ruler. In 1071 Sultan Alp Arslan inflicted a massive defeat on the Byzantines as well and most of Anatolia fell to Seljuk rule. Anatolia then became the heartland of Seljuk rule, and the subsequent 'Turkification' of Anatolia completely altered its cultural and ethnic make up. Iraq then joined Syria as provincial backwaters; henceforward the centres of Islamic civilization would pass out of the Arab heartlands to India, Persia, Turkey and Egypt.

A minor Seljuk dynasty under Emir Ridwan, subject to the sultan, was established in Aleppo at the end of the 11th century and the Fatimids, a North African dynasty ruling from Egypt, took over Palestine. In the early 12th century another minor Turkish dynasty related to the Seljuks, the Atabegs, occupied Aleppo from their base in Mosul, and ruled most of northern Syria until the 13th century. Syria and Palestine then became a pawn between these minor Turkish dynasties and the Fatimids, passing from one to the other at various times.

In the middle of all this, in the 12th century, there came a rather curious force, the Assassins. The Assassins were an extreme religious sect evolving out of Shi'ism, that originally grew up in the mountains of Persia. It was a highly secretive and very violent sect. Their name was derived from the hashish they supposedly intoxicated themselves with before carrying out their acts – mainly political and religious assassination (whence the English word). In other words, they were the Middle East's original terrorists. They moved into mountainous strongholds in western Syria and the Lebanon hills (forming a strange link between extremists in the Lebanon hills and Iran that still survives) from where the sect's grand master, known as 'The Old Man of the Mountains', directed acts of terrorism on all sides, later even making an attempt on the life of Saladin.

Into this morass of conflicting Turkish, Egyptian and Assassin interests came the Crusaders. The spectacular Seljuk advance almost to within the gates of Constantinople implied an undeniable – and perhaps irresistible – threat to Christendom. Europe, only beginning to emerge from the anarchy and chaos of the dark ages, was spurred into response. The Crusades are one of the most romanticised episodes in European history. Their ideals, it is true, were of the noblest: to recover the true cross and liberate the Christian holy places from the infidel. The First Crusade in 1097 consisted of some 150,000 men – mostly Franks and Normans – and quickly captured most of Syria, setting up principalities at Edessa and Antioch. On Christmas Day 1100, Baldwin was installed as king in Jerusalem. The Crusade, it appeared, had fulfilled the loftiest of ideals.

To the cultured Arabs, however, heirs as they were to a great civilization, the holy knights of the cross appeared as little more than barbarian pillagers. Their acts of brutality in the lands they conquered shocked even the Syrians, innured as they had been to centuries of invasions: the sadistic and treacherous exploits of Reginald of Chatillon, lord of Kerak in southern Jordan, make sickening reading by the standards of any day, let alone the ideals that the Crusaders were supposed to uphold. But it is not the barbarity of the Crusaders alone for which their ideals must be questioned. It was, after all, the Middle Ages, an age of dog eat dog, when no band of thugs had little to recommend itself over the next, and no one side had a monopoly of barbaric acts. The Crusades were a tragedy more because of the untold damage it inflicted upon the very religion it was supposed to be protecting: Christianity. Syria at the time of the Crusades still had large populations of Christians – indeed, it has been argued that Christians still formed the majority – but the Crusaders were undiscriminating: Christian and Muslim Syrian Christians alike were killed. So much so that much of the Christian population of Syria was prompted to convert to Islam simply out of self defence. When after finally losing most of their possessions in the Holy Land, the army of the Fourth Crusade in 1204 turned upon the great stronghold of Christendom itself, Constantinople, and subjected it to the most destructive sacking that even that turbulent city had ever witnessed. This was Christendom returning to its Eastern roots only to end up destroying itself.

But it was not all so one-sided. The Crusaders did after all remain in the Levant for several centuries, and this could not have been achieved without at least some co-operation from the local population. Hence, there were more than a few instances of Arab princes allying themselves with the Crusaders against other Arabs. The great Crusader fortresses, too, were administered much as their European counterparts: as feudal fiefdoms. Such an administrative network would not have been possible without the collaboration – or at least compliance – of the populations they administered. Government, throughout history, has always been a two-way process involving the co-operation of both rulers and ruled. For the Syrian peasant in any case, there would be little difference to whom taxes were paid, whether Arab, Turk or Frank.

The Crusades also produced a great leader of the Arabs: Saladin. A Kurd originally from Iraq, Saladin overthrew the last of the Fatimid rulers of Egypt in 1171, initiating the rule of his own dynasty, the Ayyubids. Having taken Egypt, he then turned on the Franks of the

Holy Land. At the great battle of Hittin, the Crusader army was utterly routed, with the king of Jerusalem himself, Guy de Lusignan, being the chief captive. One after the other, Saladin recaptured most of the Crusader strongholds until only some of the towns on the coast of Lebanon and Syria remained in Crusader hands. Contrasting sharply with the barbarity of the Crusaders, Saladin's treatment of Frankish prisoners was lenient, with most being allowed to purchase their own freedom.

The loss of Jerusalem to Saladin, however, inspired the legendary Third Crusade, attracting the participation of Europe's greatest kings: Frederick Barbarossa of Germany, Philip Augustus of France, and Richard the Lionheart of England. Great feats of arms and bravery were carried out by both sides, and much was made of the personal relationship between Richard and Saladin, but whilst gifts were exchanged and each obviously held the other in high regard, the two never met. In the end, a peace was negotiated in 1192, leaving the interior of Palestine (including Jerusalem) and Syria with the Muslims and the coastal strip to the Franks, with the rights of pilgrims being recognized by either side. Richard returned home and Saladin died of fever shortly afterwards. The Crusades struggled on for a further century, with neither side gaining the ascendant. It was in the end another ruler from Egypt, this time a Turk of the Mamluk dynasty, Sultan Baybars, who decisively defeated the Crusader kingdoms in Syria towards the end of the 13th century.

Unknown, however, to either Turk, Arab, Crusader or Assassin, there was a terrible new power threatening from the East, a power more terrible than anything that even the Middle East had ever experienced: the Mongols. They devastated everything in their path: towns, cities, entire landscapes, entire populations; genocide was practised on a scale never before seen. The world from China to Europe reeled under their impact; truly it seemed like the end of the world.

But the world did survive. The Mongols' main westward advance through the Middle East was checked in Syria. The Mongol hordes entered Syria in several waves in the latter half of the 13th century: the impregnable citadel of Aleppo was sacked for the first time in its history, and 50,000 people put to death. The rest of Syria was devastated. Nothing, it seemed, could stand in their path. But something eventually did. In the manner of fighting fire with fire, it took another equally warlike Central Asian people, closely related to the Mongols, to stop them: in the Turkish Mamluk army from Egypt, the Mongols finally met their match. The Mamluks defeated them at the battle of 'Ain Jalut (Goliath's Spring) near Nazareth in 1260 and again at the battle Marj as-Saffar, south of Damascus, in 1303.

There followed some two hundred years of Mamluk rule in Syria and Egypt. The Mamluk slave dynasty was one of the most curious institutions ever to be seen in the Middle East: they were both slaves and rulers at the same time. The Ayyubid dynasty (founded by Saladin), predecessors of the Mamluks, maintained a by-now established tradition of Middle Eastern rulers of supporting themselves by ranks of professional slave guards drawn from the Turks and Circassians of Central Asia and southern Russia. The Ayyubids became increasingly dependant upon this 'Praetorian Guard' to stay in power, until inevitably the slaves – 'Mamluk' means slave – seized power themselves, forming their own dynasty.

Curiously enough, even after taking power the Mamluks maintained their slave status: the court, most of the administration and the top ranks of the army were drawn from slaves. Indeed, slave status was essential for high office, especially under the latter line of Mamluks, when each successive sultan would be a slave specially chosen for the purpose. Under this extraordinary system, the free born – even the sons of former Mamluk Sultans – would be second-class citizens.

And by and large, the system worked extremely well, rather like the system of adopted emperors of Rome's golden age. Without the commitment to inherited lines of rulers, each Mamluk sultan would be chosen largely on talent – or at least strength. That the system succeeded is demonstrated by its length of rule, from 1250 to 1517 – nearly 300 years, the longest any dynasty had remained in power in Syria since the Byzantines. The Mamluk achievements were correspondingly impressive: external threats such as the Mongols, the Crusaders and, in 1400, the invasion of Tamerlane, were finally and decisively beaten, the Mamluk borders were extended southwards to the Sudan and Yemen and westwards to Cyrenaica, and with the stability that their rule brought, Syria and Egypt enjoyed a very high degree of new found economic and cultural prosperity. Syria especially enjoyed a cultural renaissance, with the arts, architecture and sciences, dormant since the Umayyads, flourishing once more.

Inevitably, however, the Mamluks were seen as rivals by an emerging new power on the Middle Eastern scene who were to dominate the region down to modern times: the Ottoman Turks. Following the collapse of the Seljuks in Anatolia after the Mongol invasions, several Turkish tribes jockeyed for supremacy, with the Ottoman family eventually emerging as the dominant force in the 14th century. The capture of Constantinople, Christendom's ancient capital, in 1453, provided the Ottomans with Islam's greatest psychological victory – and lent considerable weight to the Ottoman family's claim of being the spiritual heirs to the caliphs. Thereafter, their rise as Islam's greatest protagonist and Christendom's greatest threat was almost inevitable. More important than psychological advantage, however, the Ottomans possessed technology: firearms and heavy artillery, which the Mamluks lacked. When the Mamluk and Ottoman armies finally met in pitched battle near Aleppo in 1516, the effect was devastating and the Mamluks were slaughtered. Syria and Egypt were incorporated into the Ottoman Empire by Sultan Selim I. Henceforth, the Arab lands were to be ruled once again from Constantinople, but as an Ottoman backwater rather than a Byzantine hinterland.

The modern period

Ottoman Turkey was by any standards one of the most brilliant civilizations in the history of the Middle East. Its achievements were extraordinary, both in Europe and Asia, and in many ways it represented the peak of Islamic civilization. But the seat of Ottoman power lay outside the Arab Middle East. Based at Constantinople, straddling Europe and Asia, the Arab lands merely stagnated.

The Ottomans ruled Syria for exactly four hundred years: 1517 to 1917. Their rule coincided with the discovery of the sea routes to Asia by the Europeans, so that the ancient land routes through the Middle East were simply by-passed. Added to that, Ottoman rule was aimed mainly at exploitation with virtually nothing put back into the countries they ruled. It was four hundred years of stagnation, exploitation and maladministration, when Arab civilization was all but forgotten – and came on top of nearly five hundred years of Seljuk and Mamluk rule before then. Four hundred years of Turkish rule is an immensely long period by any standards – something that is often forgotten with the obsession over relatively brief European rule in the first half of the 20th century – that endowed the Arabs with problems of identity that continue to concern them to this day. Europeans who become impatient of the extreme forms that Arab nationalism often takes today would do well to bear in mind that until the 20th century, the Arabs have been without statehood for some nine hundred years – something that few European nations ever experienced.

The Ottoman province of Syria included parts of what are now southeastern Turkey as well as Jordan, Palestine and Lebanon. It was administered by three governorships, based at Aleppo, Damascus and Tripoli. Enforcement of the governorships – and the raising of taxes, which was their main purpose – was largely in the hands of the Janissaries, the Ottomans' elite force of mercenaries. The Janissaries suppressed dissent with extreme harshness: when a revolt in Damascus in the early 16th century, for example, was suppressed, about a third of the entire city and its surroundings were utterly destroyed – more destruction, in fact, than the city suffered in Tamerlane's invasion.

The Ottoman period also saw a re-awakening of European presence in Syria – Venetian, Genoese, French and English – with the establishment of trading colonies in Aleppo, Alexandretta, Tripoli and other Syrian cities. Foremost amongst European claims in Syria were the French – a prerogative the French have always assumed, ever since the Crusades. Indeed, after 1535 France not only assumed almost a monopoly of commercial power, but claimed protection over all Catholics in Syria as well. This culminated in French military intervention in Lebanon in 1860, ostensibly to protect Christian communities there from Druze depredations.

The trade that the European factories controlled, however, remained solely in European hands, and rarely did any of the wealth filter down to the Syrian population. The main Syrian family that did rise to prominence was a Damascus family, the Azems, who ruled parts of Syria under the Ottomans in the 18th century. They amassed considerable fortunes, mainly through control of the pilgrimage routes, and embellished Hama and Damascus with sumptuous palatial residences.

In the beginning of the 20th century, the interests of a new European power became focussed upon Syria: Germany. As part of the alliance formed with Ottoman Turkey, Germany sought increased economic and military influence in the Middle East. Thus, the construction of the Hejaz Railway and subsequently the Berlin to Baghdad Railway was carried out with considerable German aid, and by the outbreak of the First World War, the Turkish army contained many German advisers.

The European involvement in Syria reached its culmination with the defeat of the Ottoman Empire at the end of the First World War, and its replacement with French and British mandates. This was a cynical betrayal of the Middle East. The Arab Revolt, led by the Emir Feisal of the Hejaz, played no small part in bringing about the Turkish defeat – indeed, it is perhaps worth noting that the greatest victories achieved by the Allies in the Middle East, such as the captures of Jerusalem and Damascus, were when Arab forces were fighting alongside, whilst the greatest defeats, such as at Kut al-Amara in Iraq, were when there were none.

The fall of Damascus in 1918 and the formation of a provisional government of Syria under Feisal, proclaimed King of Syria in 1920, was therefore the crowning point of the Arab uprising against Ottoman rule. Indeed, so dormant had been the Arab national consciousness for so long that it was perhaps one of the greatest moments in Arab history since the caliphate. An achievement only to be cruelly dashed by the French and British who, betraying Arab help in winning the war turned round and robbed them of the fruits of peace. The betrayal broke T E Lawrence, Britain's most famous Arab sympathiser, but more importantly it created problems that still dominate Middle Eastern politics – indeed world politics – to this day.

After the war, the British and the French proceeded to divide up the Middle East to suit their own interests, with Arab interests, if considered at all, relegated very firmly to second place. This was a result of the Sykes-Picot Agreement of 1916, a secret agreement between the French and British recognizing their respective claims to the Middle East in the eventuality of Turkish collapse. The matter was further compounded by the notorious Balfour Declaration of 1917 promising Palestine as a Jewish state.

The first move was that Arab forces under Feisal were evicted from Damascus, and the French took over. Under the terms of the agreement, Syria was broadly recognized as a French claim and Iraq as British, but more important for the Syrians was the partition of Syria into separate states: the southern parts of the old Ottoman province of Syria were separated off as Palestine and Transjordan, under British mandates; much of the coast and the Lebanese mountains were formed into a separate state of Lebanon, under French rule; parts of northern Syria – the traditionally Syrian cities of 'Aintab (now Gaziantep), Urfa and Diyarbakir and surrounding areas – were returned to Turkish rule; and the much reduced state of Syria itself was subject to French rule. On the eve of the Second World War, the city of Antioch and its surrounding area, the Hatay, was also handed back to the Turks, to 'buy' Turkish neutrality in the forthcoming war. A cruel stab indeed: Antioch is as much an ancient capital of Syria as Damascus itself, and to this day Syria refuses to recognize Turkey's rule over Antioch and the Hatay.

The cynicism of the Sykes-Picot Agreement was bad enough, but the short-sightedness in implementing it simply made matters worse. It is perhaps worth recording at this point the recommendations of the United States on the matter. Such was US concern at Versailles for the limited vision of British and French aims that they set up their own investigation, known as the King-Crane Commission on Syria. This US commission recommended that a 'Greater Syrian' state should be maintained at all costs, and under no circumstances should be divided up. The Commission conceded the possible need for a limited mandate, but with the US or Britain as mandatory power, not France. It further recommended that any moves to create a Jewish state in Palestine would be a 'gross violation . . . of the people's rights' and under no circumstances should be entertained; Palestine was to remain a part of a united state of Syria.

The recommendations of the King-Crane Commission were

suppressed by the British and French. The Sykes-Picot Agreement instead was implemented, a French army occupied Syria, Feisal was forcibly ejected from Damascus, and Syria apportioned out between the British, French and Turks, only being reluctantly handed over to Arab rule in a greatly reduced form in 1946. The Syrians saw themselves as victors in the Great War, only to be treated as losers by the very allies whom they had helped to win. Their territories were forcibly seized and large parts of it made over to the very power they had fought so hard to defeat: Turkey. It comes as no surprise that there is bitterness amongst Arabs in the Middle East for this sell-out; small wonder that Arab governments hold Western policies towards the Middle East with such mistrust. It is even greater wonder that the traveller in Syria today encounters so little of this bitterness, experiencing rather courtesy and kindness whenever he goes.

CHAPTER 3

Architectural Background

Nine thousand years or so of one of the Middle East's greatest storehouses of architectural remains cannot be covered in a book of this size. Attention will be concentrated more on just covering the main architecture that the visitor encounters today, and outlining some of the broader themes so as to place it into context. In this way, periods may be passed over, not because they are intrinsically less important, but merely because the average visitor will see less of them.

Pre-classical

Many of the great monuments of the classical and later periods had their origins in the pre-classical past. Of the great ancient civilizations of Syria, the modern visitor will see very little. There are not the immense monumental stone remains that the ancient civilization of Egypt, for example, boasts, or even the more modest pre-classical remains that can be seen in Turkey. For on the plains of Syria which saw the beginnings of civilization, the main building material was mud – a notoriously impermanent material.

The main type of early monument that the visitor will encounter is the palaces, with particularly impressive ones excavated at Mari, Ugarit and Ebla. Of these, perhaps the most spectacular – and certainly one of the earliest – is the great palace at Mari (figure 31). Being Sumerian in origin, Mari belongs essentially to the architectural traditions of ancient Mesopotamia. But the courtyard which forms such a prominent feature of the palace – and the temples – at Mari is one of the main architectural elements that was to dominate Near Eastern architecture for thousands of years. This was the architectural concept of the open space. Unlike Western architecture, which conceptually is concerned more with enclosed spaces (reaching its height in, for example, the great cathedrals of medieval Europe), that of the Near East is dominated by the open space. This is evident at nearly every level, from the modest, traditional Near Eastern courtyard house to the immense enclosures of religious architecture (figure 34). Indeed, places of worship more than any other were dominated by this concept, culminating in the immense enclosures of the Temple Mount in Jerusalem and the other great classical temples of Syria. Its form continued as the open courtyards of the first Arab mosques (figure 3).

The use of the open space as an architectural feature can be seen at the Royal Palace at Ebla, built about 2400 BC, which has a part-colonnaded facade overlooking a large square (figure 21). This imposed a monumentality on the palace, as well as a division between the jumble of the residential area of the lower town and the formal public areas of the palace and acropolis above. Symbolically, the palace – and the king – acted as a go-between for the people and the gods. The Ebla palace has a more formal, ordered arrangement than at Mari, with its monumental entrance way, colonnades and ceremonial stairway. Whereas Mari appears little more than a jumble of rooms – a house merely enlarged on a massive scale – at Ebla one senses the existence of monumental architecture as a concept in itself. In other words, at Ebla architecture was beginning to be rather more than merely four (or four hundred) convenient walls to house a specific function.

The palace of Ugarit is also dominated by several large courtyards surrounded by a jumble of rooms seemingly in no apparent order (figure 16, plate 41). The sheer sizes of these ancient palaces appear today to be completely out of keeping with the comparatively small size of the kingdoms they ruled – sometimes little more than city-states. But palaces then performed very different functions to their later counterparts in Europe. In addition to being royal residences, they were also the centres of government, administration and trade: they housed the civil service, offices, state archives, customs and virtually all other state functions apart from military.

The use of mudbrick is a continuing Near Eastern tradition, but at Ebla ashlar blocks were beginning to be used as foundations, the beginnings of a Syrian mastery of monumental stone architecture that was to culminate in the great stone monuments of the Roman and Byzantine periods. At Ugarit the fine ashlar walls of the fortifications and stone-vaulted tombs were the finest of their day, and show links to Mycenaean architecture.

Massive urban fortifications spread across Syria after 2000 BC.

These can be seen as far apart as Tell Leilan (Shubat Enlil) in the far northeast to Ebla in the west. Those in the east are characterised by largely mud construction, in the Mesopotamian tradition, whilst those in the west have an increasing use of stone, characterised by monumental 'Cyclopean' masonry. Here we see the first evidence of a purely military style of architecture in the use of casemate walls, glacis for protection against battering rams and mining, multi-chambered gates, reinforcing towers, etc. At Qatna, for example, the walls still stand up to 20 metres high, enclosing an immense square about a kilometre across (plate 18). The huge ramparts of Ebla also still stand nearly 20 metres high. Although both Qatna and Ebla are largely earthworks, they have stone foundations and revetments. The southwest gate at Ebla is a complex series of successive entrances flanked by massive buttressing – the forerunner of the heavily defended entrances of Arab and Crusader military engineering (figure 21). Thus was initiated a very strong tradition of Syrian fortification building, that reached its height in the great castles of the Crusaders.

Despite the links that pre-classical Syrian architecture had with Mesopotamia, that most quintessential of Mesopotamian monuments, the ziggurat, is conspicuous by its absence in Syria, even though the concept behind them – that of a sacred high place – is a common theme in Syrian religious architecture. A rather amorphous mass of mudbrick at Mari, associated with one of the temples and a similar mudbrick structure at Tell Leilan, are the only structures that have been identified as ziggurats. At the other great Syrian cities, they appear to be absent.

At Ebla we also see the beginnings of the most ubiquitous Syrian architectural feature: the monumental colonnade which formed the facade of the palace. Although this concept was to become one of the most predominant features of Roman architecture in Syria, its existence at Ebla suggests that it was the Syrians who gave the idea to the Romans rather than the other way round. This is also seen at the colonnade surrounding the temple enclosure at Amrit, a Phoenician sacred site on the coast (plate 36). Here, the very block-like, almost 'cubist' form of the colonnade shows affinities with earlier South Arabian architecture, which again suggests an ancient Semitic origin for the Syrian love of colonnades.

Graeco-Roman architecture

Many of the great cities of the Roman East were founded by the Greeks: Antioch, Laodicea (Latakia), Apamea, Gerasa (Jerash in Jordan). Many others were re-founded and given a Hellenistic 'gloss':

Aleppo, Damascus, Hama. However, there is virtually nothing to be seen of Greek architecture in these cities, mainly because they were heavily overlain in Roman times. With virtually the sole exception of Beirut, no new cities were founded by the Romans, and the Roman period was largely one of consolidation upon the foundations laid down by the Greeks.

Traces of the Greek foundation of these cities can be seen in their layout: the Greek town planners imposed a rigid grid system on the towns and cities of Syria (figures 5, 12, 29). This contrasted sharply with the more haphazard, organic layouts of traditional Near Eastern cities, a pattern dictated by the immensely long period of growth and continuity that lay behind them. This essential grid pattern, dominated by a central temple complex of the town's guardian deity, characterised all of the cities the Greeks founded, from Antioch in Syria to Ai Khanum in Central Asia. It survives to this day in much of the street plan of the Old City of Damascus, with many of its streets still in the same position first laid out by Greek engineers (figure 2).

The first important monuments of Roman Syria were a number of temples built in the 1st century AD. These were dedicated to gods that were usually pre-classical Semitic deities, located at places that were already sacred to their cults and merely equated with Greek and Roman gods. It was in the 2nd and 3rd centuries AD, however, that the architecture of Roman Syria reached its peak. Not only the great temples and cities, but even small country towns were embellished on a massive scale. This was partly a result of the great wealth generated by Syria – brought about as much by its control of the lucrative trade routes as by the centuries of stability enjoyed under the Pax Romana – and partly by the rise to power of Syrian families in Rome itself. Such families were able to bring the full weight of the Empire to bear when they endowed the country of their birth (figures 8, 9, plate 16).

The Roman remains in Syria – and one includes Palmyra as 'Roman' from the architectural point of view – are amongst the most spectacular anywhere in the Roman world. When viewed at first the Western visitor feels immediately at home amongst familiar architectural forms: columned porticos, Corinthian capitals, and standard systems of architectural layout and decorative treatment that have dominated Western architecture from the time of the Romans down to the late 19th century. In other words, the architecture appears entirely – almost overbearingly – Roman; a foreign transplant that has more in common with Italy than with the ancient Near East in which Syrian civilization is rooted. But what appears at first sight so Roman, so familiar, becomes on examination more Syrian, more Oriental and alien, with Roman forms merely a veneer over predominantly Syrian architectural forms, as native Syrian elements began to reassert themselves.

The colonnaded streets, for example, that most characteristic feature of the Roman cities of the East that march so dramatically across the ruin-fields of Syria, seem to proclaim the domination of Roman civilization over Syrian in no uncertain terms (plates 27, 85). But they had details that were very un-Roman. At Apamea they were often fluted in spirals (plate 29) – a very unusual feature – and columns throughout Syria were usually on high pedestals, generally an eastern feature. The columns too often carried brackets to hold statues, such as at Apamea and – most famously – at Palmyra (plates 92, 94). But as well as such details, the concept of the colonnaded street itself was quite un-Roman: no colonnaded streets are found in the Roman homeland in Italy, or even in Greece, the origin of so many Roman architectural ideas. They are found only in the Roman cities of Asia. The reasons for this are disputed, but it is possible that the colonnaded street can be linked to the 'Eastern' concept of the bazaar or street market. In the West the forum served the function of the marketplace, but in the East (which has few forums) its function is replaced by the colonnaded street or street bazaar, merely being given a Roman 'veneer' as it became expressed in Roman monumental terms.

Another purely Eastern architectural concept is that of the vast temple enclosure, or temenos, that takes up whole quarters of the town plans of the Roman East (figure 32, plates 37, 86). These too have their origins in ancient Near Eastern traditions as we have seen. Much of the emphasis on open spaces was linked to the place of altars in Syrian architecture. They were usually situated outside in the middle of the temenos opposite the sanctuary entrance – indeed, often forming as much a focal point to the temple complex as the sanctuary itself. This was for mass participation in the worship of the deity – hence the vast sizes that so many of the temple enclosures reached. In addition, many of the temples had tower altars as well, either incorporated into the sactuary roof or in towers in the temenos wall. This has no counterpart in Roman architecture, but is related to the ancient Semitic religious use of high places of worship. Such was the Semitic predilection for sacred high places that they later became almost the main universal feature of Islamic religious architecture: the minaret. Indeed, the first minarets of Islam were the corner-towers of the temenos of the Jupiter-Haddad Temple at Damascus.

It was not just in the exteriors of the temple complexes that Syrian architectural forms re-asserted themselves. The interiors were quite different from Roman temples found in the West. Sanctuaries were dominated by a raised platform at one (or occasionally at either) end, usually approached by a flight of stairs covered by a canopy, often receiving particularly elaborate decoration. For interiors were the throne room of the deity and platforms his throne where he received his worshippers in audience, unlike the simpler interiors of Greek or Roman temples which were merely rooms to house his image.

Roman architectural decoration, highly formalized in the West and following a rigid set of formulae to the point of severity, becomes in Syria something far more relaxed, where the rules are often discarded and the natural Syrian love of flamboyance and elaboration allowed free rein. This more exuberant form of Roman architecture is often described as 'Roman baroque'. The most distinctive Syrian features of Roman baroque are the ubiquitous statue brackets on the columns of Palmyra and Apamea (plates 30, 94), and a decorative feature known as the 'Syrian niche'. This is a niche set into a wall – often to house a statue – framed by a pair of engaged colonnettes supporting a miniature pediment (plate 87). They were used to great – and elaborate – effect to decorate long facades.

Whereas the architecture of the Roman West is characterised by the increasing use of rounded forms and of brick and concrete building materials, in the East stone remained the main building material throughout, particularly in the use of the traditional column-and-lintel style. Indeed, many of the great trabeated – column-and-lintel – stone buildings in Rome itself seem to have been built with the help of craftsmen from Syria. The Syrian preference for trabeated architecture and its development on a massive, civic scale (such as the colonnaded streets) might have its roots in traditional Semitic architectural concepts, with its preferences for square, almost cubist forms. The origins of this concept can be seen in the Phoenician temple enclosure at Amrit (plate 36) or South Arabian architecture, as well as the religious iconography of the 'god block' at Petra that culminated in the Ka'bah of Mecca.

It is not just the great urban ruins and immense religious monuments that make the Roman period remains in Syria so memorable. In Syria we can walk into the small towns and the very houses where the people lived as well, for they are in a remarkable state of preservation (figure 26). In the Hauran, in southern Syria, for example, one can find the small country towns, the villages, the farm houses, and all the trappings of a prosperous, albeit little known, corner of the Empire. In the towns of Shahba, Bosra, Qanawat, and any one of the dozens of Roman sites scattered through the Hauran there are very few other places where one can get such a feeling of everyday life in Roman times: one can wander along paved streets still bearing the impressions of cartwheels, past shops, across courtyards, into houses, peering into ruins which were once kitchens, stables, servants quarters and master bedrooms. With the noise of everyday life of the Druze and Arab communities forming a living background, the past comes alive as it rarely does in the dusty ruins of Asia (plates 11, 16, 17).

1 General view of Damascus towards Qasyun Hill

2 The courtyard and facade of the sanctuary of the Umayyad Mosque

i

3 The mosaics on the 'treasury' and arcades of the Umayyad Mosque

4 Detail of the mosaics over the prayer hall of the Umayyad Mosque

5 Courtyard of the Umayyad Mosque

6 Stone inlay inside the east entrance of the Umayyad Mosque

7 Courtyard of the Azem Palace

8 The reconstructed facade of Qasr al-Hair forming the main entrance of the National Museum

9 The black basalt of the Hauran

10 Typical landscape of the Hauran, near Hit

Syria

11 Part of the Cardo at Bosra

12 The auditorium of the theatre at Bosra

13 The upper colonnade of the theatre at Bosra

14 Courtyard of the 'Seraglio' at Qanawat

15 Fragment of the temple at Slim

16 The Decumanus at Shahba

17 Roman house at Inkhil

18 The ramparts of Qatna

19 Krak des Chevaliers from the West

20 The upper courtyard over the main magazine at Krak des Chevaliers

21 Facade of the Great Hall of Krak des Chevaliers

22 View over the plain towards the northeast from the battlements of Krak des Chevaliers

23 The waterwheels of Hama

24 The castle at Misyaf

25 The castle of Shaizar from the north

26 The castle of Mudiq with the Orontes Valley in the background

27 Apamea from Mudiq Castle

28 The Cardo Maximus of Apamea

29 Detail of the spiral columns along the Cardo at Apamea

30 A monumental
column marking the
intersection of two
colonnaded streets at
Apamea

31 Qasr Ibn Wardan, with the Barracks in the foreground, the Church on the left, the Palace on the right, and the desert beyond

32 Inscription over the entrance to the Palace at Qasr Ibn Wardan, showing the construction

Little has been said so far of the most spectacular set of Roman ruins in Syria, if not in the world: Palmyra (figure 32). In many ways, despite its Roman Imperial overlay, Palmyrene art and architecture can be described as the most quintessentially Syrian: its love of flamboyance, the avenues of columns, the temple enclosure as big as a stadium. The monuments are described in more detail in Chapter 11, but mention must be made here of the most notable feature of Palmyrene architecture that has no parallel with the Roman architecture of the West: the tower tombs. These strange monuments provide one of the vividest memories of Palmyra. Long after one has left Syria when memories of the great temples and theatres, the colonnaded streets, the vast courtyards have all begin to dim, it is these least Roman of Syria's Roman past that one is left with. The haunting memory of those stark tomb towers standing in the desert behind Palmyra remains one's most enduring image of Syria's architectural heritage (plate 96).

Byzantine architecture

It is worth examining Byzantine architecture at some length because so much of it is in Syria. Byzantine architecture is overwhelmingly a Christian architecture. For whilst secular architecture naturally existed (and nowhere more so in Syria, where entire Byzantine towns are in a remarkable state of preservation), the religious architecture predominates over all others.

There are a number of reasons for this. The Byzantine period was, as we have seen, an ecclesiastical age above all, with all the arrogance of a newfound religion adopted as the state religion of the world's greatest power. Little wonder it left so many buildings behind to remind us of this. Apart from religious architecture, the Byzantine period is not marked by the need for new types of public buildings, styles of architecture or even administrative centres and towns: Roman Syria merely continued.

Yet there is a subtle but significant change in tone between Roman and Byzantine architecture. Roman architecture has a grandeur – a scale and massiveness – that Byzantine architecture, for all its newfound religious certainties, never even approaches (except in Constantinople itself). Roman architecture – the great temple complexes, the ordered streets, the massive baths, the forests of columns – states an arrogant self-confidence, an unquestioning belief in the superiority of its own culture in a way that Byzantine architecture cannot match. For whilst the religion that gave Byzantine civilization its definition was new, the culture itself, that of Rome, was a tired one, a culture that had long since begun its decline. Hence, Byzantine churches never matched the great temples of the Roman period; they were not as big, not as grand. Even much of the building materials they used were second-hand, taken from the earlier Roman buildings; construction was often second-rate, even shoddy.

There is a further difference, subtle but again important. Underneath the Roman architectural veneer, native Semitic and Syrian forms come through, as we have already seen. But in Byzantine architecture, these elements seem to disappear once more. The bold, probably native, trabeate forms that feature so prominently in the architecture of the Roman East give way to the very un-Syrian, rounded arceate forms of Byzantine church architecture, and the great open spaces of the Romano-Syrian temple complexes give way to the equally un-Syrian enclosed, internal spaces of the Byzantine basilicas. Despite the Syrian origins of the religion, the architecture of Christianity seems to lie uneasily beneath Syrian skies.

The reasons for this apparent paradox probably lie in the nature of Christianity and Christendom itself. Paganism by its very nature could allow for many alien beliefs: Roman gods were simply equated with native Syrian ones, and Roman architectural vocabulary could co-exist with Syrian architectural concepts quite harmoniously. But the monotheistic nature of Christianity was by definition far more exclusive: other religions – and religious forms – could not be embraced. With the adoption of Christianity by the Roman emperors, the capital of Christendom would no longer be Jerusalem or even Damascus or Antioch, but Rome and Constantinople. It then followed that the architectural forms of Christendom emanated from Rome and Constantinople as well, particularly with the adoption of the Roman basilical form as the main architectural expression of Christianity. Whilst the religion itself may have been Oriental, its architecture was overwhelmingly Roman.

For before its adoption as the official religion of the empire, Christianity had virtually no architecture. In its earliest years, Christianity was, at best, a private religion, and at worst a savagely suppressed one. Hence, the very first 'churches' were nothing more than private houses, being simply meeting places for members of a Christian community. A little later on, when Christian architecture became more formalized, the first churches were almost indistinguishable from private houses. Indeed, the world's very first definitely identified church has been found in Syria: not in the holy places of Palestine or even the urban centres of Damascus and Antioch where one might expect, but in the rather provincial, desert frontier town of Dura Europos on the Euphrates (figure 30). This church is dated 231 AD and follows almost exactly the form of the ordinary houses of the time.

It was this demand for a meeting place – a congregation – that first shaped the more monumental forms of Christian architecture. Pagan temples – at least at first – could not be converted to Christian places of worship. Apart from the natural abhorrence the first Christians would have felt for the temples of their oppressors, there would have been an immense resistance from the still strong pagan establishment, even after Christianity was made the official religion. But more importantly, the demands of a pagan temple were quite different to those of a Christian church: a temple was merely the earthly house of a god, requiring only a cella to house the image and associated ritual functions, but a church had to be an assembly room for the congregation, a place where the entire community could meet and worship, therefore requiring far more space than most temples. The only public building in Roman cities that met this requirement was the basilica, a secular assembly room for public and government meetings, usually located next to a forum or market place. In some places, these pre-Christian Roman basilicas achieved massive proportions the size of a cathedral and more modest sized ones survive in Syria at Bosra and some of the Dead Cities of the north. The basilical form then became the standard, virtually universal form of Christian religious architecture.

The form of these Christian basilicas adhered to a fairly strict layout with little variation. Thus, the 'standard' basilica consisted of a nave flanked by two aisles with an apse facing east at one end and an entrance room or narthex at the other (figures 24, 28). Outside the entrance there would usually be a small courtyard or atrium – a far cry from the great temple enclosures of an earlier age – and the interior would often be lit by clerestory windows, formed by the greater height of the nave above its flanking aisles. This basic layout formed the standard pattern of churches for many hundreds of years, in some cases – particularly in the East – to this day.

But these 'rules' only became set in about the 4th century. Before that the earliest basilicas did not adhere so rigidly to these forms, and displayed a refreshing experimentation. Naves could be single or double, divided down the centre or undivided; they could be aisle-less or could have four or more aisles; there could be two or even three apses, at either or both ends or even along the sides; orientation could be north, east or west, and so forth. But the Church, as soon as it became established, seemed to impose as rigid an interpretation on its architectural forms as it did on its dogma, so that by the end of the 4th century most churches followed the same general pattern, with even cathedrals differing from small country churches only in scale. The basilica assumed its conventional form, subject only to minor local variations, largely dictated by liturgical custom (plates 33, 54, 66, 69, 82).

Most Byzantine churches in Syria adhere to this pattern (though very often the narthex is left out, especially in the north, where the entrance is often in the long southern wall instead of directly into the aisle). Little wonder that the Byzantine architecture of Syria suffers from an overall sameness after the Roman.

There was, however, another type of religious building in the Christian East less staid than the basilica: the martyrium. With the founder of the religion Himself being martyred – not to mention the innumerable subsequent martyrdoms during the Roman persecutions – buildings commemorating martyrdom naturally assumed considerable importance as a separate type. In architectural and functional terms, this represented an entirely new departure that, unlike the demand for meeting halls and the evolution of the basilica, had no precedents in either the secular or religious architecture of the pagan past: entirely new forms had to be developed. Hence, the martyria are often architecturally far more refreshing than the basilicas, representing more new ideas and experimentation. Since they represented a particular holy spot, rather than merely a convenient area for the faithful to assemble, the place itself becomes the focal point of the architecture, i.e., martyria usually followed a central plan. Such a central plan allowed for far greater innovation. In the end, this central plan was adopted for many churches and cathedrals as well, providing a welcome variation on the more conventional basilical theme. They were often – indeed usually – domed, which in itself called for the development of new concepts and techniques culminating in the immense domed structures of Constantinople. Plans could be a simple circle, or more elaborate variations: octagonal, quatrefoil, square, or even combinations of all three. The quatrefoil plan became especially popular in 6th century, and survive at Bosra, Ezra'a, Apamea, Aleppo (the Madrasa Halawiya), and Resafeh. Combinations were particularly popular: inner and outer octagons such as St George's at Ezra'a (figure 10) have exedrae on four sides of the outer octagon to give a quatrefoil impression; the cathedral at Bosra has an inner octagonal colonnade in an outer circular plan with four exedrae to provide a quatrefoil, the whole encased in a square structure; the Church of St Simeon Stylites is based on an octagon (probably domed) in a square with small exedrae at each corner to form a quatrefoil, which in turn is surrounded by four basilicas to form an immense cross (figure 23). The tradition of inner and outer central plans in Syrian Christian architecture might have been related ultimately to the ritual circumambulatories common to much of Asian religious architecture. The tradition continued into the Islamic period: the circle-in-octagon plan of the 8th century Dome of the Rock in Jerusalem is directly inspired by the martyria plans of Byzantine architecture in Syria.

In leafing through the many books on Byzantine architecture there is an overwhelming preponderance of churches, and the reader receives the impression that Byzantine architecture was almost solely religious. It was, it is true, an immensely ecclesiastical age, but whilst by no means denigrating the importance of religious architecture in Byzantine civilization, its preponderance has tended to obscure the importance of domestic, civil, military and funerary architecture as well. Nowhere is this imbalance more apparent than in Syria where whole cities have survived from the Byzantine period.

If the religious architecture of the Byzantine period sometimes suffers from an overriding sameness, the domestic architecture shows a refreshing variety, particularly because there is so much to see: the Hauran, the Dead Cities of the north, the desert areas to the east. One can still walk along the streets, into the markets, through villas, taverns, houses, stables, barns and shops much as the original inhabitants left them over a thousand years ago (figure 26, plates 74, 75). This domestic architecture, however, shows considerable regional variety, so is discussed in more detail in the regions they occur, particularly the Hauran (Chapter 4) and the Dead Cities (Chapter 9) below.

Byzantine military architecture leaves no less a mark on Syria's landscape than its religious, particularly in the 6th century when the threats from the east became more pressing. Many – probably most – of the great Crusader fortresses were built on sites already fortified in the Byzantine period. Indeed, they often incorporate earlier Byzantine fortifications in them – at Qal'at Salahuddin (Saladin Castle, Sahyun), for example, the Byzantine sections of the castle form some of its main defences (figure 20) – and Crusader military architecture owes more to Byzantine Syrian traditions than it does to European. But the Byzantine architecture in the Crusader castles is heavily obscured by later overbuilding; to see more intact examples one must go eastwards to the immense Byzantine fortresses of the desert frontier, such as Resafeh and Halebiye (figures 27 and 29).

Byzantine military architecture is often seen as a European tradition, emanating from Constantinople. It is certainly true that the city walls of Justinian at Constantinople itself are the greatest in the ancient world, and Qasr Ibn Wardan and Halebiye may have been built by architects from the capital. But there is equally no doubt that such architects would have found in Syria a highly developed and immensely ancient tradition of building great fortifications in stone. The great urban fortifications of Resafeh and Halebiye – and perhaps even Constantinople as well – may be seen, therefore, as the architectural link between the ancient Syrian urban fortifications of Qatna and Ebla and the later great fortresses of the Crusaders.

45

If religious and military forms of building make the architecture of Byzantine Syria very homogeneous, the funerary architecture was far more idiosyncratic, and we see an immense variety of tombs surviving, particularly in the north. Columns in the classical style were popular, either in pairs or as a tetrapylon, as were pyramids in the more Semitic style (plates 70, 71). Often the latter would sit on top of the tetrapylon, forming a very curious stylistic hybrid. Domes were also fairly common, again occasionally capping a tetrapylon, reminiscent of the *chahartaqs* (domed four-way arches) so popular in Persian architecture, whilst gabled mausolea sitting on the tops of high plinths are reminiscent of Anatolian forms. Simple rock-cut tombs and facades were also extremely popular, part of a Semitic tradition that previously reached its height in the great rock-cut tombs of the Nabateans. In life, the Byzantine church imposed a rigid sameness to the religious architecture of Syria, but in death the immense variety of forms and styles of the funerary architecture reflected Middle Eastern civilization as a whole and the cosmopolitan nature of the inhabitants of Syria in particular.

Islamic architecture

Many of the basic principles of Islamic architecture apply not just to Syria but to the entire Islamic world. Hence, a mosque – in basic design – will be much the same in either Damascus or Delhi, Baghdad or Bukhara, and adhere to much the same pattern from the 7th century to the 20th. All religious architecture is, of course, subject to certain overall rules, but Islamic architecture, like the religion it embodies, is more universal than most. Any mosque, for example, from whatever period or place, comprises certain basic elements: it faces Mecca; it contains a *mihrab*, or prayer niche (plate 55), in the centre of the *qibla* wall, the wall oriented towards Mecca, to indicate the direction of prayer; it has a minaret, or some sort of elevated position outside, from where the call to prayer can be made; it contains an ablution area where ritual washing before prayer can be carried out (plate 51); and the floors are covered since praying involves touching the floor with one's forehead. To these elements can be added several more features which, whilst not necessarily universal, are now usually taken to be essential to mosque architecture: the *minbar*, or pulpit from which the imam addresses the congregation, to be found to one side of the *mihrab*; a courtyard for open air gatherings (plates 2, 51); and an indoor sanctuary area immediately in front of the *qibla* wall, often with a dome in front of the *mihrab* to provide further emphasis. These basic elements can be found everywhere in Islamic architecture.

Having recognized the essential unity of Islamic architecture, it would be folly to ignore its immense regional, chronological and cultural diversity as well. A minaret, for example, whilst essential to all mosques, may be anything from a simple megaphone affixed to a pole to the slim, pencil-like spires of the minarets of Istanbul or the elaborately decorated towers of Isfahan; a *mihrab* may be completely unadorned or be completely covered in elaborate inlay, tilework, painting, stucco, or carved brickwork depicting abstract designs and verses from the Koran; floor covering may be simple rush mattings or valuable carpets.

The mosque is the most universal element in Islamic architecture, but Islam has given rise to a number of other religious monuments as well. Chief amongst these is the *madrasa*, or Koranic school, the development of which figured largely in Syria. There are also tombs which, though abjured by Islam (which frowns upon any glorification of the dead or the marking of burials apart from plain, uninscribed stones), is one of the most famous features of Islamic architecture, from whole 'cities' of the dead in Egypt to immense mausolea such as the Taj Mahal.

Whilst not necessarily religious, there are a number of other buildings in Islam that are often directly related to mosques, mainly because they are financed by religious endowments. Included in this may be hospitals, libraries, charitable kitchens, drinking fountains and mental asylums. In the later periods, especially under the Ottomans, these might form parts of a large single complex that includes a mosque, religious school and tomb of its endower as well.

In secular architecture, Islam naturally boasts as wide a range as any other civilization. Thus, houses, palaces, bridges, fortifications and whole planned cities form as much a part of Islamic architecture as mosques do. But in concept, such architecture is not unique to Islamic civilization. A medieval Arab castle for example, hardly differs from one built by the Crusaders; the main difference between a Muslim house in Damascus and a Christian one is its location; and whilst an Islamic palace might differ from its Western counterpart in the divisions into public and private quarters, the difference is social rather than religious. The differences between a mosque and a church, however, are fundamental. For this reason, more emphasis is placed here on religious architecture than secular.

There are two categories of Islamic architecture, however, which, though not related to religious purposes are nonetheless found mainly in Islamic countries. These are the *hammam*, or public bath, and the *khan*, or caravanserai. The origins of the public bath in the Middle East owes much to the popularity of them in Roman and Byzantine times, and indeed much of the design and layout is based on Roman prototypes. But the demand in Islam for ritual cleaning before prayer, as well as the endowment of public works for the common good practised in Islam, at least ensured that public baths continued to play a very important part in society after Islam. Like the Roman baths before them, these often reached highly elaborate and monumental proportions. The caravanserai on the other hand, cannot be related to Islamic religious practice even indirectly, not do they occur in Western architecture. Caravanserais are merely a direct product of the great land routes across Asia, used to house and distribute both the goods brought by the trade and the traders themselves who brought them. A caravanserai would often be nothing more than a simple walled enclosure or compound, but with the great wealth they generated, they could just as easily be great monumental structures subject almost to as much elaboration and decoration as a palace (plates 49, 50).

There are two more 'universals' that Islamic architecture was subject to. The first concerns the use of the courtyard. This is almost an essential feature in the layout of any Islamic building: mosques, *madrasas*, houses, palaces, caravanserais (plates 2, 58). With the mosque, it derives from the very first mosque, which was the Prophet Muhammad's own house in Medina, a conventional courtyard house like most in the Middle East. Indeed, the use of open spaces has a very long history in the Near East as we have seen, especially in religious architecture; when mosques ceased being 'external places' as they were under the Arabs and became 'internal places' comprising the vast roofed areas they became under the Ottomans, a courtyard would still usually be added, even when not strictly necessary. A palace, such as the Azem Palace in Damascus, would revolve around a courtyard or series of courtyards (plate 7), much as a house functions though on a larger scale. Hospitals, charitable kitchens, schools, shrines, tomb complexes and caravanserais were similarly based on a courtyard principle.

The second concerns decoration. Islam forbids human and animal representation to prohibit the worship of graven images (though as in the erection of tombs, this rule was often flouted). This has meant that Islamic art and architectural decoration has excelled in the abstract, displaying an infinite variety of geometric and floriated patterns (plates 3, 4, 49, 55). It has also meant that the art of calligraphy has received greater prominence.

Crusader architecture

Chronologically – and to a large extent stylistically – Crusader architecture overlaps with Arab architecture: differences between a Crusader castle and an Arab castle of the same period are minimal.

They do, however, figure very largely in the Western mind and are one of the main attractions in Syria, so are treated separately here.

Crusader castles never occur in isolation, but are intimately connected to the landscape surrounding them: routes, rivers, passes, anchorages, heights, and all the general dictates of strategic planning. For they were above all else military strongholds imposed by outsiders. Hence, they almost never occur in towns and cities, but are usually a feature of their hinterlands, of the countryside they were attempting to control and the military positions (mainly on the coast) that they were attempting to defend (plates 22, 35, 39, 42).

The First Crusade gathered in the late 11th century beneath the walls of Constantinople; its first successful capture was the walled city of Nicaea on the Anatolian mainland. Both Constantinople and Nicaea had massive Byzantine fortifications; there was nothing remotely like them anywhere in Europe. With nothing more sophisticated in the way of military architecture than the simple keeps of the Normans – which were sometimes of wood – the Crusaders had never seen anything like these massive urban fortifications of the East.

The earliest Crusader castles, therefore, such as Safita, resembled the Norman multi-storeyed tower or keep, such as those found in England and France, rather than the more sophisticated Byzantine and Arab fortifications they encountered in Syria (plate 35). When these older fortresses were captured, the Crusaders simply took them over – but they were quick to learn. Not having vast armies of engineers and stonemasons with them, the Crusaders relied almost entirely upon the local artisans, who naturally built what they were already familiar with. They were able to draw upon a strong local tradition of military architecture already thousands of years old. Combining these Syrian traditions with the new demands made by the Franks with their Norman architectural traditions, a 'Crusader architecture' was beginning to emerge.

In the heady years of the First Crusade, these castles were essentially offensive in nature: built as strongholds from which to attack the Saracen, or to guard trade and pilgrimage routes. They were dominated by the donjon, or fortified tower of Norman tradition, but little is known of the early forms of these castles because they were usually extensively altered in 12th and 13th century rebuilding. The main thrust of Crusader building activity at this time in any case consisted simply in modifying existing fortifications that they took over. Towers and buttresses were usually square (plate 39), continuing the design widespread under Byzantine military architecture, with circular buttresses generally becoming more widespread later (plate 19).

With the Arabs more on the offensive under the Nurids and then

Saladin after the middle of the 12th century, the Crusader castles became increasingly defensive. There was a spurt in building activity, mainly in strengthening and re-fortifying existing positions, with many of the Crusader castles becoming massive strongholds built to contain large forces, large stores, and withstand long sieges. The most famous of all, Krak des Chevaliers, was built at this time by the Knights Hospitallers (figure 11, plate 19).

Crusader architecture reached its height during the Third Crusade in the 13th century. They were usually elaborate defensive systems consisting of several lines of walls, ditches and outworks, with heavily defended gateways (figures 11, 15, 18). Harbour defences – generally the Crusaders' lifeline to the West – were specially well provided, often with harbour forts or towers at the end of moles, from which the harbour entrance could be closed off by chains. In addition, new defensive techniques were built into fortifications as protection against bombardment, scaling or sapping: tapering walls and glacis to limit access, columns within walls to bond the wall-face well back to its core, increased use of semi-circular (as opposed to square) buttressing for added strength. The latter, round buttressing, is often seen as Armenian influence; indeed much of the work – on both sides – may have been undertaken by Armenian craftsmen, whose reputation in the mastery of stone masonry spread all over the Near East. Loopholes, often in several tiers, would be carefully positioned to allow for overlapping fire covering all directions. In addition, a new Arab innovation (though its origins lay in the Byzantine architecture of north Syria) came into widespread use: machicolations, or projecting galleries. These highly decorative additions at the top of battlements or over weak areas, such as gateways, were devastatingly effective in preventing any attacker from getting close to the foot of the walls (plate 47).

Gateways came in for particularly careful attention, drawing upon a tradition of well defended gateway architecture that we have already seen in the ancient walled cities such as Ebla. The bent entrance, such as at Krak des Chevaliers and Aleppo, became almost universally adopted, preventing any attacker from being able to bear directly upon a gate. They would in addition be surrounded with elaborate systems of guard towers, multiple barriers, overlooking galleries and multiple hazards (figure 20, plates 40, 46, 47). So effective were the gateways that they became the strongest part of most fortifications, with attackers rarely even attempting them but concentrating instead on piercing curtain walls – few fortresses were taken by direct storming of a gateway. Even when a defensive system fell, there would often be a second or even a third inner system of fortifications upon which the defenders could fall back upon – again, Krak des Chevaliers is a good example of the double, completely independent defensive system (figure 11).

With so much effort expended simply upon maintaining their precarious hold on Syria and the Holy Land, there was little left over for non-military building and any embellishments that did not have a direct military purpose. Hence, the few differences between Christian and Muslim military architecture: stern military function overruled religious differences when it came to building. The only uniquely Crusader features were their religious architecture – and there is very little of that, despite religion being the ostensible reason for their presence in the Near East. Most castles contained a chapel, with almost intact examples surviving at Krak des Chevaliers and Marqab, but with the exception of Safita, such chapels were usually very subordinate to the predominantly military function of the castles. Outside Jerusalem, about the only religious building that was not a strict adjunct to military architecture was the cathedral of Tortosa (modern Tartus). Unlike the castles, here the Western European influence is instantly recognisable, fitting in to the more familiar context of Late Romanesque and Gothic architecture, though the presence of Byzantine capitals and other decorative details betrays at least some local influence as well. The chapels of Marqab and Krak des Chevaliers also fit into the context of the Late Romanesque of France, though being essentially military chapels the architecture is naturally rather more severe than Tortosa.

Apart from Tortosa and other religious buildings, virtually the only place where decoration was added to the strict military demands of the architecture was in the 13th century great hall at Krak des Chevaliers. Here, the vaulted interior and the elaborate windows display a richness of ornament that is almost unique in the Crusader architecture of the Holy Land, but is entirely in keeping with French Gothic (plate 21).

CHAPTER 4

Damascus and Environs

History

D amascus claims to be the oldest city in the world – a claim that a pedant may certainly quibble with, but which ultimately can only be respected in view of its immense history. Its origins lie in remotest antiquity, and its development owes much to complex regional factors. But it is as a meeting place of many different caravan routes, one of the great market places of history and as Islam's first great capital, that Damascus is remembered. Already a great city when the Romans conquered it, the Romans made it their capital of Syria because of the trade routes it controlled. The famous 'Street Called Straight' of the Bible – its main market street – is a direct reference to the commercial activity for which Damascus was already famous, activities that reached new heights under the Umayyad caliphs in the first centuries of Islam. Even after the Arab capital moved to Baghdad, Damascus maintained its importance as a caravan city, mainly because of its links with the coast. Today, its miles of markets and bazaars make it one of the most colourful cities of the Middle East, and although no longer the terminus of an overland trading system, its markets are the survival of traditions thousands of years old.

Old, Damascus undoubtedly is. In an oasis as well-endowed by nature as Damascus, there were numerous prehistoric settlements taking advantage of the plentiful water supplied by the Barada River, such as the 5th millennium BC Chalcolithic settlement excavated at Salihiye or the 7th millennium Neolithic settlement at Ramad, both on

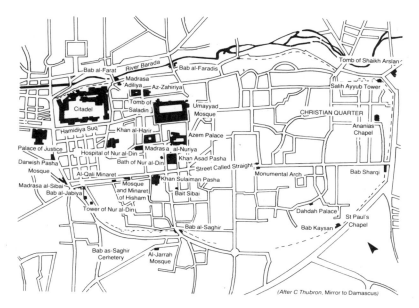

Tomb of Shaikh Arslan

Bab al-Farat · River Barada · Bab al-Faradis

Salih Ayyub Tower

Madrasa Adiliya — Az-Zahiriya

Tomb of Saladin

Citadel

Umayyad Mosque

CHRISTIAN QUARTER

Ananias Chapel

Hamidiya Suq · Khan al-Harir

Azem Palace

Palace of Justice · Hospital of Nur al-Din · Madrasa al-Nuriya

Darwish Pasha Mosque

Khan Asad Pasha

Bath of Nur al-Din

Street Called Straight

Monumental Arch

Bab Sharqi

Al-Qali Minaret

Madrasa al-Sibai

Mosque and Minaret of Hisham

Khan Sulaiman Pasha

Bab al-Jabiya

Bait Sibai

Tower of Nur al-Din

Dahdah Palace · St Paul's Chapel

Bab al-Saghir

Bab Kaysan

Bab as-Saghir Cemetery

Al-Jarrah Mosque

(After C Thubron, Mirror to Damascus)

Fig. 2 The Old City of Damascus

the outskirts of the city. In legend, Damascus was supposedly founded by one of the grandsons of Noah, but the first written testimonies to a town in this locality are in the Ebla texts of the 3rd millennium and Egyptian texts of about 1500 BC, which refer to it as Dimeshq (virtually identical to the modern Arabic version of the name: Dimashq). There are subsequent references to Damascus in Assyrian annals and in the Old Testament. But it was in the Aramaean period of the early 1st millennium BC that Damascus first emerged as a regional centre, as the capital of Aram, one of the more important Aramaean city-states. Damascus has maintained this status ever since, though no standing remains from this period exist today.

Following the conquest of all the Syrian city-states by the Assyrians, then by the Babylonians and Achaemenid Persians, Damascus was not to emerge with any independence again until the Seleucid period in the 2nd and 1st centuries BC, when it formed part of a loose federation of semi-independent city-states based in southern Syria known as the Decapolis. It came briefly under Nabatean hegemony in the 1st century BC, ruled from Bosra, when it does not appear to have had much importance, but following the Roman conquest in 64 BC, its naturally pre-eminent role was recognized by Hadrian, who elevated it to the status of metropolis. It was further elevated to the status of Roman colony by Septimus Severus.

Damascus played a very significant part in early Christian history, for it was outside Damascus that a little known Jew, Saul of Tarsus, whilst on his way to persecute the Christians of Jerusalem was miraculously converted to Christianity. Saul became the Apostle St Paul, joining the Christian community in Damascus. After several years preaching elsewhere in the Near East, he returned to Damascus only to narrowly escape persecution by being lowered over the city walls in a basket. These events were some of the most important in early Christianity. For in the highly cosmopolitan climate of Hellenistic and Roman Damascus, Paul was able to transform Christianity from its purely Judaean background to something far more palatable to the Romans and, by escaping, was able to take Christianity to Rome. Whilst it was Jesus who inspired Christianity, it was St Paul who really founded Christendom; it may have been at Jerusalem that Christianity was born, but it was at Damascus that it begun to take shape.

It was certainly a 'Christian era' that followed for Damascus – and for Syria as a whole. It became the seat of a bishopric, second only to Antioch, and innumerable churches were built, the most famous being the Basilica of John the Baptist built on the site of the Temple of Jupiter-Haddad, and convents and monasteries sprung up in and around Damascus, some still surviving today.

But it was also Damascus that was the first city to open its gates to the advancing Muslims in 635. It was an astute move by the Damascenes, for although it was subsequently reoccupied briefly by the Byzantines, it transformed Damascus from a provincial city ruled from distant Constantinople to the first city of the triumphant new religion; it became Islam's first capital after Medina. Whilst Mecca was the spiritual centre of Islam, in the easy-going, cosmopolitan atmosphere of Damascus Islam came of age – repeating much the same role it played in the formation of Christianity. Religion, it seems, requires a strong brush of the profane to make it work.

And from Damascus, Islam spread throughout the known world. It was a new glittering age for Damascus and the Damascenes, made wealthy not only by the resources of an immense empire, but – perhaps more importantly – by the control of the caravan routes which terminated at Damascus. Even after the capital of the Islamic world moved to Baghdad, it was Damascus' position midway between the Mediterranean in the west and the deserts to the east that maintained its importance as a caravan city. It also ensured its survival, when so many other cities similarly deprived of their central status declined into small provincial towns or vanished altogether. Thus, there was always wealth in Damascus to continue embellishing its public buildings, even after the collapse of the Umayyad dynasty. The Seljuks, who took Damascus in 1076, endowed several new *madrasas*. Under the Nurids, however, most of the new building work needed to be concentrated on fortifications – an unsuccessful Crusader attack was fought off in 1154.

But it was from the times when Damascus became a capital again that most of Damascus' monuments date, though never on the scale that it was under the Umayyads. It became a capital city under Saladin and the Ayyubid dynasty in the 12th and 13th centuries, and it was the capital of Mamluk Syria again from the 13th to the 16th centuries, which once more saw a great spate of building. Whilst the devastations of the Mongol and Timurid armies in the 13th and 15th centuries destroyed so much of this building, Damascus always rose again and monuments were rebuilt.

Perhaps the best place to view Damascus is from the top of Qasyun Hill overlooking the city (plate 1). The best time is evening, just before sunset. There are many cafes where one may enjoy refreshment and a stunning view over the entire oasis. The desert still shimmers in the distance under the setting sun, and closer to the city barren hills rise out of the oasis providing a spectacular amphitheatre with Damascus as its stage. It is a large city now that covers the entire plain, but the main features that have made Damascus legendary still stand out easily: the fertile green belt – the famous *ghouta* – surrounding the city, the Barada River that has provided this fertility, the old walled town at the centre still dominated by the roofs of the Umayyad Mosque. The sounds of the city drift up from below, providing a muted background hum that mingles with the cries of the birds in the surrounding hills. All of a sudden, these sounds stop – even the birds seem to fall silent – and an air of hushed expectancy falls over the city. Then at an invisible signal, the call to prayer comes up from the Umayyad Mosque, a call that is quickly taken up by the hundreds of other mosques of Damascus and reverberates across the oasis. For the traveller, it is the high point of a visit to Syria, a moment when the magic of Damascus becomes truly alive, remaining in one's memory forever. It is the age-old sound of the Islamic East, the sound of a great Islamic city.

The Umayyad Mosque

It seems appropriate, therefore, to begin one's tour of Damascus with the Umayyad Mosque. It is not only Damascus' most outstanding monument, it is also one of the most outstanding monuments of Islam itself – and its first great mosque (figure 2, plates 2-6). The best time to

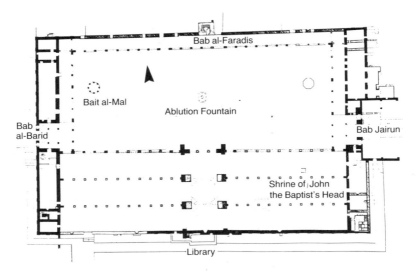

Fig. 3 The Umayad Mosque

visit is the morning before midday prayers; the afternoon is more taken up by times of prayer, when it is closed to non-worshippers. Mid-afternoon however, is the best time for photography, with the sun directly on the mosaics over the main facade (plate 4).

The mosque is set in the temenos of the Roman temple of Jupiter Damascenus, itself replacing – and largely incorporating – the earlier temple to Haddad (with whom the Romans equated Jupiter). It was built in the 1st century AD, though much of the enclosure wall we see today probably dates from the 3rd or 4th century. But it was already an ancient sacred site, as a 9th century BC basalt orthostat, probably belonging to the original Aramaean Temple of Haddad (now in the National Museum), was discovered during the course of restoration work in the northeastern corner of the temenos wall. The outer wall measures some 305 by 385 metres, built of fine ashlar blocks, with a square tower at each corner (though only the southwestern one remains). Each wall was originally pierced by Roman triple entrances. The one on the east, with a monumental propylaeum in front of it, was the main gate to the Roman temple and still forms the main entrance to the mosque today, known as the Bab Jairun. That on the west, the Bab al-Barid, is the one through which most visitors enter the mosque. It is also a Roman triple entrance, and outside one can still see the remains of the Roman propylaeum consisting of part of an elaborately decorated pediment resting on four Corinthian columns. The north entrance to the temenos, the Bab al-Faradis, is much later, but the south one is an original Roman triple entrance now walled up, with the *mihrab* of the mosque fitting into the western doorway.

The outer temenos walls are all that is left of the original Temple of Jupiter, apart from the Corinthian columns re-used in the construction of the mosque's arcades. The original temple proper would have been placed in the centre of the enclosure, much like the Temple of Bel at Palmyra or the Temple of Artemis at Jerash. This, however, was destroyed in the Byzantine period when the enclosure was used for a basilica dedicated to John the Baptist. Apart from a number of inscriptions (still preserved over the southern triple entrance), nothing remains of the Byzantine use of the temenos now, though a Byzantine colonnade can be seen outside by the north entrance. But the memory of the Byzantine use of the temenos is preserved with the shrine of John the Baptist's head inside the prayer hall, allegedly discovered in a crypt during the 8th century construction of the mosque.

The 'memory' of the Byzantine period can also be clearly seen in the architecture and decoration of the mosque itself. The Caliph al-Walid in 705 ordered the basilica of John the Baptist to be demolished to construct a mosque worthy of the first city of Islam. But the Muslims, lacking at the time sophisticated building skills themselves, employed Byzantine architects and craftsmen in its construction. Thus, a glance at the main facade of the sanctuary shows a clear dependence upon the forms of Byzantine church architecture (plate 2), whilst the magnificent mosaics that adorn the exterior walls belong to Byzantine decorative traditions. Indeed, such is the Byzantine style of the mosque that it was once thought to largely incorporate the Basilica of John the Baptist. This has now been disproved, mainly by the uniformity of the architecture which is clearly consistent with the proportions of a mosque rather than a basilica, so that what we see today is largely the work of the Caliph al-Walid in the early 8th century – the only building that still survives from Umayyad Damascus.

There are later elements as well. For the mosque underwent numerous alterations and rebuildings, the latest following a disastrous fire in 1893 when much was destroyed. Some of the arcades and all of the marble panelling in the sanctuary and inside the west entrance were rebuilt after that. The most conspicuous later additions are the three minarets. Those on the southwestern and southeastern (known as the Minaret of Jesus) corners date from 1488 and 1340 respectively, though the corner-towers they stand on were originally high places belonging to the Roman temenos. These corner towers formed the first minarets in Islam, thus forming a direct link between the ancient Semitic sacred high places and the new Semitic religion of Islam. The minaret in the middle of the north wall, known as the Bride Minaret, was built at the end of the 12th century. The ablution fountain in the centre of the courtyard is comparatively modern, as is the small cupola in the northeastern corner of the courtyard, but the curious octagonal domed structure in the northwestern corner belongs to the original mosque. This is known as the Treasury and is not usually found in mosque architecture, though its origins are uncertain – it may derive from the fountain that often stood in the courtyards of Byzantine churches.

But the sight which immediately greets one on entering the courtyard – especially in the afternoon sunlight – is the stunning array of gold and coloured mosaics that cover the facades and arcades (plates 3, 4). Although only fragments survive, it has been estimated that when completed in the 8th century it must have been the greatest surface of mosaic anywhere in the world. Even today, after the thousand years or so of warfare and turmoil that Damascus has experienced, these mosaics are an astonishing spectacle. They represent fantasy towns and rivers – which many see as Damascus itself and the Barada River – surrounded by a wealth of luxuriant foliage and stylized landscapes. Although this spectacular display represents the final flowering of Byzantine mosaic craftsmanship, it must be emphasized that nowhere are there any representations of human or animal figures, a distinctly un-Byzantine but firmly Islamic characteristic. Whilst these mosaics may be the last Byzantine work of art in Syria, they are equally the first Islamic.

Before entering the sanctuary itself, it is worth strolling around the arcades that border the other three sides of the courtyard. Not only does this enable one to appreciate the full effect of the mosaics and the space generally, it also allows one to observe the life of the mosque. It is always full of people, either solitary or in groups: families meeting to chat, individuals just resting in the shade of the arcades, having a nap, or, like oneself, simply taking in the surroundings (plates 2, 5). The Umayyad Mosque is very much a living building as well as ancient monument; it is built as much for man as for his God.

In addition to observing the life of the mosque, one arrives this way at the eastern entrance. Here can be found decoration – to my mind – even more astonishing than the mosaics. It is covered in a magnificent array of contrasting marble panels, all carefully cut and matched to provide a display of natural abstract patterns that few purely man-made patterns can match. Such a perfect blend of natural and man-made forms also make an appropriate entrance to the sanctuary itself (plate 6).

Inside one is dwarfed by the sheer massiveness of the building. Like a great cathedral, the roof and the dome soar above, held up by arcades of colossal re-used Byzantine columns supporting even more arcades on top of them. But the immense expanse of the sanctuary, with its forest of columns, give a sense of lateral space that a cathedral – with its emphasis more on verticality – never has. Furthermore, the acres of carpets that cover every inch of the floor provide a softness and warmth rarely felt in a church. But comparisons with cathedrals are perhaps out of place here, as well as unnecessary. For the Umayyad Mosque of Damascus is not only one of the first and greatest mosques of Islam, it is one of the greatest religious monuments of mankind.

The Azem Palace

This lies almost adjacent to the Umayyad Mosque, so is usually the place that most go to immediately afterwards. It is appropriate too, as it forms a complete contrast to the Umayyad Mosque: the one a religious monument, the other purely secular; the one built in the first years of Damascus' greatness, the other built in the last years of its decline. Sacred and profane, they symbolize the life of Damascus as much as they span its centuries. The Azem Palace also offers a peaceful escape from the bustle of the streets and bazaars that surround it (plate 7).

It was built in the middle of the 18th century by Asad Pasha al-Azem, the Ottoman governor of Damascus, and remained the seat of government for Syria until the end of the Ottoman period. Its buildings are of banded white limestone and black basalt, and it is a classic example of the later Islamic style of palace, divided into quarters of public reception and private retreat (the *selamlik* and *haremlik*) and surrounding an open area of courtyards, pools, running water and trees. It is these gardens that make it a lovely spot to retreat to from the noise and bustle of the streets, but it is worth examining the interiors as well, which have been made into a folklore museum. This museum not only portrays the everyday life of a Damascus now long gone, but also displays the different functions that comprised the palace and the life that was conducted in it. The interiors too are exquisitely decorated with traditional Damascene craftsmanship, which one can also see in the National Museum.

The Tomb of Saladin

This is the other monument that visitors often gravitate to from the Umayyad Mosque, as much for its associations as for its proximity. The Crusaders' greatest protagonist has always held a curious fascination for Westerners, not least for Kaiser Wilhelm II, who was drawn to it when he visited Damascus in 1898 and provided funds for its restoration – the only instance of an Islamic mausoleum being endowed by a Christian Emperor! Wilhelm found the original Ayyubid tomb neglected and abandoned – perhaps reflecting a curious ambivalence that Arabs too feel towards Saladin (who was, after all, not an Arab – but a Kurd). Be that as it may, the tomb is worth visiting, as much for its peaceful interior as its mixed Ayyubid, Ottoman and Hohenzollern architectural history.

The Citadel, city walls and gateways

Like all walled cities, the visitor is recommended to walk around the complete circuit of the walls to truly appreciate Damascus as a city (figure 2). For walls reflect the history of a city more than any other monument: the different architectural styles of its builders and rebuilders, the invasions that were held off and those that were not, the rulers that left their inscriptions above the gates and the people who leave their graffiti in more discreet places – the entire spectrum of the ups and downs of a great city that alternately stayed within and spilt beyond its walls. The walls of Damascus hold more than most.

The best place to start is the citadel. For many years it housed civil and military departments and was closed, but it is now undergoing extensive restoration with the aim of opening it to the public. It is a massive rectangular structure measuring 150 by 220 metres, with twelve towers placed at regular intervals. It probably stands on the site of the Roman praetorium, and was re-fortified by the Seljuks, but nearly all that stands today dates from complete Ayyubid rebuilding in the 13th century, with extensive Mamluk restoration. The exterior is particularly notable for the bossed masonry used in its construction and the extensive use of machicolated defences, both over the main entrance and on the towers and curtain walls. The southern facade, with its four towers, is architecturally the most complete and homogeneous part. Inside, little remains of the original apartments which formed the royal residences of Damascus until the Ottoman conquest, apart from a series of vaulted rooms in the southwestern corner.

From the citadel one can follow the northern stretch of the ramparts to Bab Touma (Thomas' Gate), which here follows the Barada River. It is not easy going, as one must cross the river several times, so an overall view of the walls is difficult. But it is the most picturesque part of the ramparts, with many old houses teetering precariously on the walls out over the river and, by continually crossing and re-crossing the

the river and passing in and out of the walls, one gets an excellent feel for the old city and its ramparts. When originally laid out in Roman (or possibly Hellenistic) times the walls enclosed a rectangular area measuring approximately 1340 by 750 metres, and the walls follow much the same line today. They have, however, been continually rebuilt through the ages, so that only the foundations or small stretches (particularly here along the north side) are Roman workmanship (though much of the masonry is re-used Roman). One passes three gates, the Bab al-Faraj, the Bab al-Faradis (Gate of Paradise) and Bab as-Salam (Gate of Peace) before reaching the Bab Touma, a particularly fine example of medieval Arab military architecture dating from the 13th century. With the Bab as-Salam, this is the only part of the Ayyubid fortifications of Damascus that have survived virtually unchanged.

From the Bab Touma one leaves the Barada and follows one of the best surviving stretches of walls skirting the ancient Christian quarter of Damascus, past the particularly fine Tower of as-Saleh Ayyub, built in 1248 at the northeastern corner of the city. This is one of the best preserved parts of the Ayyubid ramparts, and from it one continues a short distance southwards to the best preserved part of the Roman ramparts: the Bab Sharqi (the Eastern Gate; also spelt Charqi or Charki). This is the finest of Damascus' seven gates and the only original Roman one still standing. It is a standard Roman triple entrance and the central arch – the largest – is aligned exactly on the original Roman Decumanus or main thoroughfare.

The Old City

The Bab Sharqi is a good place for a diversion to explore the Christian quarter, occupying the northeastern corner of the Old City (figure 2). Some of Damascus' finest handicraft emporia are also located around here, and it is particularly worthwhile to see some of the factories just in and outside the Bab Sharqi. Most visitors, however, are drawn to the tiny Church of Saint Ananias in the Christian quarter, located near the supposed house of Ananias where St Paul took refuge. Its present form probably dates from the 7th century, and is the only one left of the numerous churches and basilicas that adorned Damascus in the Byzantine period. Other churches in the Christian quarter include the Azaria Church, just inside the Bab Touma, and the Church of St Mary, further along the Street Called Straight (see below), but these are comparatively modern.

From the Bab Sharqi one can continue a circuit of the city walls around the southern part of the old city, past the Bab Kisan, the

Bab as-Saghir and the old Jewish quarter. But the walls often get lost in the back-streets. Apart from a possible detour to visit the Chapel of St Paul near the Bab Kisan, where St Paul was supposedly lowered from a basket in his escape from Damascus, most visitors prefer to plunge into the old city following the Biblical 'Street Called Straight'. This, one of the most legendary streets in the world – and surely one of the most romantically named – is the original Roman Decumanus, now known (in the prosaic fashion of city councils the world over) merely as Midhat Pasha Street. The Decumanus was Damascus' main ancient thoroughfare originally laid out in Roman times, cutting across the Greek grid pattern from east to west. Following the manner of Palmyra, Jerash and other cities of the Roman East, it would originally have been colonnaded. Much of the gridded street pattern of Damascus today still follows that originally laid down by those rather tidy-minded Greek engineers of the 3rd century BC (figure 2). Today, it is perhaps not as picturesque as other streets in Damascus, and any stroll along it is made perilous from the traffic (which takes fullest advantage of the street's 'straightness'!). But it is still very much worth the effort: one is after all, walking through history. Some of the goods may be different and the decor may have changed, but fundamentally the shops hardly differ from those that St Paul might have passed – or Saladin or Hadrian for that matter. The street is not the picturesque museum piece of a medieval European town, but is still as alive as it ever was; the caravans may no longer arrive, but the Street Called Straight is still the legendary centre of one of the greatest caravan cities of Asia.

There are also various sights to be seen. The Church of St Mary nearly halfway along has already been mentioned, but opposite stands one of Damascus' few remaining Roman monuments: a monumental arch. Although the street now skirts it, the main archway was originally centred on the line of the street, and it probably marked the intersection of two streets. It was only rediscovered in 1947, buried in centuries of accumulation and hidden behind later buildings. It was excavated down to original street level some five metres deep, and re-erected in its present position.

At this point it might be worth making another diversion, though one that will take several hours. To the right, roughly in the area between the Christian quarter and the eastern entrance of the Umayyad Mosque, is a maze of backstreets: plunge straight into them, and simply wander around exploring them at leisure. One will almost certainly get lost, but that is part of the pleasure – the visitor is in any case never far from a landmark, and a passer-by is always happy to help regain one's bearings. These streets are the most picturesque of Damascus: narrow, winding lanes with houses that jut out at haphazard angles, occasionally even meeting overhead so that one finds oneself walking through a tunnel. Most are away from the bustle of the bazaars and are furthermore usually too narrow for heavy traffic, so it is blissfully quiet, even serene: occasional sleepy little neighbourhood shops selling household necessities, frequent tea and coffee shops to rest, glimpses of courtyards and shady interiors that have not changed for a thousand years, quiet streets adorned with vines, students pacing up and down memorising texts and women hitching their voluminous coverings to escape curious gazes. Eventually, the mighty Roman gateway to the Umayyad Mosque might loom at the end of a street to redirect one's bearings, but even then, it might be tempting to escape into the serene labyrinth once more. So much in the urban Middle East that is old or traditional has been demolished for 'development', but here is one of the few traditional areas of urban vernacular left. To experience it is to delight in an era all but gone.

Other Islamic monuments

The Street Called Straight eventually comes out at the Bab Jabiya at the western end of the old city, from where the visitor may explore the new city or return to his hotel. But before doing so, it passes through the western half of the old city, where most of Damascus' more minor Islamic monuments are located. In some ways they are more rewarding than the greater monuments, for they are islands of peace and quiet in the city and many have gems of architectural detail that are a delight to discover. There is a very large number of them, from architectural masterpieces to humble baths and caravanserais. Rather than try to guide the visitor through the maze of small streets where they are to be found, it might be easier to simply describe the main ones in turn.

Chief among them are the *madrasas*, or religious schools. Damascus saw the formative stages of the evolution of this important type of Islamic building, when they were first endowed by the Seljuk sultans to combat Shi'ism and heterodox teachings (though the *madrasa* became an important element in the Shi'a world as well). None of the original Seljuk *madrasas* remain, however. The earliest is the Adeliya Madrasa, not far from the Mausoleum of Saladin, completed in 1222. It follows a standard plan of a monumental entrance opening onto a courtyard surrounded by four *iwans* or portals, used for prayer or for teaching. Students' rooms – resembling monastic cells – are located on the first floor. Although there is much subsequent building, overall it has an air of sobriety and simplicity surrounding a peaceful garden, contrasting with the more elaborate architecture of later periods. It is very similar to the near contemporary Nuriya Madrasa to the south of the Umayyad Mosque, and may have been built by the same architect.

The Zahiriya Madrasa opposite forms an architectural unit with the Adeliya, as it both balances and contrasts with the Adeliya. It follows much the same broad plan as the Adeliya, but there the resemblance ends, for it is far more elaborate. Built in 1277, it also houses the tomb of Sultan Baybars, the Crusaders' main adversary after Saladin. The entrance is through a fine portal with a stalactite semi-dome, built of alternating layers of black basalt and white limestone. But it is the interior of the tomb which is the main showpiece. It is faced with magnificent polychrome marble panels surmounted by a mosaic frieze depicting stylized landscapes on a gold background – ample proof that the Syrian tradition of mosaic making that built the Umayyad Mosque continued until the end of the 13th century. The Zahiriya Madrasa is used for other purposes today, and Baybar's magnificent tomb kept locked up and surprisingly neglected – but then like Saladin, that other great vanquisher of the Crusaders, Baybars too was a foreigner: a Turk.

One of the more unusual Islamic buildings is the Hospital of Nur ed-Din to the south of the citadel, now housing a Museum of Islamic Science. It was built in 1154 but extensively rebuilt the following century. For Syria, its courtyard plan surrounded by four great vaulted *iwans* or halls, is unusual, as it follows a cruciform plan more common in Persian architecture, with its origins in Parthian palace plans. The larger halls were the hospital wards, with the eastern one used for consulting, while the southern one was used as a mosque, emphasizing the religious origin of such charitable foundations.

Of the secular buildings, there are a number of public baths or *hammams*, such as the Hammam Nur ed-Din, dating from the Ottoman period. But no visit to Damascus would be complete without seeing the buildings that in some ways make Damascus most famous: the caravanserais, or *khans*. Perhaps the most splendid is the Khan Asad Pasha, not far from the Azem Palace. This was built in 1702 by one of the governors of Damascus, and was used as both a storage depot for goods and a place for visiting merchants to stay. It is built to the standard courtyard pattern, with a fountain in the centre. The rooms surrounding it on the ground floor were for selling and storage, and those on the upper floor for lodging. The quality of its architecture surpasses many mosques: lavish use of striped basalt and limestone masonry was used in its construction, and it is entered through a monumental portal covered in carved decorated stonework, surmounted by a stalactite vault. Proof indeed of the high emphasis placed on the caravan trade in Damascus. Damascus has many other *khans*, which today may be little more than a walled lorry compound, but other monumental caravanserais in the old city from the days of the camel caravans include the Khan al-Harir, the Khan al-Gumruk and the Khan Sulaiman Pasha.

The New City

The Old City nowadays is but the hub around which a much larger new city revolves, now covering most of the area of the Damascus oasis. The centre, mainly dating from the periods of Ottoman and French rule (although there are earlier buildings there as well), lies immediately to the west and northwest. Occasionally behind an overgrown garden one can glimpse the faded elegance of an Ottoman or French Mandate building, evoking a more graceful and leisurely era, but there are sadly too few of these buildings left. The old Hejaz Railway Station, however, still appears much as it did in the days of imperial Ottoman might.

But most visitors are content with a visit to the National Museum and the monuments next to it. The National Museum is one of the best in the Middle East. No visit to Syria should be complete without seeing at least part of it, as it encompasses the full range of Syria's past – and indeed, much of the rest of the Near East. It is vast, and would take many days to examine every exhibit – and the remainder of this book to describe even some of them. So it is only intended to point out some of choicest. The most obvious of these is the facade of the Umayyad desert palace of Qasr al-Hair al-Gharbi, transported from the Palmyrene desert and re-constructed here as the main entrance to the museum (see Chapter 11). Also re-erected in the museum is the synagogue from Dura Europos (Chapter 10) and one of the underground tombs (hypogea) from Palmyra (Chapter 11), both in the same part of the museum. Upstairs in the Islamic wing an entire room from one of the more elaborate of the old houses of Damascus has been re-erected, covered from floor to ceiling with the traditional decorative crafts of Damascus.

Just next to the museum is a particularly graceful Ottoman complex, echoing the great mosques of Istanbul. This is the Suleimaniye complex consisting of a mosque, *madrasa* and *tekkiye* (pilgrim's hospice) designed by the great Istanbul architect Sinan between 1554 and 1560. Although it follows the standard pattern of the Istanbul mosques, it is built in black and white striped masonry in the Syrian fashion. It is also one of the loveliest gardens in Damascus. The grounds of the Suleimaniye house the Army Museum, while next door, in the former hospice quarters, is a handicraft market where one can still see the traditional crafts of Damascus being made.

In one of the streets off Khalid Ibn al-Walid Avenue in the Qanawat Quarter, just to the south of the Hejaz Railway Station, a short length of the original Roman aqueduct to Damascus could be seen a short while ago, but whilst still extant, it is now entirely concreted over. The street, however, is one of the loveliest in Damascus, with wooden houses overhanging a street covered in creepers, so is still well worth a visit.

Salihiye

To the north of the Old City, at the foot of the Qasyun hills, is the suburb of Salihiye. The area is now continually built up all the way out to Salihiye, but originally it formed a separate Kurdish enclave to Damascus, first settled by the Ayyubids (who were a Kurdish dynasty). Part of Salihiye is still called al-Akrad (the Kurdish Quarter), but the name Salihiye itself means 'holy' because of the large number of religious buildings located there – almost as many in fact as in the Old City itself. Today, Salihiye is a lovely, quiet area of old houses and semi-forgotten architectural gems, in the cleaner air above the smoke and bustle of the city below. A stroll around is both a relaxation and a discovery.

Of the lesser known mosques in Damascus, perhaps the Mozaffari Mosque (also known as the Jebel or Hanabila Mosque) in Salihiye is most worth visiting. It is the earliest surviving after the Umayyad Mosque, built between 1201 and 1213 – the first Ayyubid mosque in Damascus. Although comparatively plain, it is noteworthy as being modelled almost entirely on the Umayyad Mosque – indeed, it is virtually a smaller version, down to the Corinthian columns it re-uses for its arcades. Inside are some particularly fine examples of carved woodwork and stonework on the lintels and around the *mihrab* and *minbar*, including two columns framing the *mihrab* that originally came from a Crusader church.

A little way down the hill is the al-Qaymari Hospital founded, like the Nur ed-Din Hospital in the Old City, by the Ayyubids in the mid-13th century. Its four-*iwan* cruciform plan is very similar to the Nur ed-Din hospital. There are also numerous mausolea in Salihiye, mainly of the Mamluk period, such as the Mausoleum of Oghurlu built in 1319, several *madrasas*, and another Ottoman religious endowment, the Kitchens of Sultan Sulaiman.

The Anti-Lebanon Hills north of Damascus

Ma'alula and two nearby villages in the Anti-Lebanon hills to the north of Damascus are amongst the Middle East's more remarkable survivals. They are the only places where Aramaic is still spoken as a living language (though it survives as a purely liturgical language among many Christian communities). Finding it still spoken outside one of the main Arabic capitals, therefore, is rather like finding Latin still spoken in the Latium Hills to the east of Rome.

Ma'alula and Seidnaya are the best known of the villages tucked away in these hills, but most of the other villages in the hills also have something of interest. They are predominantly Christian, mainly Greek-Catholic. Ma'alula is one of the more attractive villages of Syria, and has an impressive monastery and church, the Monastery of Mar Sarkis, parts of which are Byzantine. From it there is a picturesque view of the village and surrounding hills, and below is a narrow fissure through the cliffs associated with the miraculous founding of the monastery.

Seidnaya also has a very famous monastery, founded probably in the time of Justinian who saw a miraculous vision of a lady whilst out hunting, commanding him to found a monastery in this position. It was famous as a place of pilgrimage in Crusader times, and houses a miraculous icon of St Luke. Perched high on a rock, many Byzantine architectural details survive in the building, which is a delightful rabbit-warren of a place: wide terraces open to the desert winds, narrow passages and stairs, quiet vine-covered courtyards, and chattering Christian families out from Damascus for the day.

Just outside Ma'alula, in the village of Berzeh to the south, is one of the traditional birthplaces of Abraham, and there is a sanctuary marking the spot in the village. Further to the north of Ma'alula, in the same range of hills, is the village of Yabrud. Yabrud was important in antiquity as a religious centre, though little remains now apart from some parts of the Byzantine cathedral, which is built of stones from the earlier Temple of Jupiter-Malek of Yabrud. There is nothing much of antiquarian interest inside. In the hills surrounding the village are many caves and funerary remains from the Roman and Byzantine periods.

At the large village of Menin, in the same range of hills but nearer Damascus, a number of minor Roman and Byzantine remains could be seen a short time ago, but it is now just a satellite town of Damascus. At Halbun, another village to the west, are some more fragmentary Roman remains, including the site of a temple, the columns from which have been re-used in the village mosque. West of Ma'mura, some distance west of the village of Rankus further north, are the remains of one of the few monuments dating from the Seleucid period in Syria: the Doric temple of Qasr Nimrud. Very little is left standing of this important building, apart from part of the cella wall and some columns, though many architectural fragments have been found nearby. A Byzantine inscription suggests it was converted to a church.

Dmeir

Some forty kilometres to the northeast of Damascus on the road to Palmyra, is the large village of Dmeir. It has been identified as ancient Thelsae, a Roman fortified post on the desert frontier. There are several ruins outside the town to the east, and inside the town many of the houses contain re-used Roman architectural fragments. But the main attraction is the superbly intact small Temple of Jupiter in the centre, preserved up to roof level. Part of the reason for this excellent state of preservation can be seen by the extent to which it was buried – one must climb down a trench some five metres deep to get to the entrance. It was completed, according to an inscription, in 245 AD.

Mt Hermon area

Mt Hermon – Jebel esh-Shaikh to the Arabs – can be seen on a clear day from Damascus or the Hauran, dominating southwestern Syria. It is a mountain rich in legend, and situated in its foothills are a number of very attractive villages rich in antiquities. The mountain itself, at 9000 feet high, is the second highest in Syria. It actually has three summits, each rather aptly overlooking Syria, Lebanon and the Jordan Valley respectively. It is mentioned several times in the Old Testament and other ancient texts, as it figured prominently in the Near Eastern tradition of sacred high places. On top are the remains of a sacred enclosure, an adjacent temple and other remains associated with the worship of high places.

In the lovely village of Arneh (classical Ornea), at the foot of the mountain, are the very fragmentary remains of a Doric temple. There are many other ancient ruins in the vicinity – temples, tombs, forts, and more unidentifiable fragments – but the most notable are at the villages of Burqush and Rakhleh in the foothills further to the north. At Burqush there are some ruins on an immense platform, partly rock-cut and partly built out over a series of chambers. On top is an arcade that – from the number of Byzantine capitals scattered about – is all that remains of a Byzantine church, though the platform itself is probably earlier. Further up the mountain at the smaller village of Rakhleh are the ruins of a large temple approximately 60 metres long, probably dedicated to the sun god Baal. Most of the columns have collapsed. Remains of other temples and funerary monuments are in the hills around Rakhleh.

CHAPTER 5

The Hauran and
Southern Syria

The Hauran is an extraordinary landscape. It is dominated by the range of volcanic hills known as the Jebel Arab (previously the Jebel Druze, and before that the Jebel Hauran), and the whole area is covered in brooding, black basalt rock and lava flows. The road from Suwaida to Damascus, for example, passes one of the most desolate scenes ever encountered, a sea of ancient, solidified lava looking more like photographs of Mars than any landscape known on Earth (plate 9). To the southeast this gives way to the strange Black Desert of eastern Syria and Jordan. But the country is surprisingly high: the central Hauran rises 1800 metres and is often snow-covered in winter, providing a stark contrast to the black lava.

Astonishingly, this area of volcanic desolation is interspersed with abundant, rich agricultural land and settlement (plate 10), and has almost more ancient remains than anywhere else in the Middle East – the remains of some three hundred ancient towns and villages have been counted in the Hauran (figure 4). For the volcanic action which produced the basalt, also produced a highly fertile soil in the valleys and plains not covered by the lava flows, making it one of the Near East's main granaries in antiquity. The basalt, furthermore, is also one of the hardest building materials known, so one can find much still standing. Virtually all building work in the Hauran until very recently used this readily available material, imparting a grimness to the landscape only softened by the contrasting greens and golds of the fields.

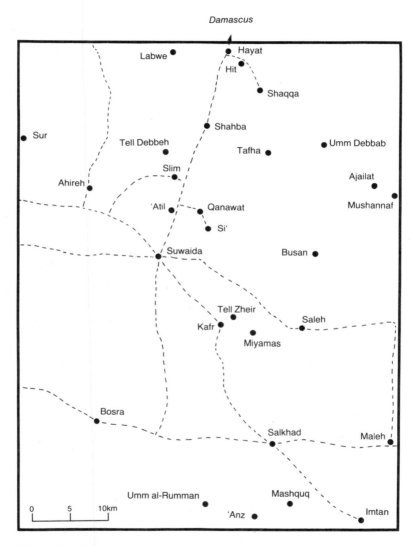

Damascus

Fig. 4 The Hauran

The settlements are not all from the classical period. Villages and towns survive from the Bronze Age and even the Chalcolithic period in the Hauran as well. From the Chalcolithic period in the 5th millennium is a deserted village at Tell Zheir and a small town with impressive ramparts at Labweh. Bronze Age settlements have been investigated recently at Rijm al-'Is and Hebariyeh, with impressive ramparts still surviving at Tell Debbeh and Tell Jubeh.

But the period of greatest prosperity was the Roman, when the Hauran particularly benefited from the 'explosion' of building activity in the 2nd century AD brought about by Roman prosperity and stability. This architectural outburst can be seen all over Roman Syria, at Jerash, Petra, Palmyra, and the Dead Cities of the north. There are several factors, however, that make the architecture of the Hauran of particular interest. The first is the black basalt building material already remarked upon. Unlike the softer stone of, say, Palmyra or Petra, this basalt is incredibly durable and rarely weathers or crumbles, so that preservation is unusually high in the Hauran. The considerable tensile strength of the basalt furthermore allowed for the development of unusual building techniques not normally possible with softer stones. Hence, it was possible to cut long basalt 'beams' or 'girders' and use them in much the same way as timber beams were used elsewhere, particularly in corbelling and cantilevering techniques to roof considerable areas – 10 metres and more. This gave rise to a distinct, cantilevered 'slab and lintel' architectural style that is peculiar to the black basalt areas of the Hauran and northeastern Jordan.

The second factor, which stems directly from the first, is the large quantity of domestic and vernacular architecture that survives: given the plentiful availability and durability of the basalt, many of the more humble buildings were built of it as well, unlike the mudbrick or rubble materials that were more common for such buildings elsewhere in the Middle East. The area is therefore, of interest to the social historian, providing details of the everyday life of the ordinary people as well as the monuments that they built.

The third factor is the Nabatean element. For two centuries before the Roman conquest the area came under the influence of the Nabateans of Petra, with their highly distinctive and vigorous architectural traditions. Indeed, towards the end of this period they moved their capital here from Petra. The architecture of the Hauran thus forms a fusion of Hellenistic, Nabatean and Roman styles.

Before moving onto the specific sites it is perhaps worth making some general comments on the domestic architecture that makes the Hauran so unique. Houses followed the standard pattern, consisting of rooms grouped around a courtyard, that is virtually universal in the Middle East both today and in antiquity, but in the Hauran they differed from the norm in one important point. Because of the immense strength of the basalt it was possible to build several storeys, with three and even four storeys still standing in parts. The ground floors were used for storage and stabling, with the upper floors for living and sleeping space, a pattern that today in the Middle East is only found in Yemen. Upper floors would often be connected by external stone staircases, jutting out from the walls on corbels – good examples of this occur at Umm al-Jemal just across the Jordanian border. Roofing, as already mentioned, consisted of long basalt slabs laid across the rooms, much the same as timber is used elsewhere. Where a space was too wide to be spanned by a beam's length, two methods would be used: either corbels would be built out at the tops of walls to narrow the space, or a series of arches would span the space and the beams placed from arch to arch, i.e., lengthwise to the room. Another peculiarity of the Hauran (though it is occasionally found elsewhere in Syria, e.g., the Palmyra tombs) was the doors, which often consisted of a single upright slab of basalt (sometimes weighing several tons) with stone hinges that would allow it to open and close surprisingly smoothly. Good examples of these building techniques can be seen in most of the ruined towns of the Hauran, with particularly fine houses surviving at Majdal ash-Shar, Jmarrin, Busan and Diyatheh, the latter an entire ruined village.

Bosra

Like so many cities in Syria, Bosra was probably laid out in Hellenistic times (figure 5). It preserves the standard grid street pattern so favoured by Greek town planners, to which the Romans added their standard east-west Cardo, or main thoroughfare, crossed at right angles by a Decumanus. The irregularity of the layout, however – particularly the eastern half – may suggest that it incorporated some earlier town plan. It remained little more than a provincial town (it does not appear to have belonged to the federation of Greek city-states known as the Decapolis) until the Nabataeans advanced from Petra to Damascus under King Aretas III in the 1st century BC. The Nabateans, ever quick to realize the commercial potential of its strategic location, closer to the rich Hellenized cities of Syria and the caravan routes to Mesopotamia, transferred their capital from Petra to Bosra. It remained here until the conquest of southern Syria and the Nabatean kingdom under Trajan in 106 AD. Trajan's conquest, far from diminishing Bosra's status, confirmed it, as it was made the capital of the Roman province of Arabia under the name Nova Trajana Bostra, as well as the garrison town of the IIIrd Cyrenaica Legion. It became a major trade entrepot, taking over much of the trade that Petra

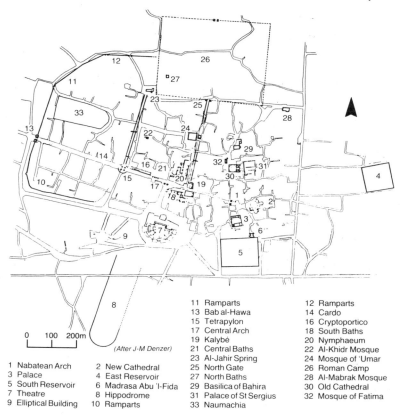

0   100   200m

(After J-M Denzer)

1 Nabatean Arch
3 Palace
5 South Reservoir
7 Theatre
9 Elliptical Building

2 New Cathedral
4 East Reservoir
6 Madrasa Abu 'l-Fida
8 Hippodrome
10 Ramparts

11 Ramparts
13 Bab al-Hawa
15 Tetrapylon
17 Central Arch
19 Kalybé
21 Central Baths
23 Al-Jahir Spring
25 North Gate
27 North Baths
29 Basilica of Bahira
31 Palace of St Sergius
33 Naumachia

12 Ramparts
14 Cardo
16 Cryptoportico
18 South Baths
20 Nymphaeum
22 Al-Khidr Mosque
24 Mosque of 'Umar
26 Roman Camp
28 Al-Mabrak Mosque
30 Old Cathedral
32 Mosque of Fatima

Fig. 5 Bosra

previously controlled, forming the head of the new road that the
Romans built down to the Gulf of Aqaba, the Via Trajana, successor to
the Biblical King's Highway. Successive Roman Emperors increased
Bosra's status: Septimus Severus greatly embellished the city,
Alexander Severus elevated it to the rank of colony and Philip the Arab
made it a metropolis.

Bosra remained an important centre in the Byzantine period, when
it became successively a bishopric then archbishopric. In the Ghassanid
period, a pre-Islamic Arab dynasty whose kingdom was centred on the
Hauran, a major cathedral was built in the 6th century – in its day, one
of the greatest cathedrals of the East. Indeed, it was the Christianity of
Ghassanid Bosra that probably played a major role in the birth of
Islam, for it was here that the Prophet Muhammad, then a caravan

leader, learnt of the elements of Christianity from the Nestorian priest Bahira at Bosra. The tradition is borne out by the veneration by the early Muslims of the supposed site of the house of Bahira, and the construction of a number of early mosques in Bosra. It remained a centre of considerable importance down to the Middle Ages, both as an important stopping place on the pilgrimage route to Mecca and as a centre for the caravan traffic. The Roman theatre was turned into a fortification during this period, and the ruler of Bosra in the 12th century, Aytekin, sided with the Crusaders. The Crusaders for a while, however, were unable to capture the fortress, despite several subsequent attacks.

Bosra is the starting point for the Hauran for most visitors. It has the most to see, and it was the ancient capital of the region (the modern one being Suweida). As a ruined city covering a vast area, Bosra is second in Syria only to Palmyra. But Bosra has an extra dimension that Palmyra does not: for interspersed amongst the ruins is a modern small town, with scenes of daily life that have not varied much since Bosra's heyday. More than most sites, therefore, ancient history comes alive in Bosra. For many visitors too, the astonishing spectacle of coming so unexpectedly upon such an enormous theatre, so marvellously intact, is the high point of a trip to Syria.

But before dashing onto the theatre as most visitors do, perhaps it is wiser to start Bosra at the gateway marking its main entry from the west: the Bab al-Hawa, or Gate of the Winds. This 2nd century AD Roman arch marks the main entrance to the city, with the paving of the Roman road passing underneath it still marvellously intact. The gateway would originally have been adorned with statues, both in the niches which flank the main arch and on projecting brackets higher up. The remains of the city walls stretch either side of the gate, though most of them were dismantled to build the castle in the medieval period. Judging from some of the immense 'cyclopean' stones that were too heavy to be carted off, the foundations of these walls might be pre-Roman, dating from the time when such Cyclopean masonry characterized urban fortifications in Syria in the 2nd millennium BC.

The gate opens onto the Cardo Maximus, the main east-west thoroughfare through Bosra. It has been excavated down to its original Roman surface, and is an attractive road, lined with trees, ruins and the remains of its colonnade in a few places (plate 11). The colonnade is all that is left of several lines of colonnades that would have lined all of the main streets at Bosra – indeed, Bosra was probably one of the most 'colonnaded' of all the cities of the Roman east. They are in the Ionic style, unlike the Corinthian which was more widely used, which may indicate that they were built earlier in the Roman period rather than later. They were used to shade the sidewalks, behind which were shops.

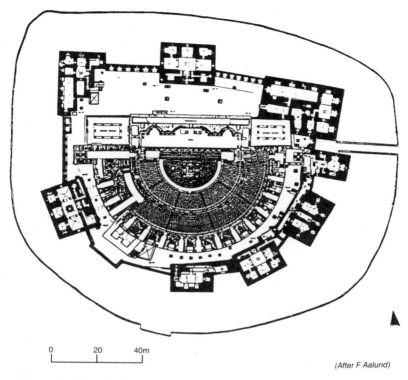

0 20 40m

(After F Aalund)

Fig. 6 The Theatre of Bosra

About halfway along an intersection with a north-south street is marked by the remains of a tetrapylon, or four-way arch, beyond which an immense underground gallery or Cryptoportico, 65 metres long, flanks the north of the Cardo.

The Cardo opens out into a central area, dominated by the Bab Qandil – the Arch of the Lantern or Central Arch – an impressive Roman triple arch of the 3rd century, around which most of Bosra's main monuments are grouped. Chief of these are four huge columns forming a Nymphaeum (a monumental fountain) and the remains of the 'Temple of the Daughter of the King' known as the Kalybeh, consisting of single tall column joined to a fragmentary wall by an elaborately decorated entablature. Both these buildings are on opposite corners formed by a street leaving the Cardo towards the North Gate. On the side street leading to the theatre are the South Baths, which follow a clear Italian design. Another bath, the Central

Baths, lies opposite to the north of the Cardo, and there is a third baths, the North Baths, on the northern edge of the city. In the area between the South and Central Baths is a large courtyard measuring 20 by 70 metres, the Khan al-Dibis, that was probably the market place or Agora.

The main monument to visit in Bosra, however – even at the cost of missing all others – is the deservedly famous theatre (figure 6). It owes its fame to its remarkable preservation, and its preservation is owed to the medieval citadel that was built up around it. Even without the attraction of the theatre, the citadel at Bosra would be a major sight, as it is one of the most intact examples of Arab military architecture in Syria. The first parts of the citadel date from the late 11th century, but most of its present form was built in the time of Saladin in the 12th century and restored by Baybars after the Mongol devastations in the 13th century. It is an impressive work of military architecture, and to wander through its rooms, vaults and galleries out onto its battlements is a marvellous experience. But most of all, it highlights the unexpected sight of the theatre within. For emerging from the dark galleries of the castle to be suddenly confronted with the spectacle of the immense black auditorium spread out above, below and around is one of the greatest sights of the Middle East (plate 12) – to be compared to the sudden sight of the Treasury on rounding the Siq at Petra.

This theatre, one of the largest ever made in the Roman world, was built in the 2nd century AD, possibly on the site of an earlier Nabatean citadel. The auditorium was filled with flimsy domestic and other buildings until it was cleared by the Department of Antiquities in the late forties, to reveal the structure in full. It has a diameter of over 100 metres, and with at least 35 tiers it would have seated some 15,000 spectators. Around the top of the auditorium a colonnade still stands almost in its entirety (plate 13). The scenae frons, or stage backdrop, has three stage entrances set in deep recesses, and was adorned with three storeys of elaborate colonnades built of white limestone, contrasting dramatically with the black basalt of the rest of the theatre. Behind the stage are two colonnaded courtyards and an immense, vaulted gallery, one of the finest pieces of Roman building workmanship that one can see anywhere. This internal gallery dwarfs the visitor much as the auditorium does outside.

To forestall the inevitable questions of so many visitors – not to mention the tales of many guides! – it is perhaps worth pointing out that theatres such as the one at Bosra were not used for gladiatorial combats, or for feeding Christians – or anybody else – to any lions or other animals. These were performed almost solely in auditoria built especially for the purpose, namely the amphitheatres, and not in theatres as such. The notorious Roman blood sports were largely a feature of the Latin West and not the more Hellenized – and more civilized! – East. It does in any case require little imagination to realize that theatres such as Bosra would have been quite inadequate for blood sports: even the least discriminating of lions would have turned up their noses at the emaciated Christians in the arena to stroll over for choicer pickings from the plump matrons and town worthies occupying the front stalls.

If the theatre was reserved for the more cultured forms of entertainment, those seeking less demanding distractions could escape to the Hippodrome, just outside the city to the south, where chariot racing and other sports would have been performed. Though much built over by modern garden walls, the outline of this immense arena and some of its seating can still be made out. Also on the outskirts of the city are three vast cisterns, to the east, west and south of the city. The latter, the Birket al-Hajj, is probably Islamic.

There are, however, many more monuments still to be seen within Bosra, though many lie amidst jumbles of ruins and recent houses (figure 5). At the western end of the Cardo is another monumental archway, the Nabatean Arch, with a Nabatean column standing nearby. The Nabatean Arch – or East Arch – is a Roman 'triumphal' arch of the late 1st or early 2nd century, built possibly in the reign of Trajan. It follows the normal pattern of such Roman arches, consisting of a large opening in the main facade and a smaller tunnel arch through its sides, but the capitals are in the pure Nabatean style. Like the West Gateway, both this and the Central Arch would have been adorned with statues.

The Nabatean Arch may have formed a monumental entrance to a palace, just to the south. This palace was the official residence of the Roman governor of Arabia in the 2nd century AD, though it may have replaced the earlier Nabatean palace of Rabbel II in the same position. It has a two storeyed portico – the lower one arcaded and the upper an Ionic colonnade – surrounding three sides of a courtyard. A series of rooms opened onto the courtyard, those on the main central block being reception rooms, with each wing being domestic and administrative quarters respectively. Unfortunately, much of this fine building is obscured by modern houses.

The other remaining Roman government building of note is the 3rd century AD basilica, sometimes called the Monastery of Bahira. It was probably a pre-Christian basilica, or Roman public assembly hall, though no doubt it was used for church purposes later on when it was associated with the Nestorian priest Bahira, who is traditionally supposed to have instructed the Prophet Muhammad in the Christian religion. It is a marvellously intact, large hall, well lit by clerestory windows, open at the front and with an apse at its end. On either side were external colonnaded porticos, and the remains of a colonnaded forecourt can be seen at the front.

Bosra also has a number of important early Christian buildings. The main one is the Cathedral of SS Sergius, Bacchus and Leontius just south of the basilica. It was built in 512 but has unfortunately much deteriorated now since it was first studied in the 19th century. It is an essentially circular building with an octagonal interior colonnade set in a square, originally covered by a large dome some 26 metres in diameter. It is thus an important building in the development of Byzantine architecture, forming the prototype that culminated in the great domed buildings of Ravenna and Constantinople. The cathedral at Bosra was also the immediate ancestor of the Dome of the Rock in Jerusalem, built less than two hundred years later. There are the remains of a Byzantine palace opposite the cathedral, and a later cathedral, also on a circular plan, has recently been discovered in the area near the Governor's Palace.

There are also a number of important Islamic buildings in Bosra. The Mosque of 'Umar is traditionally associated with the second caliph, the great 'Umar ibn al-Khattab (634-644), but was in fact built in the 13th century. It is built almost entirely from re-used Roman and Byzantine masonry, as can be seen by the mixed styles of the columns. The earliest mosque is the 12th century Mosque of al-Khidr, built next to the spring that supplied Bosra with fresh water. Other mosques are the 12th century Mosque of Mabrak an-Naqa, the 13th century Mosque of Fatima, and the 13th century ad-Dabbagha Madrasa with the Yaqut Mosque nearby. All of these Islamic buildings are distinguished by very solid looking square minarets at one corner.

Salkhad and the Southern Hauran

Salkhad, to the east of Bosra, is built on the slopes of one of the extinct volcanos that so characterise the Hauran (figure 4) – even the citadel is actually built within the crater of the volcano. The citadel is Ayyubid, but there is little else to see in Salkhad itself, even though its Biblical reference (as Salchah) suggests great antiquity. Salkhad is mainly a jumping-off place for sites in the black basalt desert, of which a fine view can be obtained from the top of the citadel.

Virtually every village in the area south and east of Salkhad contains ancient remains, but only the most intrepid of archaeological enthusiasts need cover them all. The remains include a prostyle Roman temple dated 124 AD at Mashquq, part of a Roman road at Imtan (ancient Mothana), a pre-classical small stone pyramid at Malah, an Ayyubid cistern dated 1238 at Inat (ancient Inachos), a Roman fort dated 306 AD at Deir al-Khaf, and many more Roman and Byzantine houses at Majdal and Anz, near the aptly named Umm al-Rumman ('Mother of Romans').

One of the largest areas of ruins in the Hauran can be seen at Umm al-Qutain, south of Salkhad close to the Jordanian border. This is a ruined Roman and Byzantine town, very similar to Majdal to the northeast and Umm al-Jemal and Umm as-Sarab, just across the border in Jordan. Amongst the ruins are at least three churches and a monastery, the latter quite well preserved. All of these ruined towns however – on both sides of the border – are most notable for the large number of private houses still standing to a remarkable height.

Suwaida, Qanawat, Seia and the Central Hauran

This group of ruined towns lie in the very heart of the Hauran (figure 4). The main town is Suwaida dominated by the distant view of Mt Hermon. It is now the provincial capital of the Hauran and a thriving market centre, whose inhabitants are Druze. Suwaida was the Nabatean town of Soada, an important centre for the cult of Dushares, the main Nabatean deity. Its name was changed in Roman times to Dionysias, dedicated to the worship of Dionysus, whom the Romans identified with Dushares. Very little is to be seen of Suwaida's past now, as it has been extensively built up in recent times. The fine 3rd century peripteral temple recorded at the beginning of the century can no longer be seen. There are the reasonably well preserved remains of a 4th or 5th century Byzantine basilica, and a few more fragmentary Byzantine ruins elsewhere in the town. The most worthwhile sight in Suwaida, however, is the superb museum, one of the best provincial museums in the Middle East, opened in 1991. Here, well laid-out displays document the entire history of the Hauran and its monuments.

More to see than in Suwaida itself are the remains of Qanawat, just outside Suwaida to the northeast. Indeed, Qanawat has the greatest quantity of ruins after Bosra. Like so many of the towns of the Hauran, it was probably founded in Hellenistic times, when it was known as Canatha, forming a part of the Decapolis federation of cities of southern Syria and Jordan. Since Bosra did not belong to this federation (at least at first), Canatha was probably the main city of the Hauran before the rise of Bosra in Nabatean and Roman times. Most of the remains in Qanawat, however, are Roman and Byzantine.

The ancient monuments are dotted about the modern town which is built amongst the ruins. The main concentration is a complex known as the Seraglio opening from a paved square at the beginning of the Cardo, much of which is also still paved. The Seraglio is a series of

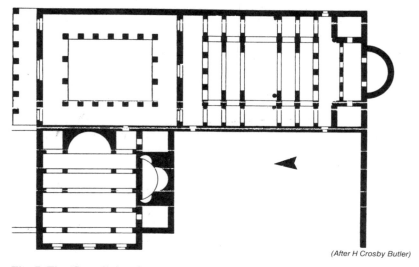

(After H Crosby Butler)

Fig. 7 The 'Seraglio' at Qanawat

buildings with a rather complex architectural history that is not easy to work out on the ground (figure 7). It consists of two apsidal structures, probably a temple complex, on the south and east sides of a colonnaded courtyard (plate 14). The western one is particularly elaborate. It is in the form of a tetrastyle temple, dating from the 2nd century AD, with a lavishly decorated entrance portal opening into a room with a trilobed apse facing south. This may originally have been a public meeting hall, but it was later converted into a church when an additional apse facing east was inserted. The eastern temple dates from the late 3rd or early 4th century and also has a south facing apse, though this too was superseded when it was later converted to a church.

From the Seraglio square a road descends towards a deep wadi that cuts the town into two. Just before the wadi is a rather stark black basalt building known as the Madrasa, roofed with long basalt slabs (though there is modern overbuilding). This may be a hall, of uncertain function, dated by an inscription to 124 AD. Across the wadi is a small theatre and the remains of a nymphaeum.

To the southeast of the Seraglio there are the remains of a peripteral temple, probably dedicated to Helios. The inner walls have completely collapsed, but parts of the outer colonnade consisting of Corinthian columns set on high pedestals are still standing.

The most outstanding monuments in the vicinity, however, used to be the sacred site of Si' further up the slopes of the Jebel Druze to the southeast. The two sites are connected by a paved Roman road, parts of which still exist, that winds up onto the plateau on which Si' lies, probably a processional way or via sacra. For Si', ancient Seia, was sacred to the Semitic gods Ba'al-Shamin and Dushares, the latter the main deity of the Nabatean pantheon. The worship of Baalshamin was practised here in ancient times well before the classical period, though the cult of Dushares probably arrived with the Nabatean conquest in the early first century BC. Both temples, however, date to the late 1st century BC, from the time of Herod the Great's conquest of the area.

The temple complex at Seia was excavated and studied in great detail by an American expedition in the beginning of the century, who were able to reconstruct the buildings by a careful study of the surviving fragments. It consisted of a sacred precinct entered through a propylaeum, or monumental triple gateway, surrounded by three temples to the south, west and north. The small temple to the south is a simple, prostyle temple of fairly conventional design, but the other two are highly unusual. That on the west is the 1st century BC Temple of Dushares, which originally had an arched entablature over the columns forming its entrance. That on the north is the great Temple of Baalshamin, dedicated in 33 BC, entered through a very elaborately decorated entrance, a restored version of which can be seen in the University Museum at Princeton, made from plaster casts of the masonry fragments found when excavating it. It had a very unusual facade, flanked by two square towers. The cellas, or sanctuaries, of both this and the Dushares temple, consist of an unusual arrangement of two enclosed squares which in turn enclose a third square formed by four columns. Today, however, apart from heaps of rubble where one can occasionally make out a decorated fragment, there is nothing to see, though a recent French expedition has been investigating various other more complete remains in the vicinity.

Despite there being so little to see, the temple complex at Seia nonetheless forms an important part in Syrian architectural history, for it contains many unusual and important elements from a variety of cultural traditions. Both the deities worshipped there place it firmly in the Semitic tradition. This tradition is given architectural expression by the twin towers that flanked the Baalshamin facade (probably related to the ancient Semitic worship of high places), an arrangement which was to achieve such popularity in the later Christian architecture of Europe. The fondness for complex and rich decoration owes much to Nabatean architecture such as at the temple of Khirbet Tannur in southern Jordan, but the overall 'language' of the decoration – the classical orders (or modified versions of it) and much of the actual decorative patterns – belongs to the Hellenistic tradition. Another

81

element, however, comes from a third direction altogether. This is the 'square in square' arrangement of the sanctuaries, which belong to an Iranian tradition that can be found in temples as far east as Hatra in Iraq, Takht-i Sulaiman in Iran, Surkh Kotal in Afghanistan and Taxila in Pakistan. This 'concentric square' concept might be the architectural origin of the concentric circle arrangement of the Byzantine martyria in Syria and elsewhere.

About 3 kilometres to the west of Qanawat are the ruins of another temple, at 'Atil, ancient Athila. This is a Roman prostyle temple built in 151 AD, with two columns in antis in a curious Corinthian and Ionic composite style. (An early morning visit is recommended to get the sun on the facade). There are the remains of a second temple as well as a church nearby. There is another very fragmentary Roman temple in an Ionic-Corinthian composite order at Slim or Suwailim, ancient Selaema, a short way further north (plate 15).

More remains can be found in the area to the south and east of Suwaida, back towards Bosra and Salkhad. At Kafr, ancient Capra, the seat of the Byzantine bishopric of the province of Arabia, many re-used ancient fragments and parts of ancient houses can be seen in the village. The ruined Roman temple to Athena, however, recorded at the beginning of the century, can no longer be seen. There are more ruins 8 kilometres east of Kafr at Khirbet Jama. At Busan, ancient Bosana, are good examples of the typical Hauran basalt houses of the Roman period. Further to the east at Saleh, ancient Salamanestha, Roman remains include a monumental fountain, and at Miyamas are the remains of two adjacent, small prostyle Roman temples that were later converted into a single Byzantine church. At Mushannaf, ancient Nela, on the edges of the desert, is a well preserved prostyle Roman temple in antis standing in a large colonnaded temenos, as well as other ruins. The architecture appears late 2nd century AD, but an inscription on its temenos wall suggests a 1st century date. It stands by a lake that is partly artificial. Just a few kilometres from Mushannaf is another area of ruins that includes some tombs at Ajailat, ancient Egla.

Shahba and the Northern Hauran

Shahba (figure 4) was the birthplace of the Emperor Philip the Arab (232-237 AD), who renamed his home town Philippopolis and elevated it to the rank of colony. Enjoying imperial patronage it was embellished with some particularly fine monuments in the 3rd century, and today Shahba, more than any other town in the Hauran, still preserves much of its original Roman character. The main bazaar street of the modern town is the same paved street that the Romans built, the modern shops

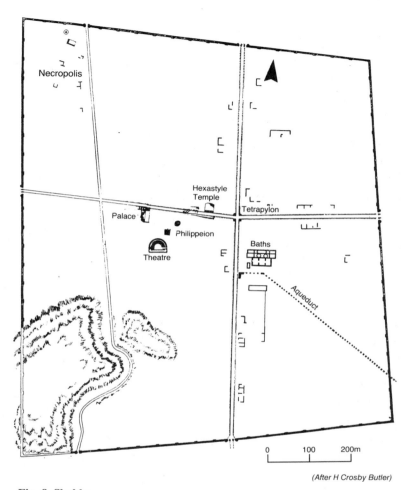

(After H Crosby Butler)

Fig. 8 Shahba

alongside are in many cases situated in the ancient ones – and probably selling much the same sort of products. Indeed, in wandering around Shahba there is a juxtaposition of ancient and modern that is sometimes confusing, but always delightful (plate 16).

The city is in the form of a walled rectangle pierced by four gateways, through which pass two paved transverse streets, the Cardo and Decumanus (figure 8). Their intersection in the centre of the city was marked by a tetrapylon, or four-way arch, of which no trace remains.

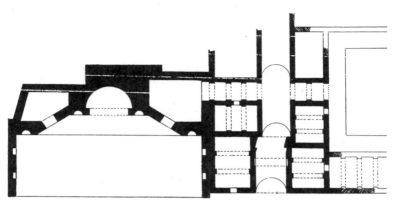

Fig. 9 The palace at Shahba
(After H Crosby Butler)

The streets were originally colonnaded in the same way as other Syrian cities. Most of the monuments are along or just off the paved street that goes westwards from the central intersection. Like so many other monuments in the Hauran, they are best seen in the early morning before the shadows fall on most of the facades. A little way along on the right is an impressive portico consisting of four large Corinthian columns. This probably led to a now vanished temple, but today leads only to a private house. Further along, the street opens onto a wide paved square dominated by a magnificent facade on a podium. This forms the east face of the 3rd century palace, most of which is further along towards the West Gate (figure 9). It has been seen as a forerunner to the great early 4th century Palace of Diocletian at Spoleto, which may have used Syrian architects in its construction. Unfortunately much of the Shahba palace is obscured by recent houses. To the left of the facade is a marvellously intact prostyle temple, the Philippeion, erected by Philip in memory of his deified father. Behind this is a small theatre, built too in the 3rd century.

Back in the centre, the two main monuments are the House of Mosaics and the baths. The former, now a museum, contains some of the finest mosaics found in Syria, and alone is well worth a visit to Shahba. The impressive baths, endowed by Philip, follow the standard Roman arrangement of rooms. It is interesting from the structural point of view for the use of light volcanic tufa in the construction of the vaults and domes, over the superstructure of standard basalt masonry. There are the remains of an aqueduct adjacent to the baths.

Like the other towns of the Hauran, the environs of Shahba are thick with more ancient remains. Most are situated to the northeast. At Hit, ancient Eitha, is a small Roman temple and some ruined houses of the Hauran style, with an even better preserved example of a two storeyed courtyard house at Hayat nearby, built in the 6th century. Hayat also has the remains of an earlier temple. Shaqqa is the ancient town of Sakkaia or Maximianopolis, a Roman town elevated to the rank of colony and later becoming an important Byzantine centre. In the centre are the remains of a large Roman public building known as the Qaisariyeh, probably the Roman governor's palace. There is also a basilica with a square tower, now a private house, dating from 176 AD. Like the Bahira basilica at Bosra, this would originally have been a Roman public assembly hall rather than a Christian church. There is another Roman town at Tafha, which has a number of large ruins, including a well preserved basilica. There are also many houses and ramparts. More Roman ruins can be found at Umm Debab nearby.

The Leijja

The area further to the north and west of Shahba (figure 4) is a sub-region (ancient Trachonitis) of the Hauran known as the Leijja, which means 'refuge' in Arabic. In many ways it is a smaller version of the Hauran itself. A refuge it certainly is, for it is a spectacularly desolate region bounded on all sides by forbidding lava flows from the Jebel Hauran. Yet Roman ruins occur throughout. Many of these are just guard-posts and milestones that marked the road that crossed it, parts of which still exist, but there are some fine monuments as well.

The capital of the Leijja is Ahireh, ancient Acrita, but little can be seen there today apart from the remains of a 2nd century public building, now housing a mosque. Mismiyeh, ancient Phaena, had a particularly fine Roman praetorium dating from 160 AD. It consisted of a central chamber of cruciform plan with intact vaulting held up by Corinthian columns, but is unfortunately no longer standing. At Buraq or Brekeh, ancient Berroka, at the northern edge of the Leijja, there were more Roman ruins, including a prostyle temple, but these also have mainly disappeared. More temple remains have been recorded at Sur or Suwara (ancient Saura) and Sahr, also in the Leijja, the former also containing a very ruined Nabatean temple.

The best monument in the Leijja is at Ezra'a or Zor'a, the ancient Zorava, that figured prominently in the Byzantine period when it was an episcopal town. The main monument is the Church of St George, a Byzantine martyrium built in 515 in a remarkable state of preservation (figure 10). It marks the supposed burial place of St George, which

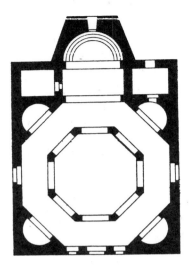

**Fig. 10 Church of St George
at Ezra'a**

probably explains its state of preservation as St George is greatly
venerated in the Middle East. The buildings follow a 'central' plan
rather than the more usual basilical plan, consisting of an octagon
within a square. This follows much the same plan as the Cathedral at
Bosra built at the same time. It is capped by a new egg-shaped dome,
rather disfigured by an ugly modern concrete bell tower. There was
another slightly later church at Ezra'a, the martyrium of St Elias, built
in the form of a cross, a plan that was to gain increasing popularity in
later periods of church architecture, but this has been entirely rebuilt as
a new Catholic church. Nearby is a ruined mosque built of re-used
ancient fragments.

At Sanamain, ancient Aere, on the main Amman-Damascus
highway, is the magnificently decorated peripteral Temple of Tyche
built in 191 AD. It is difficult to find, tucked away behind the old
mosque and almost entirely obscured by modern buildings, but it is still
one of the finest monuments in the Hauran. It is a square temple
entered through a triple entrance which faces a niche surmounted by a
conch, flanked by two decorated smaller niches. The interior has a
Greek key entablature supported by Corinthian columns standing on
pedestals – the latter a feature of Roman architecture in Syria. The rich
decoration is all the more remarkable for the extreme hardness of the
basalt into which it is carved. There are a few other miscellaneous
remains in Sanamain – some ancient houses and a much ruined tower

– amongst the modern town.

Just to the southwest of Sanamain, at Inkhil, are the 2nd century AD remains of a superb villa, now a private house (the Beit Hariri). It has a facade with an elaborately decorated doorway and conch-head niches (plate 17). Inside is a large vaulted central hall flanked by smaller rooms, beautifully decorated with busts and other sculptures, all carved from the incredibly hard black basalt of the Hauran.

The Safa and the Southern Desert

The southern desert of Syria is quite unlike the deserts of the east and north of Syria. For the desert stretching eastwards from the Jebel Hauran, known as the Safa, is a weird, utterly desolate expanse, strewn with the black basalt boulders from the volcanic activity that threw up the Jebel Hauran in the remote past. In parts these boulders lie so thickly on the desert floor that it is virtually impossible to pick a path through them; the expanse of sheer blackness seems to absorb the light even under the harshest of midday suns like some earthly black hole; viewing such a scene from one of the rare heights in the desert is an experience never forgotten.

For this reason alone the desert is worth visiting. It also comes as a surprise to learn that this desolation has supported life in the past, testified by several areas of ruins in its midst, some of them dating back to the Bronze Age and even Chalcolithic periods. For the area is crossed by several important wadis which, though dry most of the year, catch the run-off from the slopes of the Jebel Hauran. There are also several permanent water holes. Most of the remains of antiquity in this desert fall into two categories. First, are the frontier posts, mostly Roman, that guarded the wealthy areas of the Hauran from incursions by marauding nomads. And second are the large numbers of rock-cut inscriptions and petroglyphs – numbering many thousands – left by these same 'marauding' nomads. These are a curious feature of the Syrian and Jordanian deserts. They are written in the Safaitic script (which gets its name from the Safa region), an Aramaic-derived script that is one of the more immediate ancestors of modern Arabic. They were pecked onto the iron-hard surfaces of the basalt boulders by passing Arab nomads in the first few centuries AD, evidence of a surprisingly high level of literacy – and sophistication – enjoyed by these tribes. One is left wondering just who were protecting whom from what in the frontier posts!

Many of the inscriptions can be seen in the lava cliff face along the Wadi Sham near Namara, some eighty kilometres east of Suwaida, and at Zalaf nearby, in the heart of the Safa. There are also a number of ruins at Namara, probably a Roman frontier post. The best Roman frontier post can be seen at Khirbet al-Baidha near the Wadi Gharz. It dates probably from the 3rd century AD, and consists of a square fort with a round tower at each corner. Both the masonry and some of the decoration are of particularly fine workmanship. More Roman ruins can be seen at Khirbet al-Ambashi further east.

The most spectacular view of the Safa and surrounding desert can be seen from the top of the Jebel Sais, in the heart of the desert some hundred miles east of Damascus. Like the Jebel Hauran, it is an extinct volcano that has strewn the surrounding region with black basalt lava flows and boulders, and still preserves its crater at the top. From here the view is stunning. It is also covered in vast numbers of Safaitic inscriptions and petroglyphs depicting various hunting scenes. This may suggest that the mountain was venerated as a sacred high place in ancient times. At its foot are a number of Umayyad remains from the early 8th century, including a mosque and a castle.

The Golan

The Golan, or Jaulan, is in complete contrast to the Hauran. Being the southern slopes of Mt Hermon, it is watered by many streams, providing a lush vegetation in many places and a generally greener and less harsh aspect than the Hauran.

There is little to see in Qunaitra, the capital of the Golan. The main sights are a number of ruins in and around Baniyas at the source of the Jordan River, including the massive Nimrud Castle, one of the most impressive Crusader castles of Syria (though these remains are at present not accessible).

Baniyas is the ancient Greek Paneas, named after the god Pan who was worshipped in a sacred grotto that marked the source of the Jordan. It became a minor regional capital under Herod and his son Herod Philip, when it was renamed Caesarea Philippi. The town was renamed yet again as Meronias by Herod Agrippa, but reverted to Paneas in the Roman and subsequent periods. Today, little is left of these periods, though Baniyas is a delightful place of gushing streams and shady trees. The main sight is the grotto of Pan in the side of a hill, which has a number of Greek and Roman niches cut into the rock face outside it.

Just outside and above Baniyas are the massive remains of Nimrud Castle, also known as Qal'at as-Subaibeh. It was originally built by the Assassins, but was taken by the Crusaders in 1130, only to be lost to the Zengids of Aleppo two years later. It was eventually recaptured by the Crusaders in alliance with a rival branch of the Zengids in Damascus,

33 Interior of the Church at Qasr Ibn Wardan

34 The seaward fortifications of the Old Town of Tartus

35 The Castle and town of Safita

36 The temple enclosure at Amrit

37 The temple of Hosn-i Sulaiman

38 General view of Marqab from the south

39 The western defences of Marqab

40 The entrance tower of Marqab

41 View from the Acropolis at Ugarit, along the street towards the west between the Royal Palace and North Palace

42 General view of the eastern end of Qal'at Saladin (Sahyun), from the south

43 The pinnacle of rock that supported the drawbridge at Saladin Castle (Sahyun)

44 General view of the Citadel and Old Town of Aleppo from the west

45 A coffee house at Aleppo, opposite the Citadel

46 The exterior of the Citadel of Aleppo, showing the south barbican, the ditch, glacis and entrance

47 The bridge over the ditch towards the main gatehouse of the Citadel of Aleppo

48 View up the paved street in the Citadel of Aleppo, with the Mosque of Abraham on the left and the minaret of the main mosque at the end

49 A window in the courtyard of the Khan al-Wazir in Aleppo

50 Interior of the Khan al-Gumruk in Aleppo

51 Courtyard of the Great Mosque at Aleppo

**52 Courtyard of the
Great Mosque at Aleppo**

53 Interior of one of the arcades of the Great Mosque in Aleppo

54 The apse of the former Byzantine cathedral of Aleppo, now the Madrasa Halawiya

55 The mihrab of the Madrasa Sultaniya in Aleppo

56 A street scene in the Jedaideh Quarter of Aleppo, showing the traditional overhanging window, or *mushrabiya*

**57 Contrasting
traditional and modern
scene in the Jedaideh
Quarter of Aleppo**

58 Courtyard of the Achiqbash House in Aleppo

**59 Part of the central
octagon of the Basilica of
St Simeon Stylites**

60 The main entrance of the Basilica of St Simeon Stylites

61 The west wing of the Basilica of St Simeon Stylites

62 The portico of the monastery of the Basilica of St Simeon Stylites

63 Decorative detail of the Basilica of St Simeon Stylites

64 General view out over Deir Sima'an from the west wing of the Basilica of St Simeon Stylites

but eventually fell after several sieges to Nur ed-Din, who had himself conquered the Zengids, in 1164. Subsequent sieges by the Crusaders failed to retake it, and it remained an important Ayyubid stronghold in Crusader territory.

Architecturally, the castle thus reflects its various masters: Assassin, Zengid, Crusader, Nurid and Ayyubid, though it is not easy to sort all of these elements out in its labyrinthine ruins. It consists of a large curtain wall, reinforced by square and semi-circular towers, that surrounds the elongated area of the summit on which it is built, with a gateway at the southwestern end and a keep at the northeastern end. Most of the towers face the weaker, southeastern side of the castle, while the northwestern side is protected by a sheer drop down into a gully. The machicolations and battlements that would have crowned the walls have largely disappeared. There is a passageway built into the thickness of the curtain walls that provided access to the loopholes all the way around. The gateway is a surprisingly simple one in comparison with other Arab and Crusader fortifications, though it replaced an earlier one in the southeastern side, now covered by a square tower. The gate is flanked on one side by a large square tower – almost a small keep itself – that has a number of intact vaulted rooms inside it and a large cistern just outside. The keep at the northeast end is protected by a secondary line of defence cutting across the castle, consisting of a ditch and another line of walls. The inner keep has just one large room, though vaulted passageways gave access to several other rooms built in the towers that overlook the northern end of the castle.

At the square tower in the middle of the southwestern end an underground passageway led to a secret exit from the castle. Adjacent to this tower are the remains of stables and storage areas, and in the middle of the courtyard are the badly ruined remains of a chapel.

CHAPTER 6

The Orontes Valley and Central Syria

The Orontes River (in Arabic al-'Asi, 'the rebel', because it flows the 'wrong' way – from south to north) hardly ranks with the great river systems of the Middle East: the Nile, the Euphrates, the Tigris. Nevertheless, it forms the heartland of Syria, a vital backbone around which much of its history was woven and on whose banks one of the Middle East's greatest cities, Antioch, was situated. Like the Jordan – its twin river to the south – the Orontes also drains the great rift valley. This valley, known as the Ghab, is an area of lush fertility dotted with ancient tells and modern settlements. Its rich, deep red soil makes the Ghab today Syria's main market gardening area.

Homs and environs

Homs (or Hims), along with Damascus, Hama and Aleppo, was one of Syria's caravan cities facing the desert and the East, complementing the sea ports of the Phoenician coast facing the Mediterranean and the West. Like the other caravan cities, it also has a continuous history as a main centre stretching back to remotest antiquity. Its ancient name was Emesa. It was probably one of the many independent Aramaean city-states that sprang up in the vacuum left by the collapse of the Hittite Empire in Syria at the end of the 2nd millennium BC, replacing the earlier city-states of Qatna and Qadesh (see below). It was ruled by a dynasty of priest-kings, guardians of the great temple of the sun-god

Emesene Baal, becoming in the Roman period one of the main centres for this cult in Syria. Its vigorous dynasty of priest-kings were destined to become one of the foremost families of the later Roman Empire, with the marriage of the high-priest's daughter Julia Domna in 187 AD to Septimus Severus and the consequent Syrian dynasty of emperors at Rome.

Emesa accordingly flourished under such imperial patronage. Its great Temple of Emesene Baal rivalled those of Baalbek and Palmyra and the city was elevated to the rank of colony under Caracalla and Metropolis under Elagabalus. Unfortunately, virtually nothing of this remains in modern Homs, which is a large industrial town of little character. There is the citadel mound in the centre, the foundations of which are probably quite ancient, with miscellaneous walls on it and some military installations on top. There are also the ruins of a Byzantine monastery which preserves some interesting 5th century frescos in an underground chapel, but of the great Temple of Baal of Emesa not a trace remains. The only buildings surviving from this period are two ruined tomb towers of the type which can be seen at Palmyra. In the centre of the town is the tomb of the great Arab conqueror Khalid ibn al-Walid, who conquered Syria for Islam in the 7th century. Though built recently, it is a striking building in the traditional Syrian style of alternating bands of black and white stone.

Whilst lacking much of interest itself, Homs forms an important centre, both of communications and for more interesting ancient remains in the area. In particular, two of the most important Bronze Age sites in Syria are to be found near Homs: Qatna and Qadesh. Qatna lies twenty kilometres to the northeast at the village of Mishrifeh. It was founded in the 3rd millennium BC when it is mentioned in the Mari texts. At the beginning of the 2nd millennium BC Qatna formed, along with Yamhad (modern Aleppo), one of the main Middle Bronze Age kingdoms in Syria. It was eventually eclipsed by the rival Egyptian and Mitannian empires, but before that produced a flourishing culture that left some quite spectacular remains.

Chief of these are the early 2nd millennium city walls of Qatna, probably some of the most impressive anywhere in the ancient world, even in a period that saw an 'explosion' of city wall construction right across Syria and northern Mesopotamia. Those at Qatna are vast (plate 18). They enclose an area of about 100 hectares – about a kilometre across – and today still stand between 12 and 20 metres in height. They are casemated walls with foundations of massive 'Cyclopean' masonry, some of the blocks several metres long and several tons in weight. Additional protection is afforded by a smooth glacis on the outside and strong triple-chambered gateways – a clear demonstration of the Syrian mastery of fortification techniques that was to reach such heights in the medieval period. Inside, there have been some excavations by French archaeologists, though there is nothing to see now. All there is today in the enclosure are the remains of a modern village, already crumbling into dust as though just sacked by some Egyptian or Mitannian horde, but merely evacuated, it seems, in preparation for an incipient invasion by an army of pick-axe wielding archaeologists.

Qadesh, modern Tell Nebi Mend, lies about 20 kilometres to the southwest of Homs, and has been the scene of British excavations since the 1970s. It was another city state that figured prominently as a strategic goal in the campaigns of the Egyptians of the New Kingdom into Syria in the latter half of the 2nd millennium. In particular, Qadesh was the site of a famous battle between Rameses II of Egypt and the Hittite army in 1286/85 BC, of which we have conflicting accounts in both the Egyptian and Hittite official annals. Rameses claimed a great victory, but it seems that the Hittites were left in control of Qadesh, so the battle was at best an undecided one for the Egyptians, albeit with great loss of life on both sides. Thereafter, Qadesh declined, though it later became the site of the minor Roman town of Laodicea ad Libanum.

Tells, more than most ancient sites, suffer from a sense of familiar ennui. But Tell Nebi Mend has its own atmosphere. The quiet of the late afternoon is always the best time of day for archaeological sites, when the past seems to come alive more than at other times. Tell Nebi Mend is a simply immense artificial mound. From the topmost part over 30 metres high there is a fine view over the surrounding plain. At the time of the Battle of Qadesh it would have been a little lower, but not much; with nothing but the black rocks of the modern graves and the wind whipping over the summit for company it is easy to imagine the battle that took place below. It would have been a far cry from the organized, orderly troops and carefully planned tactics of the Greek and Roman professional armies that dominated the world over a thousand years later. Two armies facing each other, not as orderly drawn up lines but as a fairly disordered throng of individual foot soldiers and chariots (cavalry then did not exist) that would have filled half the plain. Battle would not have been the solid, organized charges of attacking and counter-attacking units so beloved of Hollywood irregulars, but would probably have started merely as individual challenges and insults, deteriorating into occasional combats and ragged scrimmages. Full battle, when it came, was simply two surging masses of dust, blood and humanity. Organization and planning – if it ever existed – would soon be lost in the melee, chains of command would not exist: it would simply be a mixture of chaos, individual bravery and sheer blind panic; of confused individual bashing and hacking with blunt primitive weapons, of looting and indescribable butchery. It is not surprising that full battle between strong forces in the ancient world was often avoided. Even less surprising that victory, when full battle did come, would be decided not so much by the strongest, but by the least confused. Either way, it is no wonder that battles, like Qadesh, were so often undecided; victory would only lie with whoever had the strongest propaganda for posterity.

Between Nebi Mend and Homs lies Lake Qattina, formed by a dam across the Orontes. The dam wall is built of massive Cyclopean masonry over a kilometre long, probably dating from the 2nd millennium, though it has undergone considerable alterations and restorations since. There is a fortress on an island in the middle of the lake. Further to the south, beyond Qusayr on the main Homs-Beirut road, several areas of ruins are reported, some very large. Those known as Jusiya al-Kharab are the remains of a 5th and 6th century Byzantine town, that include a church and monastery. Those known as Jusiya al-Jadid nearby may be the site of the Greek Triparadisos where Alexander the Great's generals met after his death to divide up his empire.

In the desert at Hawarin, some 80 kilometres to the southeast of Homs, are the ruins of a Byzantine fort and two 6th century churches, and a minor Umayyad desert palace built by the Caliph Yazid.

Krak des Chevaliers

The greatest of all Crusader castles, and one of the greatest sights of Syria, the Krak des Chevaliers was described by T E Lawrence as 'perhaps the best preserved and most wholly admirable castle in the world'. Here, all that was best in both European and Middle Eastern military design combined to produce a castle – *the* castle – against which, once visited, all castles are ultimately measured. Without doubt, it is one of the greatest masterpieces of military architecture in the world.

For this reason the visitor should perhaps visit Krak (Arabic Qal'at al-Hosn) before any other Crusader castle. On the other hand, Robin Fedden recommends that 'any castle after Krak is an anti-climax' so should be reserved to last. Either way, no visit to Syria is complete without it.

The first castle at this site was probably just a small fort built by an emir of Homs in 1031 to guard the pass over to the coast. He garrisoned it with Kurdish soldiers (which gave rise to one of the castle's Arabic names of Husn al-Akrad). It was briefly occupied by the Crusaders in 1099, but was captured by Tancred of Antioch in 1109 and then held by the Crusaders until 8 April 1271 – an unbroken period of 162 years

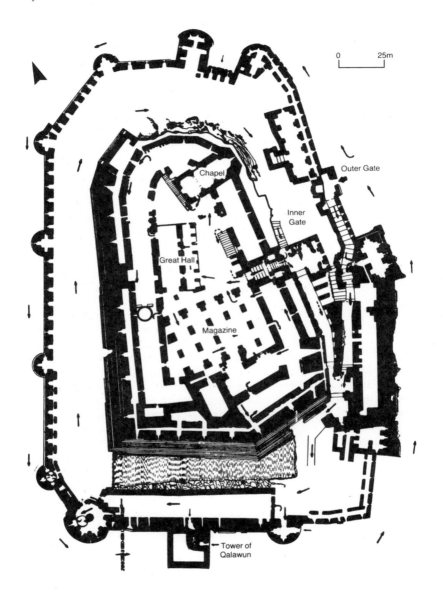

Fig. 11 Krak des Chevaliers

during which it was never once captured. It was acquired by the Counts of Tripoli in 1112, but ceded by them, under Count Raymond II, to the Knights Hospitallers, under whom it remained until the end. Saracen attacks in 1163, 1167 and 1188 (the latter led by Saladin himself) were repulsed. In the beginning of the 13th century the Hospitallers were confident enough in their stronghold to go on the offensive, leading raids deep into the interior of Syria. More sieges by the Ayyubid rulers of Aleppo were repulsed between 1207 and 1252, but it was the great Mamluk Sultan of Egypt, Baybars, who finally captured the immense Hospitaller stronghold. Even then, however, it was not taken by storm, but the knights were forced to surrender and hand over the castle virtually intact in 1271. It then became a Mamluk stronghold, and remained in intermittent use until the early 19th century.

The first castle, the original Castle of the Kurds, was probably razed by the Crusaders. After it came into the hands of the Hospitallers in 1142 a massive programme of building was embarked upon that was to last until the end of the century (figure 11). Much of this was probably to repair earthquake damage rather than to guard against particular military threats: the three main phases of building work occurred immediately after the earthquakes of 1157, 1169-70, and 1201-2, the latter being when the outer ring of defences was constructed. A fourth spate of building activity occurred in 1285 after its capitulation to the Mamluks when the great south tower was constructed. The final works were carried out after 1927 by the French government and subsequently the Syrian Department of Antiquities, who cleared out the village that occupied the interior and carried out restoration work.

In attempting to describe this fortress one finds oneself quickly exhausting one's stock of words for size: words like immense, massive, huge, and solid keep tumbling from a rather dazed vocabulary, but such words sound weak and hackneyed when attempting to convey its sheer size. On approaching, its strategic position is immediately apparent, situated high up on a spur and dominating the surrounding countryside for miles in all directions. This is reinforced when standing on the topmost tower with the birds wheeling below and the plain stretched out even further below that – indeed, it is in visual contact with Safita Castle some 20 kilometres to the west, and thence with Tortosa and the Crusader castles of the coast.

But before entering it is worth continuing up to the hill that overlooks the castle from the west, to fully appreciate both the strategic location and the size of the castle itself (plate 19; it is extremely unfortunate that a modern concrete building has been allowed to encroach on this view). For on subsequently reaching the foot of the walls one's over-riding impression is of sheer immensity: it is simply huge – and massively solid. Krak des Chevaliers was not the largest Crusader castle by any means, but being the most intact it conveys a far greater impression of size than the more ruinous larger ones. It comes as no surprise at all to learn that it held a garrison of some 4000 troops, and the sheer solidity of its massive stone walls leaves one wondering why it ever capitulated, when even modern artillery would have difficulty in dislodging a well-stocked garrison.

It is easy to see why it could never be taken by any straightforward storming of the gateway, for on entering, one immediately turns a sharp angle to climb up a long, steep narrow tunnel, built within the thickness of the walls, that would force any attacker into a single vulnerable file to be picked off with ease. Such an entrance could surely never have been penetrated. Even if the impossible was achieved and attackers did manage to run the gauntlet of murderous fire from all sides and successive traps and barriers of this entrance, they would only have reached the outer courtyard – another equally impenetrable tunnel entrance awaited them into the main castle. For the visitor, it is perhaps worth diverting here awhile to walk the full circuit of the battlements of the outer defences. Here one can gain the fullest view of the inner castle from all sides, and also properly appreciate its defences: the rock-cut fosse at the southern end (which served as a reservoir of rather greenish water as well as an additional obstruction) overlooked by the three massive towers that guarded the castle's weakest side to the south; the sloped glacis at the foot of the walls; the arrangement of the loopholes that provided interlinking fire at all points.

The second entrance into the main castle is through a massive gatehouse and then an inner gate – a system of defences even more formidable than the first. This opens onto the inner courtyard, divided into upper and lower parts (plate 20). Beneath the upper courtyard is an extensive vaulted magazine, that would have kept the garrison amply supplied for almost any siege. Surrounding the inner courtyard on all sides were a series of cavernous, long vaulted rooms that served as additional magazines as well as stables, stores and barracks for the garrison. But immediately opposite the entrance one is confronted by a structure that appears almost out of place in such a severely functional castle where every single stone is strictly subordinate to its military role. This is the great hall and cloister, a beautifully decorated building in Gothic style that would be more in place in the cathedral towns of medieval France than in a fortress high above the Orontes Valley in Syria (plate 21). As if to remind us, however, of the military rather than religious nature of the Crusades, we leave the great hall to enter the chapel adjacent: no elaborate Gothic decoration here, the strict military architecture of the castle sternly re-asserts itself in this rather cold, severe room.

It is perhaps best to simply spend a few hours to wander at will through the castle: along passageways, up staircases, out onto windy towers and battlements (plate 22), through into immense echoing halls and poky guard chambers. Saladin was repulsed below these walls, the king of Hungary dined in the great hall, Geoffrey de Joinville died somewhere within the walls. Names such as Tancred, Guillaume de Cratum, Hughes Revel, Armant de Montbrun, echo along the passages; medieval sounding names that have no place in today's world. And yet the whole massive thing is so solid, so intact, so empty, yet as if the Hospitallers walked out only yesterday.

Before leaving, it is worth examining several minor buildings in and around the village of al-Hosn below its walls. The mosque in the village dates from the time of Baybars' capture of the Krak, but almost certainly incorporates parts of an earlier Crusader church. Four kilometres below the village is the Monastery of St George, a Greek Orthodox monastery that is largely recent. Its foundation, however, dates from the time of Justinian, and the monastery preserves parts which go back to medieval times and earlier.

Hama

Hama in some ways is the most quintessential of Syria's cities of the Silk Route: it faces the desert, it is immensely ancient, it was an important caravan centre, it is a famous silk producing centre, and it is highly picturesque. It is also on the Orontes – and of it, unlike Homs which turns its back to the Orontes. This is Hama's great attraction: it is a city of gardens, of picturesque riverside houses, of shaded walks, and – most famously – of enormous waterwheels. But this idyllic setting also hides a history of religious conservatism, extremism, and violence. Its drabber sister city – and rival – of Homs perhaps has more to recommend itself after all.

Its origins are very ancient. They are certainly Neolithic, and important Chalcolithic (5th millennium) remains have been excavated by Danish archaeologists on the citadel mound. Along with Ebla and Qatna, it was one of the important central Syrian kingdoms that flourished in the late 3rd millennium and early 2nd millennium BC, enjoying its greatest prosperity in the middle of the 2nd millennium as an Amorite principality dependent upon the Mitannian empire. It disappears from history for a while with the collapse of Mitannian power. But it re-emerged with the rise of the Aramaeans in Syria round about 1100 BC, when it formed one of several important Aramaean and Neo-Hittite states in Syria known as Hamath. This was perhaps the period of Hama's greatest prosperity, but its independence was abruptly extinguished – along with the rest of Syria – with its conquest in 720 BC by Sargon of Assyria, when the city was totally destroyed and its inhabitants transported. There was a revival of fortunes under the Seleucids, probably presaged by the return of its inhabitants under the Persian Empire. A new town was founded, named Epiphania after the Seleucid Emperor Antiochus IV Epiphanes, and it remained a prosperous town under the Romans. It never underwent an Aramaic revival, however, as the Syrian cities further north did, and the subsequent periods of Byzantine, Umayyad, Ayyubid, Mamluk and Ottoman rule were periods of purely local, albeit prosperous, significance. It did, however, form an important trade terminus to the caravan routes in the Middle Ages, when it was a silk producing centre, a product for which Hama is still famous.

Hama today is a pleasant town to explore, more for its domestic architecture than its historical remains. The famous water-wheels are quite spectacular, some of them hundreds of years old (plate 23). Whilst these are depicted on many postcards and posters of Syria, no postcard conveys the deep, mellifluous grinding sound – like a cathedral organ – that the waterwheels emit. Less publicised but equally spectacular are the high, graceful aqueducts that march off behind the waterwheels.

The principal ancient monument was the Great Mosque, though nothing is left standing of it today. It was one of the earliest mosques in Islam, founded in 636-7 by the usual custom then of simply converting the existing Byzantine church, which in its turn replaced a Roman temple. The mosque still incorporated much of the Byzantine structure.

The other main building in Hama is the Azem Palace, now a museum. Like its more famous namesake in Damascus, it was built as a pasha's residence in the 18th century by the Azem family. Inside, as well as exhibits from excavations in and around Hama, there are superb examples of traditional Syrian architectural decoration, particularly wooden panelling and inlay work.

The citadel mound, now a public park, is where most of the excavations into Hama's past have taken place, though there is little to see today apart from the fine view over the town. The mound is an artificial tell, representing first the successive settlements of the town itself, and then, as it became higher and the town spread over a greater area, just the monumental and military centre. Traces from every period of Hama's long history were excavated, particularly parts of the Neo-Hittite palace and citadel from the Aramaean period in the early 1st millennium.

There are also several 18th century caravanserais, such as the Khan Asad Pasha and Khan Rustam Pasha in the souq area, the Zengid mosque of Nuri near the river, and several other minor Islamic monuments in Hama.

The Orontes Valley and the west of Hama

The area of Hama is in many ways Syria's heartland. For it is a pivotal area around which much of Syria's history has revolved; it is midway between Damascus and Aleppo, as well as midway between the desert and the coast. It is also watered by the Orontes, Syria's main river. Furthermore, the area boasts some of the most impressive remains in Syria: Greek, Roman, Byzantine and medieval.

Monuments of the latter period, the medieval, dominate the Orontes Valley – known as the Ghab – to the west of Hama, though numerous tells dotting the valley floor attest to considerable earlier settlement as well. The Ghab is close to the Crusader possessions of the coast, so three of Syria's main castles are located here: Misyaf, Shaizar and Mudiq. Misyaf, at the foot of the mountains on the edge of the Orontes valley to the southwest, is a walled town as well as castle (plate 24). The castle has a complex history, probably originating in the Byzantine period, but it first comes to notice as an Arab fortress in the 12th century, though the Crusaders may have held it briefly. It came under the possession of the Assassins in 1127, becoming the seat of the grand master of the sect, the Old Man of the Mountains. Because of this Saladin besieged it as retaliation for several assassination attempts against him by the Assassins, but lifted the siege after a reconciliation. The castle and town were eventually captured in 1270 during Sultan Baybars' suppression of the order.

The town is still an Isma'ili one and Isma'ili shrines dot the hilltops around. Several gateways survive. The castle itself is an impressive fortification with no less than three sets of defences: an outer curtain wall and two inner fortresses, dominated by a large gatehouse. The many different styles of the towers in the walls reflect the many rebuildings that the castle went through, and large quantities of re-used classical masonry indicate the existence of a Roman town nearby.

Further north along the edge of the Orontes Valley is the small Crusader fort of Laqoba, modern al-Laqbeh. Still further along the foothills is the picturesquely situated Assassin castle of Abu Qubais, known as Bokabeis Castle to the Crusaders, and there is a third castle further north still at Barzieh. The latter is probably the best preserved of these castles. It was originally Byzantine, and contains extensive Crusader and Arab additions, being taken by Saladin after a particularly fierce four-day battle in 1188. Misyaf, Laqbeh, Abu Qubais and Barzieh all overlooked the rich valley of the central

Orontes, but the main strongholds within the valley itself were Shaizar and Mudiq. Shaizar (plate 25), the first of these, derives from Caesara, a Roman town at its foot. This was in turn a continuation of the Seleucid military settlement of Larissa, colonised by Thessalonians, though nothing remains of the Greek and Roman town today. The castle was first built by an Arab dynasty of emirs in the 11th and 12th centuries, the Munqids, who were a constant threat to both the Byzantines and Crusaders in northern Syria. Its most colourful emir, 'Usama ibn al-Munqidh, left behind a lively series of memoirs of his life and times. Despite many attempts, Shaizar never fell to Christian forces. Both Tancred, Crusader prince of Antioch, and John II Comnenus, the Byzantine emperor, failed to take it in successive sieges in 1108 and 1138, despite the massive and elaborate siege engines used by the Byzantines. In the end it was natural forces rather than either Frankish or Byzantine that dislodged the Munqid lords of Shaizar: the castle fell to a terrible earthquake in 1157, that killed the emir and his entire family. Even then, however, the Crusaders missed taking it by a narrow margin: the Assassins got there first, though they were dislodged by Nur ed-Din of Aleppo a few years later, after which it remained in Muslim hands.

The castle itself occupies a long ridge overlooking the Orontes, which is crossed here by a stone bridge, not far from a waterwheel. There is a large modern village at the foot of the castle. Entry is up a stone bridge at the northern end of the castle through a large square gatehouse, which is dated by an inscription over the gate to Sultan Qalawun. The great two-storeyed donjon stands at the southern end of the castle, which is here isolated from the rest of the ridge by a deep fosse. This donjon is built of particularly deeply bossed masonry which, with an elaborately floriated window overlooking the valley, makes a superbly textured facade. The ends of columns taken from the classical ruins can be seen embedded into the walls for additional strength.

The castle of Mudiq (plate 26) dominates the ruins of the main town on the Orontes in antiquity: the Greek and Roman town of Apamea, from whence the Arab and Crusader name for the castle derives, Afamia. Before moving onto Apamea, however, it is worth describing the castle to complete our survey of the fortifications of the Ghab. The castle was presumably the acropolis of the ancient town, so would already have been fortified when the Arabs arrived on the scene. It fell to Bohemond of Antioch in 1106, after a particularly long siege, who made it over to the Hospitallers. It then became one of the Crusaders' most forward bases, used to carry out raids deep into the interior of Syria, until it was finally taken by Nur ed-Din in 1149. Afamia remained in Saracen hands, apart from a possible re-occupation by the Crusaders after the earthquake of 1157. The Saracens in turn used it as

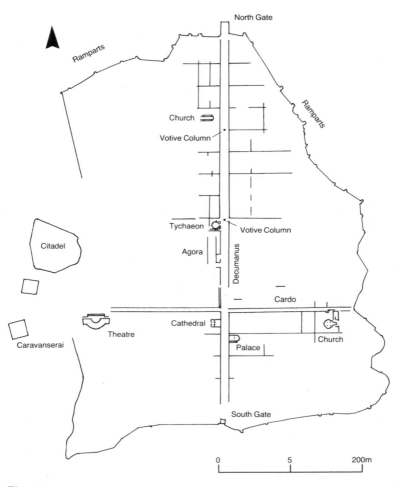

North Gate

Ramparts

Ramparts

Church

Votive Column

Citadel

Tychaeon

Votive Column

Agora

Decumanus

Cardo

Theatre

Cathedral

Church

Caravanserai

Palace

South Gate

0   5   200m

Fig. 12 Apamea

a base to harry the Crusaders and to dominate the Ghab, until it lost its military importance after the 14th century.

Mudiq Castle does not have the elaborate systems of defence that characterise so many of the other castles, but consists mainly of a simple, though well-preserved, curtain wall that surrounds the perimeter of the rock which formed the ancient acropolis. The curtain wall is reinforced by rectangular towers at regular intervals, with the gateway to the south flanked by two larger towers. The interior is fully occupied by the modern village. At the foot of the castle is a splendid Ottoman caravanserai, now a museum.

The vast ancient town of Apamea itself stretches to the east of the castle (figure 12, plate 27). It was founded in the wake of Alexander's conquest when it was called Pharnake, but was soon renamed Pella, after Philip the Great's capital in Macedonia. It was renamed yet again, however – presumably to avoid confusion with the town of Pella on the Jordan River – by Seleucus Nicator, who renamed it Apamea (one of three cities he so named) after his Bactrian wife Apama, daughter of the Persian commander Spitames. Apamea then became the third city of the Seleucid Empire, after Antioch and Seleucus on the Tigris, becoming particularly prominent as the imperial army headquarters. The main bulk of the Seleucid army was stationed there rather than at the capital in Antioch, where they might meddle with government, yet still within easy call just in case government should require a little meddling with. With such excellent pasturage in the surrounding valley, Apamea was also ideally situated for a stud farm, training area and supply centre generally for the army: 30,000 mares, 300 stallions and some 500 elephants are recorded as being stationed, raised and trained there, as well as the war treasury. It fell to Pompey in 64 BC, who destroyed its citadel, but the town continued as a prosperous, albeit less military, centre for many more centuries: its population was recorded as numbering 117,000 free inhabitants shortly after the conquest. Its oracle and Temple of Baal were famous as far away as southern France, and its wine was particularly famous for mixing with honey! This prosperity continued into the Byzantine period, when it became the centre of an important bishopric. All this ended dramatically in 540 AD, however, with the invasion of Chosroes I Parviz of Persia, who completely destroyed Apamea. Thus, ironically both its beginning and its end were linked with the Persians.

Apamea's lovely rural setting and its astonishing colonnaded Cardo (plate 28) – probably the longest and widest surviving from the Roman East – make it in many ways as impressive as Palmyra. Much of what there is to see has been exposed by a long programme of Belgian excavations and subsequent restorations, still in progress. Virtually nothing survives of the Seleucid city, apart from odd fragments built into Roman monuments, though the actual layout of the city itself is presumably Seleucid. This consists of an immense, roughly rectangular walled enclosure over a mile long, divided into four quarters in standard Hellenistic pattern by two main thoroughfares, the Cardo and Decumanus. Smaller side streets subdivided the city in a grid pattern. The Antioch Gate to the north is the only one of the city's four gates that is relatively well preserved, albeit consisting of just a great pile of masonry blocks.

The Cardo and Decumanus were colonnaded between about 116 and 160 AD in the manner of other cities of Roman Syria, though with important architectural quirks all of its own. The columns were of the Corinthian order, but the entablature above them combined Doric, Ionic and Corinthian orders. As if this were not enough, many of the columns have curious, floriated bulbous bases inserted between the foot of the shaft and the column base proper, and many more have spirally fluted column shafts (plate 29). Furthermore, many of the columns have projecting brackets from their shafts to hold statues, a feature that is also distinctive of the Palmyra street colonnades. The centres of intersections are marked by tall single columns on elaborate plinths (plate 30), rather than the more usual tetrapylons. Although not as famous as the colonnaded streets of Palmyra and Jerash, the great colonnaded avenues of Apamea must have surpassed all others in sheer elaboration – as indeed they still do. The forms of classical architecture – usually laid down in ancient Greece – were rigidly dominated by strict rules of order and proportion that were almost invariably adhered to. In Syria however – and especially at Apamaea – anything goes it seems: the rules were refreshingly relaxed and set formulas happily disregarded, lending the monuments a spontaneity and humour so often lacking in the purer but colder classical monuments further west.

Although many of the street colonnades are being re-erected, most of the remaining monuments are very fragmentary or still largely buried. The 2nd century theatre at the foot of the citadel was the largest in Syria – larger even than Bosra – and one of the largest in the Roman world. Parts of the Temple of Tyche and the Temple of Dionysus – two favourite gods of the Greek east – have been excavated, though only the former preserves a few fragments of the original Greek structure. Traces of the forum lie behind the Temple of Tyche, and very fragmentary remains of a baths and palaestra have also been found. The main Byzantine monument of importance is a 6th century church existing only in foundation. It has a distinctive, and architecturally important, quatrefoil plan.

The desert fringes east of Hama

Although the rich valley of the Orontes is Hama's hinterland, the city itself is one of Syria's 'desert ports': it faces the East, not the West. To the east lies the desert and the great caravan routes, the source of Syria's wealth in antiquity. The desert, therefore, is as much a part of Hama as the Orontes; the camel as much a symbol as the waterwheel, so it is to the desert we turn next.

The fringes of the desert hold mainly Byzantine remains – indeed, whole Byzantine towns. The existence of these remains in fact belies the term 'desert': though certainly dry and sparse by European standards, it holds sufficient water in wadis and wells which can, when properly conserved, support settlement and agriculture. The first of the Byzantine towns is Salamiya, now a sizeable provincial centre. Outside the modern town is an extensive area of ruins, ancient Salamias, that stretches for several kilometres. The ruins are built mainly from the ubiquitous black basalt, and include a basilica and many houses. Although most of these ruins are Byzantine, there are some later Arab remains as well, mainly from the time when it was one of the first Isma'ili centres in Syria in the 10th century. Indeed it was here that 'Ubaidullah, the first caliph of the Fatimid dynasty of Egypt, was born (the Fatimids belonged to a Shi'a sect related to the Isma'ilis). Ruins from this time include a mosque and the citadel of Qal'at ash-Sham, the latter built on top of a volcanic crater to the west of the town.

By far the most important of the desert remains is Qasr Ibn Wardan. There are three buildings: a palace, a church, and a barracks (plate 31). They stand on a slight rise, surrounded and extended by three levels of artificial terraces. These buildings form a part of a Byzantine imperial desert outpost, built between 561 and 564 during the time of Justinian, probably as a major defensive post against the Sasanians. They are unique in all Syria for their building style, for they are built entirely in the Byzantine imperial style of Constantinople, rather than in the local Syrian style. Hence, construction is of alternating bands of small stone masonry and brick (plate 32), identical to buildings in Constantinople, rather than the large masonry blocks that were almost universally used in Byzantine Syria. In a country where even modest domestic buildings were of stone, the use of brick was very exceptional – and presumably unnecessary. Indeed, the bricks themselves are identical in size to the standard bricks of Constantinople. Whilst they were presumably at least made on site, the actual moulds were probably imported. With such a clear disregard of local building practices, the design, the architects and even some of the skilled workmen of Qasr Ibn Wardan were also presumably imported.

The ruins of the palace cover an area measuring some 50 metres square, surrounding a courtyard. The entrance is through the north side, and the east and west wings were probably private apartments and administrative offices. Most has collapsed apart from a range of rooms along the south, which were the state apartments and reception rooms, still standing to a height of two stories. In layout, therefore, Qasr Ibn Wardan bears a strong resemblance to the 2nd century governor's palace at Bosra. The main feature of the state wing is the large, trefoil

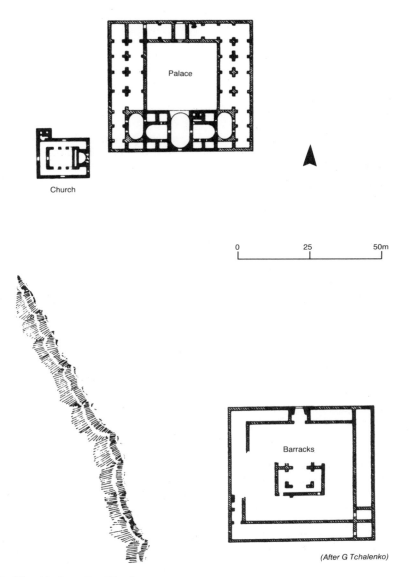

Palace

Church

Barracks

(After G Tchalenko)

Fig. 13 Qasr Ibn Wardan

105

shaped audience hall on the second floor.

The church immediately adjacent is also in a good state of preservation (plate 33). It is small – only some 13 by 17 metres – but is fairly ambitious in design, originally having a dome over the centre of the nave, surrounded by aisles and galleries separated by three-storeyed arcades which meet across the front to form a galleried narthex. This plan, like the construction technique, may also have been imported from Constantinople as it does not copy local Syrian models. Because of its compact size it probably formed a chapel or private church to the palace, rather than a congregational church or martyrium in the conventional sense.

The fortified barracks opposite is the largest building, but is almost entirely ruined apart from a few standing fragments. It consisted of rooms surrounding a central courtyard, in the centre of which is a two storeyed building. The whole was surrounded by a defensive wall. Some scattered column drums indicate a colonnade.

The complex at Qasr Ibn Wardan is something of an anomaly. It has no associated town, city or religious centre (which was at least as important in Byzantine times), so was a self-sufficient complex. Yet its strong architectural associations with the imperial capital indicate that this was no mere desert outpost under local control. Clearly, its construction must have been of considerable strategic planning of international importance to the Byzantine court. It was presumably a part of the extensive re-fortification and general re-organization of the empire carried out by Justinian, such as the massive fortifications at Halebiye on the Euphrates, in response to the increasing Persian threats from the east. Yet whilst the barracks suggest a military function, the church and the palace stand isolated and unprotected. The complex is more in the nature of the desert palaces, such as Qasr al-Hair or the ones in Jordan, but these did not appear until much later in the Umayyad period. Perhaps it was built in preparation for a visit from an emperor who never came.

Some 10 kilometres northeast on the desert track to al-Andarin are the remains of another Byzantine desert fortification: Qasr al-Antar. This is slightly earlier than Qasr Ibn Wardan, being built in 557-8, and consists again of a square fortification measuring some 88 by 82 metres, strengthened by square towers at each corner and flanking the entrance.

At al-Andarin itself, some 25 kilometres northeast of Qasr Ibn Wardan, are the ruins of the Byzantine town of Androna, perhaps the town that both Antar and Ibn Wardan might have been protecting. The ruins of Androna cover a large area, forming a fortified town that probably formed a part of Justinian's re-fortification programme, but abandoned soon after the Arab conquest. Unlike Qasr Ibn Wardan, the public buildings are of large, well-made masonry blocks in the normal Syrian fashion, but most of the private buildings and houses are of mudbrick, which becomes more and more common further in the desert regions until it becomes almost the only building material used in the east of Syria.

The town is laid out in a square with two intersecting main streets, surrounded by ramparts reinforced at regular intervals by square towers. In this way it follows the standard form of Byzantine fortifications, such as at Rasafeh and Halebiye on the Euphrates. The possible military nature of al-Andarin is emphasized by a large barracks about 85 metres square that dominates the centre of the town. Nearby are the very fragmentary remains of the cathedral which, unlike the contemporary Qasr Ibn Wardan church, follows the standard layout of north Syrian church architecture in the 6th century. There is a better preserved church to the south, probably part of a fortified monastery, and there are two more churches near the barracks dedicated to the archangels.

CHAPTER 7

The Coast

Crossing the ranges that separate inland Syria from the coast, one passes from one world to another. Behind is the Near East: the caravan towns and deserts link Syria with Mesopotamia, Persia and ultimately Central Asia. In front is the Mediterranean, a different world altogether whose destiny is intimately bound up with the sea and the other countries whose shores it laps. A world open to influences from the West which someone from the coasts of Spain – or Greece or Tunisia – would find familiar. Assyrians, Persians, Amorites, Palmyrenes, Mongols – all seem very alien here. This is the world of the Phoenicians and Crusaders, of Greeks, Romans and Venetians. The sea, in separating so many peoples and nations, also binds them intimately together. A Mediterranean world.

It is only a narrow strip never more than a few miles wide. Yet this strip holds an immense wealth of history, and remains of every period can be seen here. For if Syria is the 'gateway to Asia', its coastal strip is the gateway to Syria – and the gateway to the West. Remains from earliest history, such as Ugarit, coexist with modern Isma'ili tombs dotting the hilltops and the silent colossi of the Crusader era: Yahmur, Marqab, Saladin Castle (Sahyun). Terraced hills richly scented with wild-flowers give way to forests and green pasture land higher up. The forests face the glint of the Mediterranean, providing a contrast with the interior of Syria as much as a rest for the eyes. The ports of Latakia and Tartus – not to mention Tripoli, Byblos, Tyre, Antioch and Alexandretta to the south and north – are part of the network that span the Mediterranean. They are linked to Smyrna, Marseilles, Carthage and Genoa, much as Damascus and Aleppo are linked to Samarqand and Isfahan.

Tartus and Arwad

Tartus is a twin city consisting of the town of Tartus itself on the mainland facing the island of Arwad a few kilometres offshore. Both formed major centres of maritime power, and their history is inextricably entwined.

Even their names are interlinked. In ancient times the island was known as Aradus, with its counterpart on the mainland known simply as Antaradus, both eventually evolving to Arwad (or Ruwad) and Tartus (or Tortosa) respectively. Of the two, Arwad is probably the more ancient in foundation. It is mentioned in Genesis as well as in Egyptian documents as one of a number of Canaanite settlements on the coast in the early 2nd millennium. Like Tyre, it was an island city-state with an economy based almost entirely on trade, creating a network that later under the Phoenicians would span the Mediterranean. Arwad in fact formed the head of a minor Phoenician maritime empire, consisting of a federation of coastal city-states which were mostly founded and colonised up and down the coast from Arwad itself. Such trading colonies were Baniyas, Amrit and Jeble, but the most important – at least for the Aradians – was their foothold on the mainland: Antaradus. Aradus however, remained the more 'senior partner' until the Roman period.

As the head of its federation of city-states, Arwad treated separately with both the Egyptians and Hittites, sending its own contingent to fight on the side of the Hittites in the Battle of Qadesh in 1285. With all the other Phoenician city-states of the Levant, Arwad and Tartus came under the nominal overlordship of the Assyrians at the beginning of the 1st millennium, followed in turn by the Babylonians, Persians and Greeks. But it was in these conquerors' own interests to allow at least some independence to the coastal cities: they did after all, make money, a commodity that no wise conqueror ever suppresses!

Arwad passed peacefully to Alexander the Great, having the wisdom to submit rather than try to match the famous siege – and spectacular defeat – that the other Phoenician island-city of Tyre underwent in 232. Because of this, it enjoyed newfound prosperity, but with the coming of the Romans its fortunes passed to Tartus on the mainland. Under the Pax Romana the natural defences of an island were no longer necessary, whilst on the mainland there was at least room for growth and expansion, so Tartus grew at the expense of Arwad. It underwent a major programme of rebuilding in 346 under Constantine, probably because of its ancient shrine dedicated to the Virgin Mary. It was for a while consequently renamed Constantia, though it soon reverted to its ancient name of Tartus. It is under this name – or its Latinized form of Tortosa – that it became famous in Crusader times as one of the main Crusader towns – as opposed to just fortresses – in Syria, mainly as the headquarters of the Knights Templar. It was first captured from the Arabs in 968 by the Byzantine Emperor Nicephorus Phocas, and in 1099 was captured by the Crusaders on their way to Jerusalem, but lost again almost immediately until its recapture three years later by Raymond de St Gilles. Tortosa then achieved fame as a pilgrimage centre to the sanctuary of the Virgin, around which was built the cathedral in the middle of the 13th century, remaining almost continuously in Crusader hands until their final eviction from the Levantine mainland in 1291. Apart from a brief occupation of Tartus by Nur ed-Din in 1152, the main threat to the Templars came from Saladin in 1188, who captured nearly all of the town including the cathedral. The Crusaders managed to just hold on in a single heavily fortified tower, from where they were eventually able to retake the rest of the town. After the final loss of Tartus in 1291, the Crusaders were never able to re-establish a foothold on the mainland again. They managed to hold out on Arwad for a further eleven years until 1302, taking the celebrated image of the Virgin Mary with them from the cathedral, and re-occupied Arwad briefly in 1518. Arwad, therefore, is the Crusaders' 'last stand' in the Near East.

Although heavily built over, a surprising amount of the Crusader town and fortifications still exists in Tartus (figure 14). But one has to look for it in the maze of narrow alleyways and squares that make up the old town. The streets are in any case a delight to explore, coming across medieval fragments at every turn. The warm yellow sandstone of the older buildings contrast with the dull concrete of the new. They also preserve a true medieval flavour, but not the scrubbed, sanitized medievalism of European 'heritage centres': this is the real thing, so visitors be warned!

The original Crusader fortifications consisted of the city walls, the harbour walls, and the citadel. The latter stands at the northwestern corner of the walled town overlooking the sea (plate 34). On the landward side it is heavily protected by a triple line of defences consisting of an outer curtain wall, a ditch, and an inner wall reinforced with rectangular towers. The heavily defended entrance is on the north side protected by a large square tower in the outer wall. Immediately inside the inner wall is the great hall, though completely built over by modern houses, with a small chapel adjacent. Over by the sea are the very badly ruined remains of the great donjon, or keep, from where the knights withstood Saladin's siege in 1188. Massive vaulted undercrofts

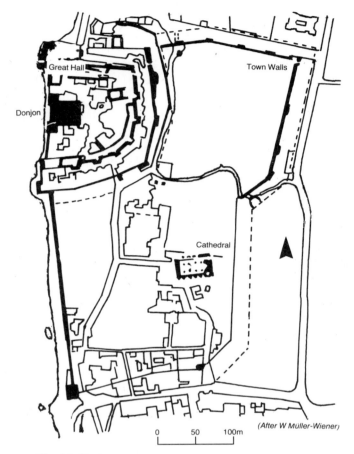

Fig. 14 Tartus

can still be seen, though above them modern housing has all but obscured the keep. On the seaward side can still be seen the postern gate from which the last of the Knights Templar escaped to Arwad and Cyprus in 1291.

In the middle of the town the Cathedral of Our Lady of Tortosa is preserved virtually intact. The site was already a famous centre of pilgrimage in the Byzantine period, and several fragments of Byzantine masonry have been found re-used in its construction. As it stands, however, it is a remarkable example of French early Gothic architecture, with its facade almost exactly as the Crusaders would have left it. The interior, now a museum, preserves virtually all its original appearance. Its austere appearance, however, lacks the grace of contemporary churches in France, as if to remind us that this was still a garrison church subordinate to military purposes.

Arwad is only a tiny island some 900 by 550 metres in extent, 3 kilometres off Tartus. Not long ago it was one of the gems of the eastern Mediterranean. But today it is a slum, jam-packed from shore to shore – taking fullest advantage of the lack of cars on the island to make streets even more narrow and noisome – that is slowly sinking under its own garbage. It is with relief that the visitor comes across the thriving boat-building industry at one end of the island, providing the only note of colour.

The island is roughly U-shaped, with a fishing harbour at its open, southern end. Sea walls survive in occasional fragments by the shore around the other sides. Nothing survives of the great Phoenician city of Aradus, though a very fine 8th century BC alabaster relief was found on the island. The Lusignan coat of arms can still be seen over the gateway of the castle overlooking the harbour, and the larger castle in the centre of the island today houses a small museum. The museum is poorly maintained and the exhibits are unlabelled, though some appear intriguing, such as some Parthian statuettes probably from Hatra in Iraq.

Crusader Castles inland from Tartus

With Tartus being one of the Crusaders' main possessions, its landward approaches were naturally heavily guarded by several castles: Yahmur, Safita, Araimeh and Khawabi. The first three are to the southeast of Tartus on the route to Homs, part of the chain of fortresses defending this route that included Krak des Chevaliers. Araimeh Castle (known as Arima in the Crusader annals) is the most ruinous of this chain. It was a Templar castle that was linked to both the Homs and the Tripoli lines of fortifications east and south of Tartus. Its early and later history is obscure, only being mentioned for the first time in the middle of the 12th century in connection with Tripoli, with no mention of when the Crusaders finally vacated it, though sources refer to a brief occupation in 1166-7 by Nur ed-Din. Though heavily ruined, its impressive defences are still apparent, consisting of a triple line of walls with an inner, rectangular keep situated high up on a ridge.

Qal‘at Yahmur – known as Chastel Rouge to the Crusaders – is in visual contact with both Tartus and Arima. The site is an ancient one, with Roman remains in the vicinity, so may have been a fortress before the present one. This is mainly 12th century, having been captured by the Crusaders at the beginning of the century. It is a fairly simple castle consisting of just a single enclosure wall surrounding a square, originally three storeyed, vaulted donjon – perhaps a real Norman keep. Two towers were added, at opposite corners of the outer wall, after its capture by Sultan Qalawun in 1289.

Yahmur's 'sister' castle of Safita – the Chastel Blanc of the Crusaders – is further east towards Krak (plate 35). It too consists of a central donjon surrounded by an outer wall, but on a larger scale than Yahmur with the oval shaped outer walls encircling part of a very picturesque small town. Much of the walls are now built over, but the main entrance is dominated by a large two storeyed tower on the eastern side, with the remains of vaulted rooms still visible. The castle changed hands several times between Crusaders and Saracens, belonging to the Knights Templar for most of the time, who substantially rebuilt it after its recapture from Nur ed-Din and the subsequent earthquake in 1170. It again suffered considerable earthquake damage in 1202 requiring further rebuilding. The massive donjon dominating the hill appears to be a classic keep in the Norman tradition. Inside, most of the space is taken up by a splendid chapel dedicated to St Michael on the ground floor – today still the parish church of Safita – and a magnificent vaulted hall on the first; in effect, Safita Castle was a fortified church. Most of the donjon probably dates from after its last rebuilding, following the 1202 earthquake, but the chapel might be earlier. The castle resisted Saladin in 1188, and finally fell to Sultan Baibars in 1271.

The fourth castle that overlooked Tartus was Qal'at al-Khawabi near the road to Misyaf. It was known to the Crusaders as Coible Castle, but for most of its history it was probably an Assassin stronghold – who were allied to the Hospitallers – dating from about 1160. It is impressively situated on a crag dominated by the surrounding mountains, and consists of outer and inner defences.

Phoenician sacred remains in the Tartus region

A few kilometres south of Tartus is the site of another colony founded by the Phoenicians of Arwad: Amrit, ancient Marathus. Indeed, the island of Arwad lies about the same distance from Amrit as it does from Tartus itself, though the latter had far closer connections with Arwad. Amrit in fact tried to break free from Arwad's domination in 219 BC, which probably explains why it declined in the Graeco-Roman period while Tartus rose at its expense.

This meant, however, that Amrit escaped the subsequent Romanization which all but eclipsed the Phoenician remains of Arwad and Tartus. It therefore preserves some of the most important

Phoenician monuments on the entire Levantine coast. They are remarkable for preserving pre-classical forms of Semitic religious architecture, without the classical veneer that nearly all Semitic monuments were subsequently subjected to. They lie in three groups in the site, known as al-Ma'bid, al-Maghazil, and Burj al-Bazzaq, scattered over nearly three kilometres. The first, to the north, lies next to the Amrit River. It is known as al-Ma'bid, which simply means 'the temple', and is probably the strangest monument the visitor will encounter in Syria (plate 36). This was probably the main sanctuary for the whole group of ruins at Amrit. It is certainly its most impressive, as it consists of a large court measuring some 65 metres square – the by now familiar Semitic sacred 'open space' – cut entirely out of the rock. In the centre is a small cella raised on a high, rock-cut cube surmounted by a crow-step frieze. The rock-cut enclosure was flooded by a nearby spring, turning it into a sacred pool and the cella an island. This pool is surrounded by a colonnade consisting of simple, square upright slabs of stone that is very reminiscent of the much earlier Sabaean architecture of South Arabia – ample evidence of the Semitic origins of the colonnaded enclosures that achieved such popularity in Roman Syria.

Further south on a small ridge is al-Maghazil (which means 'the spindles'). They are probably funerary monuments, consisting of square pedestals surmounted by huge monolithic cylinders, 13 and 23 feet high respectively, and each further surmounted by a pyramid on the smaller one and a half sphere on the larger. The area is surrounded by ancient quarries and more funerary monuments, including a free-standing monolithic mausoleum carved entirely out of the bedrock and containing several chambers, and another cube-shaped mausoleum surmounted by a pyramid.

The third group, Burj al-Bazzaq, lies further south again. Both this and the Maghazil are in a military area, so access is not possible. It consists of a great black mausoleum in the shape of a cube. Its name – rather mysteriously – means 'Tower of the Snails'. It has two super-imposed burial chambers and was originally surmounted by an obelisk, the remains of which have fallen below. Another cubic block is nearby, and another fallen obelisk lies further to the south.

The whole Amrit area is now largely wasteland and military zones on the outskirts of Tartus, with rapidly expanding beach-side development along the coast, so it is difficult to obtain an overall impression of the site. There is a tell near al-Ma'bid representing the ancient town of Amrit. The monuments probably date from the 5th or early 4th centuries BC. The cube form, pyramids and obelisks have obvious affinities with Egypt. More important, however, they recall ancient Semitic worship of abstract forms – particularly the cube – that can be seen as far apart as Mareb in Yemen and Nabatean architecture in

Petra, with its emphasis on 'god-blocks' and obelisks to represent its deities in abstract form. Indeed, the ancient Semitic idea of the sacred cube reaches its culmination in the centre of Semitic worship to this day: the Ka'bah (which is Arabic for 'cube') at Mecca.

Further inland to the northwest of Tartus, high up in the valleys and hills of the Nusairi ranges, are the magnificent remains of the ancient Phoenician sanctuary of Hosn as-Sulaiman, ancient Baetocecea, a great temple complex in some ways almost as impressive as Baalbek. This was a high place dedicated to the worship of Baetocecian Baal, the patron god of the Phoenicians of Arwad, sacred since the earliest times, though the present sanctuary dates from the Graeco-Roman period in the 1st and 2nd centuries AD. Set high up in the clouds within a natural amphitheatre, surrounded on all sides by the hills and the heady scent of wild flowers, the setting has a wild beauty that befits a great pagan god.

The sanctuary consists mainly of a vast open space, or temenos, in the ancient Semitic tradition, as large as the great urban sacred enclosures of Damascus or Palmyra (plate 37). It measures some 160 by 100 metres, and is walled with huge stone blocks up to 10 metres long. It is entered by four pylon gates on each side, with bas-reliefs representing the morning and evening stars, Phosphorus and Hesperus, on all four gates and additional reliefs representing Victories on the south and west gates. A dedicatory inscription dated 171 AD on the east gate declares the temple to have been built by public subscription. Another inscription of the Emperors Valerian and Galienus dating from 250 AD is on the north gate. In the centre of the enclosure is an Ionic temple now mainly a great tumbled mass of masonry, with an open-air altar in front. Lion sculptures decorate the facade of the temple as well as the north facade of the enclosure. There is another small temple to the northwest of the enclosure, as well as the remains of a massive building of unknown purpose, built in superb quality masonry blocks.

Baniyas and the Central Coast

The foothills of the Nusairi Mountains facing the sea between Tartus and Latakia must contain the biggest concentration of medieval castles anywhere in the world. Yahmur, Safita and Khawabi we have already seen, and further north, castles abound, both Crusader and Assassin.

The greatest of these – indeed probably the greatest in Syria after the incomparable Krak – is Qal'at al-Marqab, known to the Crusaders as Margat Castle (plate 38). It is also the first to be encountered on leaving Tartus to the north, just before Baniyas, part of the chain that stretched up to Antioch. The castle is 'announced' by a small advance tower, the Burj as-Sabi, overlooking the sea that was probably an outlying fort of Marqab guarding the coastal road. Marqab itself is a vast fortress occupying a dramatic position on a hill overlooking the sea, commanding the coastal plain for miles in both directions. It is a complex castle of many different building periods, reflecting its complex history. The first castle – probably just a small fort – to be built on this site was one belonging to a local Arab chief in 1062, and this was probably the one occupied briefly by Byzantine troops under John Cantacuzenus in 1104 before it reverted to the Arabs. It was made over by negotiation to Roger of Antioch in about 1117, who presented it as a fiefdom to the Mansoer family. The upkeep of such a fortress, however, was too much for a small family, particularly after the massive repairs required after the earthquakes of 1157, 1170 and 1186, so it was handed over in 1186 to the powerful Hospitaller order. It was apparently so strong that Saladin did not even attempt to attack it in his campaign along the coast two years later, and it successfully resisted a long siege in 1204-5 by the emir of Aleppo. The surrender of the great Hospitaller fortress of Krak in 1271, however, must have sent ripples throughout all of the Hospitaller possessions in northern Syria, and Marqab was forced to give up much of its land. Finally, in 1285, it fell to Sultan Qalawun, and remained a major Mamluk stronghold until the 15th century.

Marqab was one of the largest Crusader castles built, and today its awesome size with views far out to sea are quite stunning. It also had some of the most formidable defences (figure 15). Situated high on an extinct volcanic cone in the form of an immense triangle, it consists of an outer and an inner fortress. The outer fortress is protected by a ditch and double line of walls, the inner separated by a further ditch and surrounded in parts by another double wall – truly an impregnable stronghold (plate 39). Small wonder that Saladin simply by-passed it. The first enclosure wall in the outer fortress is reinforced by semi-circular towers, though the entrance is through a large rectangular tower (plate 40). The second enclosure wall is largely ruined, as are most of the buildings in the outer castle, which is now just a wilderness of snakes and hollyhocks. The main defences are concentrated in the great triangular citadel at the southern end of the enclosure walls. It is dominated at its southern tip by an immense, three storied circular tower overlooking a semi-circular salient in the outer walls. The inner courtyard is surrounded by the remains of barracks and vaulted storerooms, now very ruined, and is divided by the castle chapel. This chapel, still in an excellent state of preservation, is a good example of the high Romanesque architecture of France, and was used by the bishop of Valenia (Baniyas) during times of insecurity.

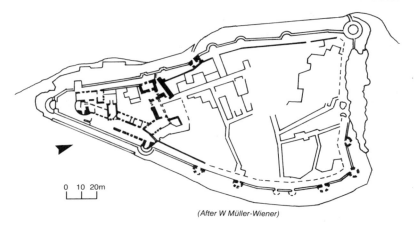

(After W Müller-Wiener)

Fig. 15 Marqab

For Baniyas, on the coast below Marqab, was the town that the castle was guarding, though it possessed its own fortifications. Originally a Phoenician colony founded by Arwad, it became a minor sea port in Roman and Byzantine times under the name of Balanea. It became a more important port and a bishopric under the Crusaders, when it was known as Valenia, forming the boundary between the kingdoms of Tripoli and Antioch. Apart from a few fragments virtually nothing remains of its past in the modern town.

High in the Nusairi Mountains inland from Marqab are a chain of Assassin castles stretching northwards towards Latakia. The Castle of Khawabi, to the south behind Tartus, we have already discussed, as well as the castles of Misyaf and Abu Qubais inland overlooking the Orontes Valley. Continuing northwards along the coast from Khawabi are the Assassin castles of Kahf, Qadmus, 'Alaiqa, Qusaibeh and Bustwar. Qal'at al-Kahf is only a few kilometres further inland from Marqab, though there is no road. It was one of the first castles in Syria to come into the Assassins' possession, in 1134, and was the last Assassin castle to fall to Baybars in 1273 in his suppression of the order. It is very well protected by the natural terrain, though there is little left standing of the castle itself apart from a tomb just outside which is the reputed burial place of the Old Man of the Mountain himself. Qadmus Castle, further inland on the main road from Baniyas to Misyaf and Hama, perches dramatically on a crag overlooking the village like a central Italian hill town, though almost nothing survives of its walls. It was taken from the Assassins by Bohemond II, who made it over to the Hospitallers of Marqab in 1186.

117

North of Qadmus lies Qal'at al-'Alaiqa, another Assassin castle, on top of a steep-sided small plateau. The outer walls surround the edges of this plateau in the shape of a triangle, enclosing a massive inner keep. A few miles north is Qal'at al-Qusaibeh, or Maniqeh, a better preserved Assassin castle that in 1168 was also made over to the Hospitallers. It stands on the end of a ridge, part of which has been cut away to isolate it on all sides. A number of well-preserved towers and some underground vaults survive inside. Another Assassin castle, of which very little remains, is Qal'at Bustwar a few miles further north.

Back on the coast, the village of 'Arab al-Mulk marks the site of Paltos, another Phoenician port that became a minor town in Roman and Byzantine times. Under the Crusaders a small castle was built there by the Hospitallers of Marqab, though nothing is left today.

Jebleh, ancient Gabala, further north was another ancient Phoenician colony founded from Arwad. In the 5th century BC Gabala became a Greek colony of the Dorians, the only one on the Levantine coast. It continued as a prosperous seaport under subsequent Seleucid, Roman and Byzantine rule when it was the seat of a bishopric. It changed hands several times between Muslims and Byzantines, until 1098 when Raymond de St Gilles captured it from the former, making it part of the principality of Antioch under the name of Zibel. It again became a bishopric, and the Crusaders fortified the town and restored the harbour, but it was captured by Saladin in 1188, only to be abandoned four years later. The Prince of Antioch then ceded it to the Hospitallers, though rival claims were made by the Templars, until it was finally taken by Sultan Qalawun in 1285 after the capture of Marqab.

There are few remains left today, the most important being the impressive Roman theatre – one of the few free-standing ones in Syria – and parts of the rock-cut harbour, which is probably Phoenician work. A few remnants of the Crusader fortifications can be made out behind the harbour, albeit heavily built over. Near the theatre is the Muslim shrine to Ibrahim ibn Adham, an 8th century Persian mystic – one of Islam's first sufis – from Balkh whose early life closely resembled that of Buddha.

Inland from Jibleh is the very ruined Crusader castle of Qal'at Bani Isra'il or Bani Qahtan, probably the Hospitaller castle of Chateau de la Vieille, captured by Tancred in 1111. Another small castle, Qal'at ar-Rus (Castle of the Bride) lies by the sea a few kilometres north of Jibleh where there also used to be traces of a bridge and the old Roman road between Tartus and Latakia, but these are now in a military area.

Latakia and environs

Latakia is the ancient Laodicea, so-named by Seleucus I Nicator after his mother, shortly after Alexander the Great's conquest. With Antioch and Apamea, it was one of the three main cities of Seleucid Syria, forming the main harbour for the latter, linked by a road across the Nusairi Mountains. But Laodicea already had an ancient history long before Alexander. In the 2nd millennium BC it was the Canaanite port of Ramitha, part of the kingdom of Ugarit just up the coast. As Ugarit declined, the better natural harbour facilities at Laodicea increased its importance, becoming a major port second only to Antioch in Greek and Roman times – indeed, Antioch itself was even subordinated to Laodicea for a while under Septimus Severus. It flourished under the Romans: the slopes behind the city were covered with gardens and vines (Laodicea's wines were famous), Herod the Great – in order to curry Roman favour – endowed the city with an aqueduct, and Septimus Severus endowed the colonnaded streets. It continued to prosper under the Byzantines, becoming the seat of a metropolitan in the 6th century. After the Byzantine period, however, its history is generally one of repeated devastation, either by the earthquakes of the 5th, 6th, 12th, 13th, 18th and 19th centuries, or by constant invasions: Persians, Arabs, Byzantines, Seljuks, Crusaders, Mamluks and Ottomans, with many returning for repeat devastations. Few other cities in the Levant had quite such a chequered history.

But despite such a catalogue of devastations there are still some monuments standing in the city. There is a 14th century Mamluk tower at the end of a jetty in the harbour, though no traces remain of any of the fortifications from the time of the Crusades, when Latakia was a Latin bishopric called La Liche. Surprisingly, some Roman remains survive. There is a fragmentary Corinthian colonnade, probably a part of the Temple of Adonis, and not far from it, the remarkably impressive tetrapylon, a monumental four-way arch that would have marked the junction of two colonnaded streets. In the streets, the occasional re-used classical fragment or row of columns buried almost up to their necks attest to further remains below ground, whilst parks and roundabouts in the modern city are often adorned with re-erected colonnades discovered in the course of building work.

More remains can be seen on the coast on the northern outskirts of Latakia, opposite the Meridien Hotel near the small peninsula of Ra's Ibn Hani. This is the site of Diospolis, a town of the Seleucid period, though recent French excavations have also uncovered parts of a Bronze Age town as well. Its ruins cover a wide area, though they are mostly buried, with only occasional foundations protruding from the debris where the archaeologists have uncovered them.

On the next peninsula a few kilometres further on from Ra's Ibn Hani is the site of Ra's Shamra, ancient Ugarit (Ra's means 'peninsula' or 'headland'), most famous of all the ancient Canaanite/Phoenician city-states along the Syrian coast. Famous indeed it was: ancient references to Ugarit have been found as wide apart as Mari on the Euphrates, Bogazkoy in central Anatolia, and Tell el-Amarna in Egypt, dating back to the 2nd millennium BC. The history of Ugarit, however, goes back many thousands of years before that, back to the Aceramic Neolithic period in 8th millennium BC. Then it was probably little more than a small village, but finds at Ugarit of obsidian tools from both Chiftlik, south of Konya, and Suphan Dagh north of Lake Van in eastern Turkey, show that already trade was beginning to figure prominently. Ugarit rapidly gained an edge in trade, which became its economic mainstay over the subsequent millennia. Thus, from the many different levels of its immense history, goods from all over the ancient world have been discovered in the excavations: from Egypt, Cyprus, Crete and Greece in the west to Mesopotamia and Persia in the east. The evidence for this trade has come mainly from pottery and cuneiform documents, but occasionally the evidence is more unusual: a shipment of a thousand Cypriot perfume flasks, for example, was discovered in one of the harbourside warehouses. Ugarit was the first of Syria's great caravan cities.

Ugarit flourished as one of the Mediterranean's main trading entrepots for many thousands of years, sometimes coming under the domination of one major power, sometimes of another: Egyptian, Hittite, Mitannian. Like all good businessmen, however, the people of Ugarit generally managed to maintain a balance of good trade relations with all powers. Its height was in the latter half of the 2nd millennium, having particular control over the trade of metalwork, timber, grain, wine, and the 'Tyrian' purple dye, which they manufactured locally. The archaeological record has found evidence of many ups and downs throughout this immensely long history: invasions, conflagrations, earthquakes and even tidal waves. To relate it all, together with its complex relations with the super-powers, would be to relate much of the history of the Near East, and would take far too long here. Ugarit always rose again, always as a trading and intellectual centre. But after the invasion of the 'Peoples of the Sea' mentioned in the Egyptian texts in about 1200, Ugarit never recovered, its place taken over by the Phoenician city-states further down the coast.

It was a chance discovery in 1928 that led to the discovery of Ugarit, and excavations have continued intermittently ever since by French archaeologists. A vast amount has been uncovered: a rich art, many thousands of cuneiform texts, and large areas of the site. It covers a

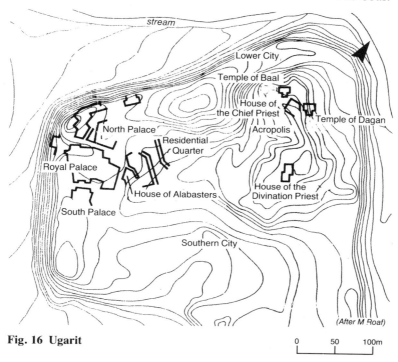

Fig. 16 Ugarit

0   50   100m

very large area, stretching down to the ancient harbour of Minet al-
Baidha. The two main areas of excavation, however, comprise the
acropolis where the main temples are located, overlooking a palace
area to the south (figure 16). The whole was surrounded by stone
ramparts that are entered through an unusual trapezoid-shaped
gateway that is reminiscent of Mycenaean work. The royal palace is an
immense, rambling affair of over 90 rooms and six courtyards, covering
many different periods from about 1600 to 1200 BC (figure 17, plate
41). It also dates from many periods of excavation over the past 60
years, with some parts excavated and others overgrown, so it is not easy
to find one's way around. In fact this probably gives a fairly accurate
impression of what it must have been like originally: a rather confusing
rabbit-warren of a place easy to lose one's way in, with some parts
bustling with courtiers, scribes, ambassadors and merchants, other
older wings lying quiet and semi-derelict, a prey to whispers and
intrigue.

The acropolis is dominated by temples to the two chief deities of
Ugarit: Baal and Dagan. The latter is a massively constructed stone

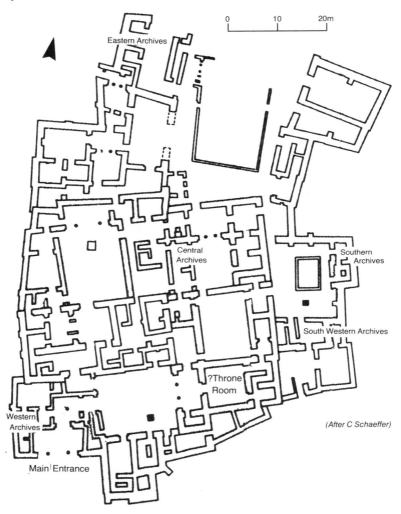

Fig. 17 The palace at Ugarit

structure with an underground vaulted burial chamber, again reminiscent of Mycenaean architecture. One of the largest subterranean pits here, however, is a simply massive sounding excavated by the archaeologists. Many vaulted burial chambers can be seen elsewhere on the site, usually underneath the floors of private houses. From the top of the acropolis is a good view of the lower town

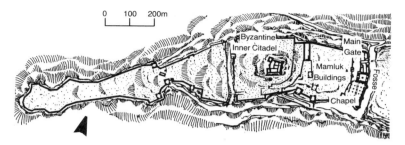

Fig. 18 Qal'at Salahuddin (Sahyun)

to the west, with street lines, house ruins and miscellaneous bits of walls
– some standing several metres high – discernible.

Further north along the coast, not far from the present Turkish
border, is another peninsula, the Ra's al-Basit. This is the site of the
ancient Seleucid harbour of Posidium, though the present fortifications
are probably Arab.

Qal'at Salahuddin (Sahyun)

Inland from Latakia are two more Crusader castles. The lesser of these,
Qal'at al-Mahelbeh or Balatonos (deriving from Platanus) was built by
the Arabs in the early 11th century but taken by the Crusaders in 1031
before it was finished. It became a fiefdom of the great castle of Saladin
(Sahyun) just to the north under the princes of Antioch, falling to
Saladin in 1188 just a few days after the fall of Castle Saladin. Today it
is difficult of access, standing high up on top of a mountain. The
mountain top is surrounded by a curtain wall reinforced by round,
square and polygonal towers, though it is very badly ruined.

The main stronghold of the entire northern coast, however, is the
great Qal'at al-Sahyun, now known as Saladin Castle (Qal'at
Salahuddin). Along with Marqab and Krak des Chevaliers, Saladin
Castle was one of the main Crusader castles of Syria, occupying a
strategic position on the route from Latakia to Aleppo. The site is an
ancient one, probably first fortified by the Phoenicians of Arwad, but
the first castle of any size there was built by the Byzantines in the late
10th century as part of their campaigns against the Hamdanids of
Aleppo. It came into the possession of the Crusader princes of Antioch
after their conquest of Latakia in 1108, when it was known as Saone,
and was the scene of one of Saladin's greatest sieges in 1188. Saladin

123

was able to take control of a hill overlooking the castle and bombard it with immense mangonels, with the garrison capitulating after its numbers became more and more depleted. It remained a major military and administrative centre under the Mamluks, being abandoned and falling into decay after the Ottoman conquest.

Saladin Castle is huge. It is superbly well situated, occupying a long, needle-shaped ridge nearly a kilometre long with gorges on two sides meeting at the west in a point (figure 18, plate 42). All around are the rich, heady scents of the wild flowers and pine forests that surround its walls. The eastern end has been isolated from the ridge by cutting a deep, sheer chasm across from one gorge to the other to create what must by one of the most impressive – and impregnable! – castle entrances anywhere: the castle walls rise sheer from this man-made chasm, and a thin pinnacle of rock rises out of the centre of it to support a drawbridge (plate 43). The gateway above this is flanked by two circular towers, but the present entrance is through a smaller gate in the south wall. Inside, the ridge is divided into a succession of terraces defended by a series of defensive walls. The middle terrace is dominated by the original Byzantine fortress in the centre, though most of the buildings around it are remains from the long Mamluk occupation. These include a mosque and a bath-house. The main Crusader works are those overlooking the ditch at the eastern end. This is dominated by the massive multi-storeyed donjon, each floor consisting of just a single vaulted room surrounding a central pillar. Adjacent to this is a large vaulted magazine. Between this and the central fortress is an immense underground cistern cut out of the rock, as big as a great hall in itself. There is a tiny chapel halfway along the outer bailey towards the west.

It is difficult to conceive of the immense scale of these Crusader colossi – as with Krak des Chevaliers, one's vocabulary is quickly exhausted of its stock of words for size. There are simply no fortifications to compare with them in Europe, they are more like the great hill fortresses of Central India. The great cavernous halls, the sheer massive, solid, military functionalism of the Crusader buildings, built to stand a thousand years, leave one utterly overawed. Besides them, the more decorative Mamluk buildings inside seem almost frivolous and entirely out of place. Barbarian and unimaginative the Crusaders may have been, but one cannot but help be awed by them.

CHAPTER 8

Aleppo and Environs

Aleppo is everything that the popular image of an Arab Middle Eastern city ought to be. It has one of the best bazaars in the Middle East, it is dominated by a magnificent citadel, it has an immense history, it has colourful people, it has old, picturesque quiet backstreets and great monuments. But there is so much more as well. Without the burden of government shouldered by its rival, Damascus, Aleppo is far more care-free, developing a sophistication that makes it one of the most cosmopolitan and relaxed cities in the Middle East. Hence, it also has a vibrant cafe life, the best cuisine in Syria, pleasant modern streets, and a relaxed outgoing atmosphere. In short, there are few better places to visit.

Historical background

The northernmost of Syria's desert ports, Aleppo is ideally located for a great city. Lying midway between the Mediterranean coast and the great bend in the Euphrates, it was a northern pivot for much of the ancient world's trade for many thousands of years. Like Damascus, its origins are very ancient, and we first read about it in Eblaite texts in the 3rd millennium under the name Hal-pa-pa, though its history may well go back long before. But it is in the early 2nd millennium that it first begins to emerge as a major centre in the north, particularly following Naram Sin's sack of Ebla in the Akkadian period. This was as the capital of the Amorite kingdom of Yamhad, gaining particular renown as an important centre for the worship of the great storm god Hadad.

Syria

Along with Qatna and Carchemish, Yamhad was the main power in northern Syria before the arrival of the Hittites and Mitannians in the mid-2nd millennium. There followed a period of instability for Aleppo, as the rival great powers of the ancient world – Hittites, Egyptians and Mitannians – all fought for influence in Syria. Aleppo came most, however, under the Hittite sphere, so much so that after the final collapse of the Hittite Empire in about 1200 BC, Aleppo re-emerged as one of the more important Neo-Hittite city-states in northern Syria. These city-states – the other important ones in north Syria were Carchemish, Til Barsip and Guzana (Tell Halaf) – probably had Aramaean populations but were ruled by descendants of the Hittites, and so had an overlay of Hittite culture. Whilst this overlay may never have been much more than a veneer (it was, after all, northern rather than southern Syria that experienced the Aramaic revival over a thousand years later) it was a manifestation of the rival pulls between the highland peoples of Anatolia and the desert peoples of Syria that continues to dominate northern Syria to this day.

With the centres of power much further east, Aleppo declined once more under Assyrian, Babylonian and Persian domination. But after the creation of the new Near Eastern capital nearby at Antioch, there was a revival under the Seleucids, who renamed it Beroea after a city in Macedonia. With the trade routes from the Hellenistic East coming up the Euphrates via Dura Europos and across to Antioch, Aleppo, midway on this route, was able to profit enormously. Such prosperity continued throughout subsequent Roman and Byzantine periods.

Aleppo declined with the Muslim conquest when the centre of the country shifted from Antioch to Damascus, but its fortunes recovered somewhat with the decline of Damascus and the move of the Caliphate to Baghdad. For whilst Syria as a whole became a backwater, Baghdad was able to tolerate more independence in Aleppo than it would in its arch-rival Damascus. Hence, the 10th century saw the rise of a brilliant new dynasty in Aleppo: the Hamdanids. Originating in the upper reaches of the Tigris in northern Iraq, the Hamdanid family extended their power westwards across the Jazira into Syria. From their capitals in Aleppo and Mosul they were able to maintain a balance between the 'Abbasid caliphs to the east, the new Fatimid dynasty of Egypt exerting its sway over Palestine and southern Syria to the south, and the new Paleologi dynasty of Byzantine emperors to the north. Indeed, the Hamdanids were a particular threat to the latter: Saif ad-Daula, the greatest of the Hamdanid rulers, posed the first real threat to the Byzantine Empire since the Umayyads. Under him, Aleppo enjoyed a renaissance of Syrian arts and literature.

Sadly, virtually nothing remains of the brilliant Hamdanid court in Aleppo. The buildings we see are mainly from the Zengid and Ayyubid rulers in the 12th and 13th centuries, who to a large extent continued the Hamdanid embellishment of Aleppo. With the Crusading kingdoms of Edessa and Antioch to its north and west, Aleppo came under continual threat, but the impregnable citadel of Aleppo was able to withstand several Crusader sieges. Indeed, both Reginauld de Chatillon, Prince of Antioch, and Joscelin, Count of Edessa, were captured by Nur ed-Din Zangi of Aleppo. Aleppo's mighty citadel, however, was not able to withstand the Mongols under Hulagu in 1260 and Tamerlane in 1400, though in the case of the former it fell by ruse rather than assault. Nevertheless, both times Aleppo was devastated, and most of its citizens either butchered or carted off only to die more slowly in captivity in the wastes of Central Asia. Never, it seemed, could a city survive such utter devastation.

But survive it did, even regaining some measure of prosperity under the Mamluks – devastated or not, Aleppo's position still ensured it remain the natural centre of the north. Its commerce revived with the arrival of the first European merchants in the 16th and 17th centuries: Venice opened a consulate there in 1548, followed by France in 1562, England in 1583 and Holland in 1613. Once more, Aleppo became a trade entrepot as in the days of old, with links that stretched throughout the Middle East. The various treaties following the First World War, however, dealt more of a blow to Aleppo than it did other Syrian cities, for it lost much of its hinterland to Turkey, first 'Aintab (modern Gaziantep) in 1923 and then Antioch and Alexandretta in 1939. Even the railway that connects Aleppo to the Syrian Jazira to the northeast was mainly ceded to Turkey.

The Citadel

The gigantic citadel dominates Aleppo like few other cities. The approach to Aleppo from the west in the setting sun is one of the greatest approaches to any city: one can see the citadel long before one sees the city itself, dominating the city like a Pacific island, with the city as its lagoon (plate 44). It also dominates Aleppo's history. Built only partly on a natural elevation, most of its present height represents thousands of years of accumulation. Excavations have revealed remains belonging to the time of the Neo-Hittite kingdom of Aleppo, when it formed an acropolis to the town, although there are far earlier remains locked within its immense bulk. This tell continued as the religious and military centre of the city throughout the Greek and Roman periods. It was heavily fortified by the Byzantine period, for we hear of it withstanding the siege by Chosroes I Anushirwan of Persia in 540 AD. Virtually all of the present remains, however, date from the

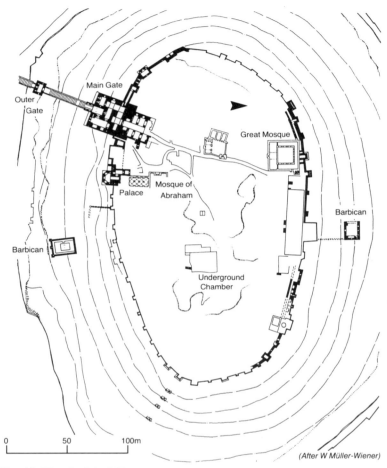

Fig. 19 The citadel of Aleppo

Zengid and Ayyubid periods of the 12th and 13th centuries, the acme of Arab military architecture. The Aleppo citadel is the crowning glory of this peak.

Perhaps the best place to begin a tour is not at the citadel itself, but in one of the cafes opposite its entrance. Here one can sit back and appreciate not only the superb architecture of the place but also the life of the city that goes by its walls: all of Aleppo seem to pass by, beneath, in, out and around the citadel, providing it with a living context that the great Crusader citadels of Syria lack. There are also few nicer places to experience that great lifeline of the Middle East: the coffee house (plate 45)!

Before entering, it is worth walking around the outside of the citadel. It is in the shape of an oval, measuring 500 by 350 metres (figure 19). Impregnable it certainly appears, surrounded by a ditch and a steep glacis. On top, the walls rise sheer, punctuated by over forty rectangular towers spaced evenly around the perimeter (plate 46). The glacis, at an angle of 48°, not only prevented an attacker from being able to bear directly against the foot of the walls above, it also enabled the defenders to roll huge boulders down against anybody who approached. It is completely lined with stone to provide a smooth – and slippery! – surface, bonded deep into the hillside by columns embedded into the masonry at regular intervals. As if these defences were not formidable enough, it is further defended by two barbicans, linked to the main citadel by underground passages, on the north and south sides.

The great entrance on the southwest side is almost a separate castle in itself. It consists of a first gatehouse outside the ditch, which is then crossed by a bridge supported on eight massive arches, then the main gatehouse itself (plate 47), through which the entrance makes no less than six right-angle turns to prevent any direct frontal attacks. The outer gatehouse is dated by an inscription over the entrance to 1507. It was closed by two heavy doors, which can still be seen, beyond which there was once a drawbridge, forming a third barrier. The main gatehouse was built over several periods between the 13th and 15th centuries. The outside is protected by several sets of machicolations and loopholes, through which defenders could pour a murderous crossfire upon an attacker from all sides. Above the entrance are two inscriptions, one Koranic and the other recording its repair by Qalawun in 1291-2, mentioning his full titles as 'Lord, the greatest ruler, the most noble king, the learned, the just, the victorious, the warrior, the guardian of the frontiers, the helper, the triumphant, the victorious, the probity of the world and religion, the foremost of kings, helper of Islam and the Muslims, pillar of the state, support of the faith, protector of the people, aid of the caliphate, ally of the imamate, lord of kings and rulers, rulers of the armies of those who proclaim the oneness of God, protector of the right by proofs, giver of life to justice in all the worlds, destroyer of apostates, suppressor of rebels, killer of infidels and heretics, vanquisher of oppressors and renegades, suppressor of worshippers of the cross, the Alexander of his time, conqueror of capitals, conqueror of the armies of the Franks and the Armenians and the Tatars, destroyer of Acre and the countries of the coast, giver of life to the illustrious 'Abbasid state, protector of the

Mohammedan community.' Doubtless, he was a great lover and a kind father as well! In case one should forget, there is a second inscription of Qalawun's a little further on summarizing his attributes. Over the gate to the right is a relief of two, inter-twined double-headed serpents. A second gate a little further on has a relief of two lions and a fleur-de-lys above it, and reliefs of two more lions guard the third – and final – gate after the last right-angled turn. All three gates were closed by immense wooden doors sheathed in iron. Smaller doors within the entrance passage give access to guard rooms in the main gatehouse above.

Once through the gatehouse, the interior of the citadel appears a rather confusing jumble of ruins and mounds, much still a result of Tamerlane's devastations. It is crossed by a paved street which leads up to the mosque and a late barracks on the north side of the citadel (plate 48). Immediately to the right of the entrance is a vast underground vaulted room of Byzantine construction, in the bottom of which is a rock-cut cistern somewhat macabrely known as the 'Prison of Blood'. Beyond are the remains of a 13th century *hammam* and palace, entered through an elaborate portal. The palace surrounds a courtyard and has a graceful throne room entered through a second portal, dating from the 15th century. Halfway up the street on the left is the so-called 'Mosque of Abraham' associated with the tradition of Abraham's wanderings from Ur to Harran, though the present structure was built by Nur ed-Din in 1179-80. Just beyond this mosque on the opposite side of the street, archaeological soundings revealed parts of a Neo-Hittite monumental building, including a relief of the sun and moon gods, now in the Aleppo Museum. The Great Mosque at the end of the street was restored in 1213-14 after a fire, and its square minaret was also used as a watchtower. Another vast underground Byzantine room lies to the south of the Great Mosque in the centre of the citadel. It was probably built as a cistern, and used for storage in the Middle Ages.

The city walls and gates

After the superb fortifications of the citadel, the actual city walls of Aleppo come as rather an anti-climax (figure 49). Much of them have disappeared – only those parts surrounding the southern half of the old city are still standing – and much else has been built over. Perhaps the best view of the surviving stretch of city walls can be obtained from the cemetery opposite the Qinnesrin Gate at the southwestern corner of the old city. The foundations and parts of the base of the walls probably date from the Roman and Byzantine period, but most of what can be seen today was built in the 12th and 13th centuries, with extensive additions – mainly of the towers – in the Mamluk period. The 13th century Qinnesrin Gate is probably the best preserved of the city gates, though the 15th century Maqam Gate, with its market, is the more picturesque. The Antioch Gate to the west is probably the oldest still standing. It was built in the 12th century, although heavily restored in the 15th.

The bazaars and caravanserais

Aleppo is renowned for its bazaars. And justly so, for it was as a caravan city that Aleppo achieved its wealth. And the labyrinth of vaulted bazaars – they are said to total over 15 kilometres in length – are certainly the best in the Middle East. A visit, therefore, might well take most of the day. Even without buying, simply wandering around a great Eastern bazaar – and this is one of the greatest – is like nothing else in the world. Experiencing it is to experience the East at its most romantic: it is the stuff that travellers' tales are made of. Even to the most jaded, entering a great bazaar never loses its excitement.

The bazaars comprise several lines of mainly covered streets and alleys that stretch between the citadel and the Antioch Gate. Although appearing a maze nowadays, they follow to a large extent the original plan of the city laid out in Graeco-Roman times, occupying the Cardo Maximus of the Roman city. Although the present architecture of the bazaar is much later, the vaulted passageways – much of them decorated – are masterpieces of medieval Arab urban architecture. In it can be found goods of every description, ranging from luxury items and exquisite works of craftsmanship to the everyday necessities of life. Whilst the sections dealing with spices or colourful fabrics may be the most exotic to the Western eye, even the displays of simple plastic buckets, coils of rope or fruit and vegetables have an appeal that no Western store or supermarket can match.

Opening off the bazaars can be found some of Aleppo's great caravanserais, or *khans*. So grand and so elaborately decorated are some of these caravanserais that at first sight they might be mistaken for mosques or even minor palaces, as their architecture reflects the great wealth that they brought to Aleppo. The greatest of them is the Khan al-Wazir to the north of the bazaar, built in the 17th century. The entrance is decorated in alternating bands of black and white stone in the traditional Syrian fashion. Inside is a courtyard surrounded by two storeys of rooms, with all facades – particularly the window surrounds (plate 49) – decorated in exquisitely carved abstract patterns, with stalactite decoration above the windows. The two windows over the inside of the entrance each incorporate a cross and a minaret in their decoration, supposedly reflecting the respective religions of the two

131

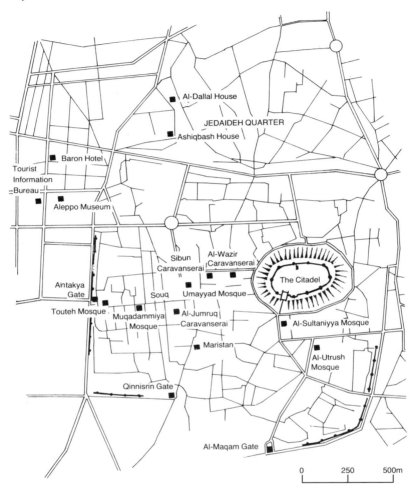

Fig. 20 Aleppo

artisans who decorated the *khan*. The Khan as-Sabun, a 16th century caravanserai not far from the Khan al-Wazir, has equally rich decorative detail, particularly around the entrance. The Khan al-Gumruk, another 17th century caravanserai to the south of the bazaar, has a fine entrance portal with a stalactite cornice. Its windows on the inside have particularly fine engaged colonettes surrounding them. The Khan al-Gumruk was the centre for the English, French and Dutch

132

merchants in the 17th century (plate 50).

A short way to the south of the Khan al-Gumruk is the Maristan Arghun, a hospital and asylum endowed by the Mamluk governor of Aleppo in 1354. It is a fairly simple building – particularly in contrast to the elaborate caravanserais – but has a serene courtyard with two unusual double *iwans* on either side.

The Great Mosque and the Madrasa Halawiya

The Great Mosque of Aleppo, with its vast expanse of paved courtyard surrounded by arcades, bears an initial resemblance to the Umayyad Mosque in Damascus. The resemblance is no superficial one, for the Aleppo mosque too was founded by the Umayyad in 715, only ten years after the one in Damascus. It was also built in the courtyard of a Byzantine church, which in turn was probably on the site of a Roman temple temenos – again a similar pedigree to the Umayyad Mosque in Damascus. But there the resemblance ends, for the Great Mosque in Aleppo has been destroyed so repeatedly that only the plan survives of the original Umayyad building. Indeed, the oldest part of it standing is probably the remarkable minaret, which dates from the Seljuk restoration of the mosque in 1090. The mosque was reconstructed again by Nur ed-Din after a fire in 1159, only to be destroyed yet again by the Mongols in 1260. Most of the existing fabric, therefore, was built under the Mamluks, albeit following its earlier style.

Despite such a chequered history, the mosque is still a lovely building. The vast open space of the courtyard is particularly pleasing, with elaborate patterns created by masterful use of black and white paving stones (plate 51). More important, it is very much a living space, with a constant stream of people coming as much to relax in the arcades as to pray (plates 52, 53). There is a shrine inside the sanctuary that houses the head of Zachariah, John the Baptist's father (a further link with the Umayyad Mosque of Damascus).

The mosque was built in the courtyard of the Byzantine cathedral of Aleppo, and surprisingly, parts of the original cathedral are still standing. This has been incorporated into the Madrasa Halawiya (the 'Sweet Madrasa'), just next door to the Great Mosque. According to tradition it was founded by the Empress Helena on the site of a pagan temple. The distinctive quatrefoil plan of the cathedral however – following contemporary church plans such as those at Apamea, Antioch and Bosra – probably dates from about 500, though it was probably rebuilt by Justinian after the destruction of Aleppo by the Persians in 540. It remained a Christian church until the time of the Crusader sieges of Aleppo, when the Muslims, fearing a possible alliance between native Christians and the Crusader besiegers, moved the Christians outside the city walls to a new quarter and converted the church into a *madrasa*.

This *madrasa* still incorporates one 'leaf' of the original quatrefoil of the Byzantine cathedral, consisting of a semi-circular arcade of Corinthian columns (plate 54). Most of the remainder of the *madrasa*, however, dates from its rebuilding in the 13th century. It has an exceptionally fine carved wooden *mihrab* with ivory inlay dating from this time.

Other mosques and madrasas

The oldest mosque in Aleppo is the Tutah ('Mulberry') Mosque, just inside the Antioch Gate. It was founded in the mid-7th century possibly on the site of a church, as parts of the west facade are Roman workmanship. The particularly fine floriated Kufic inscription on the facade, however, was added in the 12th century. The oldest *madrasa* in Aleppo – indeed the second oldest in Syria – is the Madrasa Muqaddamiyya is further along from the Tutah Mosque towards the bazaar. Again on the site of a church, the present building is dated by an inscription above the entrance to 1168.

One of the most important religious complexes in Aleppo is the Madrasa al-Firdaus (the 'Madrasa of Paradise'), which lies some way outside the old city beyond the Maqam Gate. It consists of a mosque, *madrasa* and tombs, built in 1234 by Daifa Khatun, the daughter-in-law of Saladin who was twice regent of Aleppo for both her son and grandson. Apart from the stalactite semi-dome over the entrance portal, it is a very plain building, but at the same time a very serene one, with its quiet – almost intimate – vine-covered courtyard and octagonal pool. The courtyard is dominated by an immense *iwan* on its north side, used for religious study. The sanctuary is on the south side, covered by three domes, and inside is one of the most exquisitely decorated marble *mihrabs* to be found anywhere, consisting of elaborate patterns made up of interlocking pieces of different coloured marble. Another varicoloured marble *mihrab* almost as splendid can be seen at the Madrasa Sultaniyya, opposite the main entrance to the citadel (plate 55). It was built in 1223, again as a combined mosque, *madrasa* and tomb complex.

Also near the citadel is the al-Utrush Mosque, built in 1403, which is one of the best examples of Mamluk architecture in Aleppo. The facade is particularly fine, with fine decoration and an octagonal minaret, and resembles many of the Mamluk mosques of Cairo.

The Jedaideh Quarter and the New City

The old residential quarters of Aleppo form as much a part of the city's character as the bazaars – and are equally delightful to explore. One leaves the noise and bustle of the bazaars and enters a much quieter world of paved stone streets, twisting narrow lanes, tunnels and archways (plate 56), broad courtyards and quiet cafes. It is a world of sudden turns providing strong visual images, both of the people and of the architecture that frames them (plate 57). But it is equally a very private world of high walls and courtyards where domestic scenes are occasionally glimpsed through open doors, but where even an innocent glance seems intrusive.

There are some houses, however, which it is possible to visit. These houses, mostly dating from the 17th and 18th centuries, are architectural gems, typically Syrian in design and richly decorated. All are built around a courtyard, usually with a central pool and planted with vines or citrus trees. Facing the courtyard will be a large *iwan*, used as an outdoor living room in the summers, while for the winter months each house would have a large domed reception room inside, often behind the *iwan*. The reception room of the Sayegh house – now an Armenian school – is decorated with particularly fine painted and gilded woodwork, as is the 17th century Dallal house nearby, which also has extensive use of coloured marble decorating the courtyard. One of the most splendid is the 18th century Achiqbash house, which has very elaborately carved stonework above each window and in a frieze around the top of the courtyard (plate 58).

Although not exactly an historic building, no book on Aleppo would be complete without mentioning the Hotel Baron, one of the great oriental hotels in the grand old tradition of a more leisurely age. Every room is heavily redolent of nostalgia, with posters advertising the Simplon Orient Express to Baghdad still up in the hallway. Its guest book reads like a *Who's Who* of the early 20th century: T E Lawrence, Leonard Woolley, Kemal Ataturk, Charles Lindbergh, Amy Johnston, Theodore Roosevelt, Lord Mountbatten, Agatha Christie. It is a great pity that such old hotels inevitably give way to bland, anonymous hotels belonging to international chains, and more characterful hotels like the Baron disappear.

The new city has pleasantly laid out streets dating from the French Mandate. The main place of interest is the Aleppo Museum, which houses objects from north Syrian sites such as Tell Halaf, Ugarit, Mari, Ebla and Aleppo itself. But the new city is best visited after dark, when it comes alive with strolling families, overflowing street cafes and cinema crowds. Such a relaxed, sophisticated atmosphere is much more a part of the Middle East than the bloodshed and intolerance that fill newspaper headlines, a very Levantine atmosphere. Truly Aleppo is a wonderful city in which to spend a long time.

The environs of Aleppo

The environs of Aleppo is the region of the Dead Cities, one of the richest areas of standing remains in the Middle East. But these form the subject of a separate chapter. Here we will simply look at two areas to the north and south not covered by the Dead Cities: the city of Cyrrhus to the north, including the important earlier site of 'Ain Dara, and the city of Qinnesrin to the south, including the site of Ebla.

Cyrrhus and the north of Aleppo

A number of important archaeological sites and ruins can be seen in the environs of Azzaz, the small town marking the border crossing point into Turkey due north of Aleppo. To the south of Azzaz, just to the east of the road from Aleppo, is a mound marking the site of Tell Rifa'at, the ancient Arpad. Arpad was the capital of a small Neo-Hittite kingdom in the early 1st millennium BC, one of a number of Neo-Hittite kingdoms scattered across the north of Syria that included Carchemish, Til Barsip (Tell Ahmar, Chapter 10), Guzana (Tell Halaf, Chapter 10) and 'Ain Dara (see below). Arpad was conquered by the Assyrian emperor Tiglath-Pileser III in 743 BC, along with the other Neo-Hittite kingdoms, thus bringing about the end of the Hittite 'twilight' in northern Syria. It was excavated in the 1920s by Czech archaeologists and again in the 1950s by the British.

To the west of the Aleppo-Azaz road, roughly opposite Tell Rifa'at, a small track goes across country to join the road from Qal'at Sima'an to Azaz at 'Ain Dara. Along this track a number of standing Graeco-Roman ruins can be seen near the villages of Tatmarash, Tinib, and Jubbul. At 'Ain Dara itself is a large tell, the site of another important Neo-Hittite city-state. Excavations by Syrian and American archaeologists in the seventies and eighties uncovered a very rich array of bas-reliefs and other sculptures adorning the temple of Ishtar.

The most important remains in the far northwest of Syria can be seen at Cyrrhus, modern Nabi Khouri, a ruined Greek and Roman city founded shortly after the conquest of Alexander as a fortified post guarding Antioch's northeastern flank. Like the other Greek cities of

65 General view of the ruins of Deir Sima'an

66 The southwest church of Deir Sima'an

67 A section of the Roman road between Antioch and Aleppo

68 Part of the ruins of Bamouqqa

69 The church of Qalb Lozeh

70 The ruins of al-Bara amidst the olive groves

71 One of the pyramid tombs at al-Bara

72 The ruins of Serjilla in the foreground, looking southwards towards the ruins of Rabi'ah on the horizon

73 The tavern at Serjilla

74 Looking out from the portico of the tavern at Serjilla

Syria

75 General view of Jeradeh

76 General view of the ruined villas at Ruwaiha

xxxviii

77 The temple tomb at Ruwaiha

78 The massive arch of the Church of Bizzos at Ruwaiha

79 The city walls of Resafeh, with beduin in the foreground

80 The North Gate of Resafeh

81 Detail of an acanthus capital at the North Gate of Resafeh

82 The nave of the Basilica of St Sergius at Resafeh

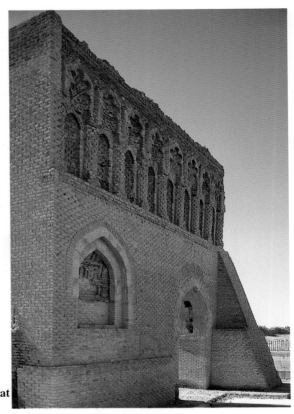

**83 The Baghdad Gate at
Raqqa**

84 Beehive houses on the Jazira

85   General view of Palmyra from the Castle of Fakhr ud-Din

86 The exterior of the Temple of Bel at Palmyra, with the palm trees of the 'Ain Eqfa Spring in the foreground

87 The courtyard of the Temple of Bel at Palmyra

88 The sanctuary of the Temple of Bel at Palmyra

89 The monumental arch at Palmyra

90 Detail of the monumental arch at Palmyra

91 The tetrapylon at Palmyra

92 The Cardo at Palmyra, with the Castle of Fakhr ud-Din in the background

93 The Funerary Temple at Palmyra, with the desert beyond

94 View along the Cardo at Palmyra from the Funerary Temple

95 The Temple of Ba'al Shamin at Palmyra

96 The Valley of the Tombs at Palmyra

Syria it was greatly rejuvenated and embellished after the Roman conquest in 64 BC, as both a military and a commercial centre. It was badly damaged in the Persian invasions of the mid-3rd century, but revived under the Byzantines when for a time it was known as Hagiopolis ('City of the Saints'), mainly because of its relics of SS Damian and Cosmas. After the Arab conquest it slowly declined, and although the Crusaders installed a Latin bishop there, by the end of the 12th century it had largely disappeared.

The city forms a rough, walled triangle along the banks of the Sabun River, which is crossed by a very fine Byzantine bridge. The outline of the city walls and acropolis can still be seen, but inside, whilst there are large numbers of remains, much is indistinct and grown over. The city was bisected by a colonnaded street, the Cardo Maximus, parts of which can still be seen, but the most intact building is the 2nd century AD theatre in the centre of the city, which was excavated by French archaeologists in the fifties. The remains of several churches can still be identified, and outside the city to the east is a fine hexagonal mausoleum with a pyramid roof.

Qinnesrin, Ebla and the south of Aleppo

Qinnesrin, about 100 kilometres to the south of Aleppo, is the site of the city of Chalcis founded by Seleucus Nicator in the late 4th century BC. During the subsequent Roman and Byzantine periods it became one of the main centres in northern Syria, surpassing for a time even Aleppo, as it stood in the centre of a very fertile plain and commanded the trade routes to the south and east. It was fortified in the mid-6th century by Justinian, but destroyed in about 637 by the first Arab invasions. In the 10th century most of its population was deported to rebuild and repopulate Aleppo, after which its sister city rapidly overtook it in importance.

There is not a great deal for the visitor to see, though the acropolis, the outline of the city ramparts, and the street pattern are fairly easily discernible. Outside is a vast necropolis and quarry area, in which are numerous very impressive underground vaults.

Tell Mardikh, just to the east of the Aleppo-Damascus highway shortly after the Latakia road branches off, is the scene of some of the most important discoveries in Near Eastern archaeology in the late 20th century (figure 21). It is the site of the ancient city of Ebla, one of the larger archaeological sites in Syria and the capital of an important kingdom and civilization in the 3rd millennium BC, which an Italian team has been excavating since the sixties. Although the existence of

Elba had been known from cuneiform sources, its site was unknown. With its location firmly established by the Italian archaeologists at Tell Mardikh, the discoveries there – particularly of some of the earliest state archives known to man – far surpassed all expectations, introducing a new civilization into the ancient Near East. The results are still in the process of being fully assessed by specialists – indeed, the excavations themselves are still in progress – but already they have entailed much of our history of the ancient Near East having to be re-written.

Much of the history and culture of Ebla has been discussed in Chapters 2 and 3, so it is only necessary to emphasize the main points here. It was founded in the latter half of the 4th millennium, but its height came in the later 3rd and early 2nd millennium BC, when it became a city of about 50 hectares in area, dominated by a large palace covering much of the acropolis in the centre. It was from the administrative quarter of this palace that over 17,000 cuneiform fragments were discovered in a hitherto unknown Semitic language now called Eblaite. These texts, amongst the earliest literature of mankind, have provided detailed information on the religion (including controversial new light on Biblical background), administration, trade, economy, history, and other aspects of the life and times of a major Near Eastern kingdom over four and a half thousand years ago. In its heyday Ebla controlled much of Syria, though its political and trading links stretched much further afield – a discovery of over 20 kilos of raw lapis lazuli in the palace demonstrated links as far off as northeastern Afghanistan. It was conquered and sacked by Sargon and his grandson Naram-Sin of Akkad in Mesopotamia at the end of this period, but revived during the early 2nd millennium – though this time, having learned its lesson, Ebla was provided with some of the most heavily fortified ramparts in Syria. It was conquered and destroyed again, however, in about 1600 BC, probably by the Hittites, after which it disappears from history.

Like so many archaeological sites of earliest antiquity, there is not a great deal at Tell Mardikh for the visitor to see today: the mounds of the city walls with one of the gates excavated, the acropolis with the 3rd millennium palace at its foot where the tablets were discovered, some temple foundations, and excavated areas of the lower town. The site is still a must, however, for any visit to Syria, if only to appreciate the great extent of these ancient cities and the sheer antiquity of Ebla in particular. Below one's feet are the fragments of a civilization so old that it was already ancient when our own cultural forbears, the Romans, walked over here 2,000 years ago. By then it was already 3,000 years old and had long vanished from memory; Ebla must have

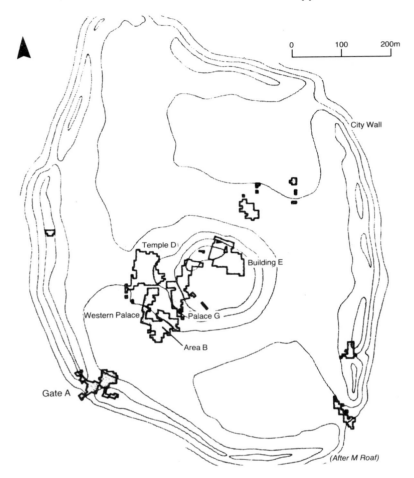

Fig. 21 Ebla

appeared much the same to the Romans – if tttthe inhabitants who occupied a very poor late Roman monastic settlement huddling at the edge of the acropolis even recognized it all – as it does to us today: an area of low mounds, fragments of potsherds, and dust. The Roman remains appear particularly mean as if in deference to the greatness that lay beneath their feet – there was, after all, otherwise nothing exactly mean about Roman building in Syria! It was a group of

139

latter-day Romans (the excavations are by the University of Rome) on sifting through that dust who finally rediscovered the astonishing story of Ebla.

CHAPTER 9

The Dead Cities of the North

The environs of Aleppo are one of the most extraordinary areas of ruins and the greatest storehouses of Byzantine architecture to be found in the ancient world. This is the region of the Dead Cities, the remains of some seven hundred deserted towns, villages and monastic settlements roughly in the area between Aleppo and Antioch stretching southwards as far as the Jebel Zawiya. So many are there that this book can only mention a fraction of them, and it is with great reluctance that some quite superb examples of architecture or even entire ruined towns must be omitted.

Today the region appears as if blasted: hills bleached white by the sun and drained of soil by wind and rain so that now it is a harsh, bare terrain of boulders and occasional spiky vegetation that blisters under the sun (plates 64, 72). It might appear strange that this area supported such a large population in the past. But it must be remembered that this was the natural centre of Syria in late antiquity: this was the hinterland of Antioch, one of the greatest cities of the Mediterranean world in Roman and Byzantine times. The region consequently saw an explosion of prosperity, and so many towns and villages flourished in the region that by Byzantine times the area was almost continuously built up. Whilst very little survives of Antioch itself, the remains of these towns forming its hinterland – the Dead Cities – still litter the landscape providing one of the best pictures of the world of late antiquity to be found anywhere.

Following the Islamic conquest, the demographic and political centre of Syria moved from Antioch to Damascus. Accordingly, the region behind Antioch declined in its wake. Whilst Aleppo was a large enough

141

centre to sustain this decline, the towns and villages in the region were not: the populations slowly moved elsewhere, leaving their towns empty. Not being destroyed by invasions or natural disasters, these towns simply became ghost towns, surviving in some cases almost intact. Consequently, it is still possible to wander along streets, into modest houses and hostelries or grander villas and churches that in many cases are almost perfectly preserved, with only their roofs missing (plates 74, 75, 66).

The term 'Dead Cities' is perhaps a misnomer: 'Dead Towns' or even 'Dead Villages', whilst sounding less dramatic, reflects more accurately the nature of the settlements. Gone are the strict urban layouts of the Graeco-Roman cities, with their standard grid patterns intersected by main north-south and east-west thoroughfares. The Dead Cities appear more haphazard collections of buildings scattered over a hillside; their growth is organic rather than planned, reflecting perhaps a re-assertion of Near Eastern traditions over classical (figure 25). Or perhaps the classical traditions simply never spread much outside the big cities. Apart from those of the desert frontier to the east, none of the Dead Cities have any fortifications, reflecting the high degree of security in the countryside.

Before moving on to specific sites, a few general observations can be made on the architecture of the Dead Cities. They are mostly Byzantine in date, but are often as representative of Roman countryside architecture as they are of Byzantine since the basic architectural forms did not change much. Indeed, few other areas in the Roman world evoke the life of the Roman provinces as well as the Dead Cities do. Apart from the arceate forms of the Christian architecture (arched colonnades, apses, domes), which we have already remarked upon as an essentially non-Syrian form (Chapter 3), the architecture as a whole reflects the Syrian predilection for bold, almost cubist, trabeate forms: simple slab and lintel construction techniques and long lines of square, almost monolithic pillars supporting porticos sometimes several storeys in height (plates 62, 65, 73). These forms appear very distant from the more flowing, rounded forms of Byzantine classical architecture (plates 59, 69, 78), and whilst the portico form might be seen as classical in origin, the monolithic almost 'cubist' vocabulary of the porticos seem to hearken back to a pre-classical Semitic past, such as Amrit or ancient South Arabian architecture, rather than Roman and Byzantine. These simple trabeate forms – allied to a Syrian mastery of working with stone – enabled domestic buildings and towers to reach several storeys (plate 62). This is similar in some respects to the buildings of the Hauran, though the corbelling techniques and external staircases so distinctive of the Hauran are virtually absent here in the north. Houses – of which a great many survive – were generally fairly simple affairs, but unlike the usual form of housing in the Middle East (which consist of rooms surrounding a central courtyard) courtyards in the north were generally just to one or either side of the rooms, with the house proper forming a central block. Roofs were generally flat and of timber, though the occasional use of gabled tile roofs marks an import from the West. The porticos, already remarked upon, were an important feature of both domestic and public building, and are probably the architectural 'cousins' of the colonnaded streets that are such a feature of the cities of the Roman East. Many houses – particularly the wealthier ones – would have a portico or 'verandah' along one or two sides, usually on two storeys, whilst longer porticos alongside streets would form bazaar shops, a tradition that survives intact today. Indeed, such 'verandahed' houses must have borne a strong resemblance to European colonial architecture, with the porticoed streets resembling the verandahed streets of the American West and Australian Outback (plates 73, 74). Like the colonnaded streets of the Roman East, the demands imposed by climate of such architectural forms are obvious.

The religious architecture probably comprises the largest number of churches surviving anywhere in the ancient world. They are everywhere. These churches were usually very small; apart from a few exceptions, such as the great pilgrimage church of St Simeon Stylites, there are few larger churches or cathedrals. Although their architecture generally follows imported forms – they almost invariably follow the conventional basilical form developed in the Roman West – there are a number of local variations. Foremost of these is the way the entrances are usually in the south wall opening directly into the south aisle, rather than in the western end opposite the apse, as is found in churches further west. This form often meant that the narthex would be omitted. Apses are usually flanked by two small square chambers, opening from the ends of each aisle, perhaps following pre-Christian temple layouts (figure 24). In addition, the centre of the nave would often be occupied by an exedra facing the apse, reflecting differing liturgical usages in the north Syrian church where the eastern half of the church would be reserved for clergy in certain services (figure 28).

If the overall forms of north Syrian churches reflect Western architectural styles, the church buildings associated with them were purely local in style. Large numbers of the churches would have monasteries, convents and hospices attached to them, which architecturally were almost indistinguishable from domestic buildings.

There are very roughly four 'concentrations' or groups of Dead Cities, corresponding to the low ranges of hills in which they are situated. Whilst these groupings are to some extent artificial, with no neat edges, they do at least serve as convenient divisions with which to describe and visit them. The groups are: the Jebel Shaikh Barakat and the Jebel Sima'an to the west and northwest of Aleppo, which include the best known of the Dead Cities comprising the Basilica of St Simeon Stylites and associated remains (figure 22); the Jebel Barisha and Jebel al-'Ala to the west near the present Turkish border, which has the largest concentration of ruins (figure 22); the Jebel Zawiya to the southwest towards the Ghab, which is mainly a little earlier than the others (figure 25); and the desert areas to the southeast. This last division forms the most amorphous 'group', as it is a part of a long chain of widely spaced, mainly Byzantine ruined cities and fortifications throughout the northwestern desert areas of Syria, that includes places far apart as Qasr Ibn Wardan and al-Anderin towards Hama (Chapter 6) and Resafeh (Chapter 10) south of the Euphrates.

The Jebel Sema'an and Jebel Shaikh Barakat

This area (figure 22) just to the west and northwest of Aleppo is the most visited of the Dead Cities, partly because it is the group nearest to Aleppo, but mainly because it includes the great monastery-church of St Simeon Stylites (Qal'at Sema'an) and its associated pilgrimage town of Deir Sema'an, which together make up the most spectacular of all the Dead Cities. If one has no time to visit even some of the Dead Cities, this is the one that should not be missed.

But before examining the ruins of St Simeon Stylites, there are a few lesser known groups of ruins on the skirts of the Jebel Shaikh Barakat just to the south of Qal'at Sema'an. At the village of Mushabbak, just to the south of the direct road between Qal'at Sema'an and Aleppo, a very well preserved late 5th century Byzantine basilica on top of the hill proclaims one's arrival into the ecclesiastical world of the Byzantine ruins of north Syria. Some funerary monuments consisting of a pair of columns (the tomb of Aemilius Reginus) and many tombs cut into a rock face, can be seen a little beyond Dairat Azzah at Qatura. These tombs are probably the necropolis of the town of Refadah just to the northwest not long before St Simeon Stylites, which contains the ruins of one of the finest villas in Syria dated 510 AD. It has two storeys of porticos, the upper one particularly finely decorated. Some other houses at Refada have superbly fitted polygonal 'Cyclopean' masonry walls, perhaps earlier construction. Between Refada and Qatura is the ruined monastery of Sitt ar-Rum ('Lady of the Greeks') and two square columns marking the 2nd century AD tomb of Isodotos Ptolemaus.

Just to the north of Turmanin, further south along the road to Bab al-Hawa, a particularly fine 5th century cathedral was still standing until quite recently. It has been demolished, but its associated monastery –

Fig. 22 Dead Cities west of Aleppo

originally a very large complex almost as big as St Simeon – can still be seen. Much of it is still extant. Some more monastic remains can be seen nearby at Tell 'Adeh, ancient Tellada, the birthplace of St Simeon. Two kilometres before the main Aleppo-Antakya road is the village of Dana, which contains an impressive Roman tetrapylon tomb of four columns. There are also some ancient towers in the vicinity. On top of the Jebel Shaikh Barakat – some 2,800 feet high – is the remains of a large colonnaded temenos of a Roman prostyle temple of Zeus. Although there is little standing, its position is spectacular – presumably it is an ancient Semitic sacred high place.

The remains of the monastery-church of St Simeon Stylites on the slopes of the Jebel Sema'an can be seen from some distance. It must have dominated the landscape to an even greater extent in the 5th century as much as it dominated the minds of the early Christians, when pilgrims flocked from all over the Christian world, at first to pay homage to the great ascetic who founded it and then after his death to visit the great monastery that grew up around his memory. St Simeon

145

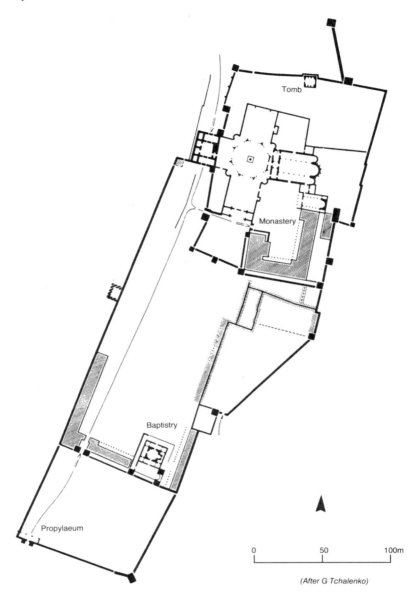

Fig. 23 St Simeon Stylites

Stylites was one of the most curious of the saints of the early church. Born about 390, the persecution of martyrs had all but ceased in Christendom, so the young Simeon had no recourse it seems but to persecute himself! Indeed, he appears to have displayed a particular aptitude for self-inflicted pain from an early age: on entering a monastery at the age of sixteen, he wore a spiked girdle that drew blood and spent his summers buried up to his chin in the ground. For Lent, mere fasting was not enough, and he would wall himself up in his cell completely. Such odd behaviour naturally attracted considerable attention, so he perched on a pillar to escape the crowds: the more the crowds came the higher his pillar would become, so the more the crowds would come – a rather self-defeating ploy perhaps, but otherwise quite a crowd-puller. His pillar eventually reached the height of 64 feet, where he spent the last thirty years of his life, year in, year out, through intense summer heat and bitter winter cold. For added discomfort he had an iron collar and chain fastened around his neck. Far from being a recluse like the more conventional, retiring ascetics of the time, Simeon therefore ended up being one of the world's great exhibitionists. He would hold court each day over the crowds gathered at his feet, and his influence – invariably reactionary and fundamentalist – spread far and wide: a humane church edict, for example, restoring the synagogues to the Jews was cancelled at his intercession. As his fame spread people flocked in their thousands, many of them pilgrims to pay homage but doubtless many more simply curious to see such an astonishing spectacle. The town below the monastery swelled almost to a minor city to accommodate so many people, profiting immensely in what became Syria's greatest tourist attraction of the time. After his death, squatting on pillars became the rage, and ascetics on pillars were dotted all over the landscape of northern Syria, while one of Christendom's most elaborate churches was built around St Simeon's own pillar.

Sadly, all that is left of Simeon's pillar now is just a stump, though the ruins of the church surrounding it are amongst the most impressive – and unique – in early Christendom. Following the death of St Simeon, such was his fame that the monastery-church commemorating him was endowed by the Emperor Zeno himself, and was built in about 480-90 AD on a scale and lavishness that had rarely been seen in Syria since the era of the great Roman temples (figure 23). The stump of his pillar is surrounded by a large octagonal chamber, probably originally domed. The octagon is then squared off by the addition of four basilical halls on each side. It thus combines three separate early church forms: the central 'martyrium' plan of the octagon, the basilica and the cross. The combination, however, does not jar; there are no clumsy transitions nor inherent contradictions, and the three quite separate elements combine most effectively, together forming one of the greatest masterpieces of early Christian architecture (plate 59). It was later fortified, probably against the Persian and Arab invasions of the 6th and 7th centuries, but such was the importance of the monastery that it maintained its independence even after the Arab conquest right down to the 10th century.

The entire complex is set within an immense enclosure, built partly on a terrace overlooking the plain, comprising inner and outer courtyards (figure 23). This seems to recall the great temple enclosures of an earlier era. The main entrance was at the south, up a sacred processional way leading from the pilgrim town of Telanissos (Deir Sima'an) below. This led into the outer enclosure next to the magnificent baptistry, a square building surrounding an octagonal inner dome chamber, built at the same time as the main church. Its unusual location next to – and in part forming – the main entrance to the church complex was probably to enable mass baptisms of the pilgrims as they came up from the town below. There followed an entrance into the inner enclosure, where the church proper and its associated monastery was situated. The main entrance to the church was through the south wing, in the manner of north Syrian architecture, though lateral entrances into the aisles existed in all other wings as well. This main entrance is one of the most splendid features of the church, consisting of a triangular pediment over the great triple entrance to the narthex, then a larger square pediment behind it pierced by clerestory windows over the entrance to the nave itself (plate 60). The east wing contains a triple apse and would have been the main part of the church, the other three functioning more as assembly halls for the pilgrims. The west wing is built out over a vaulted substructure (plate 61). The exterior is particularly graceful: the walls of each wing are pierced by alternating arched windows and doorways, and the junctions of the wings are marked by small semicircular niches; these disparate parts are then pulled together into a harmonious whole by two sharply delineated string courses, the lower one emphasizing the graceful curves of the openings.

The monastery buildings are grouped around an inner courtyard, formed in part by the arms of the church itself. The facades consist of an impressive portico, in places surviving to three storeys in height (plate 62). The bold slab and lintel technique of these porticos, with its strong emphasis on simple verticals and horizontals, contrasts starkly with the more graceful curvilinear architecture of the church itself (plate 63). These two contrasting styles probably represent a meeting – or clash – of Eastern and Western forms: the curvilinear representing a Western tradition that culminated in the Romanesque, and the trabeate being a much earlier Semitic tradition with its emphasis on simple angular forms.

This slab and lintel technique is met with very frequently in the Dead Cities. Standing at the end of the west wing of the church, one has a splendid view down onto one of the greatest of the Dead Cities, the pilgrimage town of Telanissos, modern Deir Sima'an (plate 64). One can follow the ancient pilgrimage route down via the sacred way which leaves past the baptistry of the church. The remains of a triumphal arch mark the foot of the sacred way at the bottom of the hill, beyond which is a large square where pilgrims would assemble for the ascent. From there, one is confronted by a veritable wilderness of ruins: houses, hostelries, monasteries and churches abound, some now no more than heaps of rubble but others still standing with virtually every stone intact, as though the monks left only yesterday. The most dominant features of the landscape are the great block-like porticos, many of them several storeys high, mainly belonging to monasteries and hostelries, all built to service the great monastery church up on the hill (plate 65). There are too many individual ruins to enumerate and the visitor is best left to simply explore at will, but mention must be made of a particularly intact church at the southwestern corner of the city. Apart from the collapse of its timber roof, this rather simple but graceful small basilica appears almost exactly as on the day it was completed in the early 6th century (plate 66).

Many more such ruins can be seen following the spine of the Jebel Sima'an, though most can only be reached on foot or horseback. To the southeast of Qal'at Sima'an is the town of Taqleh, that has a fine 5th century church and some well preserved village houses in typical north Syrian style. At Fafertin further to the east can be seen the second oldest dated church in Syria (after Dura Europos), a basilica dated 372 AD. More ruined churches can seen northwards along the Jebel Sima'an, at Fasufian, Burj Haidar and Kfar Nabu, while at Barad further north are the remains of the main market town for the region. It has a cathedral dated 399-402 and several other churches, as well as a monastery, a well preserved tower, and a very neat private bath building. At the north end of the Jebel Sima'an there are more remains at Dermemish, Soghanak and Kimar, the latter a small town containing ruined houses with fine examples of decorated Byzantine stonework. On the eastern slopes of the Jebel Sima'an not far off the Aleppo-Azaz road, more ruined Byzantine towns and churches can be seen at Shaikh Sulaiman, Qal'at Qalota and Kharab Shams, the latter containing a particularly well preserved basilica of the late 5th century.

The Jebel Barisha and Jebel Al-'Ala

The next group of Dead Cities (figure 22) is to the west of Aleppo, along and to the south of the present main road to Antioch. This area probably has one of the greatest concentrations of standing ruins in the world. They all belong to the Roman and Byzantine periods, but the existence of a number of walls of superbly fitted 'Cyclopean' masonry (for example, at Bamouqqa, Babisqa and Banqusa) suggests a far older date for some of them, perhaps in the 2nd millennium – or at least the survival of earlier building techniques.

Soon out of Aleppo, shortly after Urum as-Sughra where the road forks southwards to Idlib, the remains of a large tower, probably part of a Byzantine monastery, overlook the right of the road at Khirbet Shaikh 'Ali. The road soon crosses some of the finest stretches of Roman road that can be seen anywhere, parts of the ancient road that linked Aleppo and Qinnesrin (Chalcis) with Antioch – the lifeline of the Dead Cities (plate 67). To the left of the road at Tell Aqibrin are ruins of some houses of the Byzantine period. Here the road branches off to the right to Dana and Qal'at Sima'an. A Roman column tomb, consisting of two columns dating from the mid-2nd century AD, dominates the village of Sarmada just to the south of the main road. At Bab al-Hawa ('Gate of Winds') further on, remains include a Roman triumphal arch over the ancient road (now asphalted over) just opposite the modern customs post. The road then crosses the border at Qasr al-Banat, an extensive 6th century complex of monastic ruins dominated by a massive six-storey tower.

To the south of this road rise the hills of the Jebel Barisha. In the triangle formed by the Antioch road, the Harim road, and the Turkish border, access once again is mainly on foot or horseback. It is an area of ruined towns, villages, towers, houses and villas – and churches. So rich is the area in churches that it is possible only to mention the most important ones, though all of them have features that make each one unique. They are mainly centred on the town of Ba'udeh, the chief town of the district in Byzantine times, an ancient market town where it is still possible to walk along the paved bazaar streets past the two-storeyed porticos and galleries of the shops themselves. Many more porticoed galleries and villas can be seen at the ruined towns of Babisqa and Dar Qita further west. All three of these towns of course, abound in churches – the east church at Babisqa has particularly rich decoration. Babisqa also has a large, 5th-6th century bath complex, and remains of more churches can be seen at Burj Mudakhkar and Ksaijbeh to the east, Bur Deiruni to the south, and Khirbet Tizin and Qasr Iblisu to the west of the Jebel Barisha. At Serjibla the ruins include a church and public building, and a five-storey tower house.

Other remains in the Jebel Barisha can be reached from the Harim road, which branches off the Antioch road back at Sarmada. A few kilometres west of Sarmada at al-Braijjeh are the impressive remains of another monastery a little way up the side of the Jebel Barisha

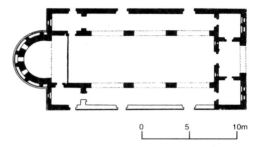

0   5   10m

Fig. 24 Qalb Lozeh

overlooking the road. It includes a staged tower still standing several storeys in height, and several large rock-cut cisterns behind. On the hill opposite is the Dead City of Sarfud. The road then winds up the Jebel Barisha to the village of Bashmishleh. At the top at Burj Baqirha can be seen the main Roman monument of the region, which comes as a refreshingly pagan break after such a bewildering surplus of Byzantine Christianity. This is the temenos of a Temple of Zeus dated 161 AD, probably occupying the site of an earlier Semitic sacred high place, which still has its monumental entrance and parts of a small prostyle temple preserved. The view from the temple is stunning, with ruins visible in all directions. Just below it to the north is the Dead City of Baqirha, with the flowing curvilinear lines of its superbly preserved east church visible from the temple. A little further west beyond Bashmishleh is the Dead City of Bamouqqa, a jumble of ruins covering an extensive area (plate 68). The most interesting remains are a particularly fine Roman villa and a monumental underground tomb of the same date next to it, presumably the mausoleum of the family owning the villa.

Some of the most impressive remains of the area are further south in the Jebel al-'Ala. The road branches off the Harim road shortly after al-Braijjeh. A few kilometres along is the Byzantine monastery of Kafr Darian standing in a large enclosure reminiscent of earlier temple enclosures. In it is an overturned column belonging to one of St Simeon's imitators. To the west within the Jebal al-'Ala is the ruined village of Qirq Bizah, which preserves houses, towers, and other buildings, including one of the earliest churches in Syria. Here it is possible to wander into courtyards, rest under the shade of the porticos, and come across many small decorative fragments that would have embellished luxury villas. But for one of the most intact monuments in all the Dead Cities, one must visit the village of Qalb Lozeh a little

151

further to the west. Here is one of the loveliest and most intact churches in Syria, a cathedral probably dedicated to SS Gabriel and Michael dating from the mid-5th century (figure 24, plate 69). The entrance is flanked by three-storey towers, a form originating with the temples at Seia and Ba'albek and culminating in the great cathedral facades of medieval Europe. Inside, the aisles are separated from the nave by three arches on thick, square piers. The solidness of these piers is relieved by the rich decoration of the capitals and arches, which also surround the doorways leading in from the narthex. The aisles are roofed by a series of ingenious interlocking stone slabs.

Surrounding Qirq Bizeh and Qalb Lozeh is an immense number of other ruined towns and villages, many of which can be seen from the ridge behind Qalb Lozeh. To visit them all would require time and resources – most have no motorable roads to them – beyond the means of most visitors, and are of interest mainly to the specialist. Many, however, contain gems of detail that would fascinate all but the most jaded, whether they are fragments of sculpture from the hand of an artist long forgotten or simply new insights into a way of life long vanished. The remains at Behyo, Kafr Qal'a, Dawwar, Kokanaya, Deir Seta and Me'ez to the south are the more important. All have ruined churches and houses, often on an impressive scale, whilst elsewhere one may stumble across isolated homesteads, ancient cisterns, faded inscriptions or undiscovered tombs that even the archaeologists might have missed. Me'ez has the ruins of a Roman public meeting hall, dated 29 AD, consisting of a gabled hall and porticos. At Benabil at the northern end of the Jebel al-'Ala, there is a superbly preserved Roman house of the 2nd century with a two-storeyed Ionic colonnade along one side. Banaqfur, also at the northern end, is a ruined town with many fine portico houses. To the east is the town of Harim, surrounding the remains of a castle that – both historically and architecturally – follows the by now usual Byzantine, Arab and Crusader pattern of sieges, rebuildings and defensive systems.

The Jebel Zawiyeh

The next concentration of dead cities comprises another hilly massif, the Jebel Zawiyeh (figure 25) or Jebel Riha, bordering the eastern side of the Ghab to the southwest of Aleppo. Historically, it comprises the line of agriculture based settlements between Antioch and Apamea. It is as rich in remains as the other areas, and is generally slightly earlier in date. The area is approached – or rather skirted, as most remains lie off these roads – by two roads: the Aleppo-Latakia road on the

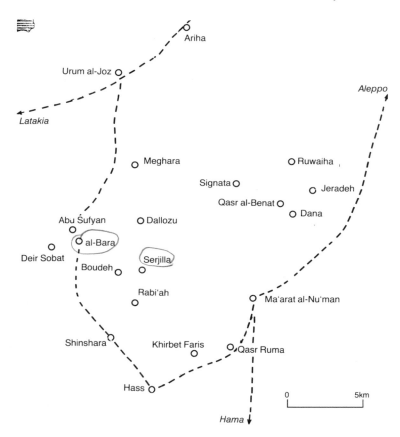

Fig. 25 Jebel Zawiyeh

northwest and the main Aleppo-Damascus road on the east.

From the northwest, the first group of ruins one comes to, soon after leaving the road at Urum al-Joz (near where there are a number of Roman funerary monuments), is Meghara to the north of the road to al-Bara. There are a number of ruins strewn over the hillside, but the most interesting are underneath: a series of superb underground monumental tombs dating from between the 3rd and 5th centuries AD. At Dalloza, between Meghara and al-Bara, there are a number of villas including one that is almost intact.

The most extensive series of ruins in the area is at al-Bara in the

153

centre of the Jebel. Here, the ruins of the ancient city of Kapropera cover a vast area, with many buildings dating from the 3rd century AD to medieval times. Dominating it is the fort of Abu Sufian, an important Arab stronghold controlling the road between Antioch and Apamea, though it was occupied briefly by the Crusaders between 1098 and 1123, who established a bishopric there. The ruins of several mosques amongst the more ancient remains, however, show that it remained an important strategic town to the Arabs long after the Crusaders had left.

From the fort one can gain a good view of al-Bara. It lies in a forest of olive groves, and the strange pyramid roofs of the tombs protruding above it give it the appearance of a Mayan city (plate 70). There are several churches at al-Bara, but perhaps the most interesting buildings are the large villas – or rather farmhouses, as many of them have olive presses, stables and barns attached to them. The best preserved is now known as Deir Sobat ('Monastery of Elizabeth') some way out of al-Bara beyond a ravine to the west, where one can obtain a very good idea of the workings of an ancient farmhouse. There are also a number of monumental necropolises surrounding the city, dating mainly from the 5th and 6th centuries, of which the most distinctive – and intact – type of monument are pyramid-roofed tombs. These are often of considerable proportions and magnificently decorated, and often perfectly preserved (plate 71).

Another superbly preserved ruined town is that of Serjilla, further to the southeast of al-Bara on the road which joins the main Aleppo-Damascus highway at Ma'arat an-Nu'man. Between al-Bara and Serjilla is also the deserted town of Boudeh. But Sergilla is the gem of the Dead Cities – indeed, in some ways the most incredible ruin in Syria (figure 26, plate 72). It is no Palmyra or Damascus with grandiose monuments that trumpet their arrogance through the pages of great tomes on architecture; what makes Serjilla so remarkable rather is its *small* size, its very ordinariness. For Serjilla is nothing more than an unassuming, everyday small country town such as can be found the world over – a town that almost anybody can identify with – yet so intact that one can still hear the voices in the wind blowing through the dry grass of the people who lived there so long ago. At Serjilla one can see virtually the full layout of a modest but prosperous country town of the Late Roman and Early Byzantine period in its entirety: here are the farmhouses with the labourers' cottages, stables and farm buildings nearby; there is the parish church and the village shops; in the central square is the town pub – looking remarkably like an Australian outback pub with its two-storeyed verandah (plates 73, 74) – and behind it the public baths; up the hill is the manor house with its olive presses. It all seems so remarkably peaceful and rural, so ordinary and everyday – as

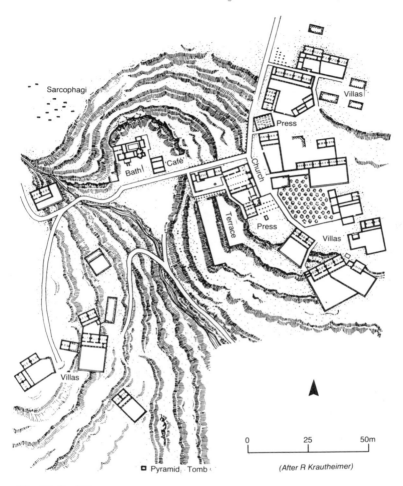

Fig. 26 Serjilla

indeed it must have been. And so alive with its past inhabitants – it seems almost fitting that the site guard at Serjilla is a deaf-mute!

Further east towards Ma'arat an-Nu'man lie several more areas of ruins: Rabi'a, Khirbet Hass, Hass and Kafr Ruma. The main one is the ruined town of Khirbet Hass or Shinsharah, a vast area of ruins that includes the remains of no less than seven churches. There are also many monumental mausolea and many other domestic and public buildings, including a public assembly hall with a courtyard lined by doric porticos. The other ruined town of Khass, across a ravine that contains several tombs, has been much reduced by stone quarrying in the 20th century. Kafr Ruma consists of a ruined castle of the 10th century, some tombs, a Roman reservoir, and a rather curious trabeate bridge made of stone slabs – rather than the more usual series of arches – resting on square piers.

The main Aleppo-Damascus highway is joined at Ma'arat an-Nu'man, a town of some importance in Byzantine and medieval times, though its somewhat turbulent history has left little standing apart from the 12th century Madrasa an-Nuriyeh and the Mosque of Joshua of the same date. The very ruined medieval citadel is situated on a steep, paved mound and surrounded by a moat. There are two impressive Ottoman caravanserais facing each other. One is now a museum with a particularly fine collection of mosaics, mainly from the Dead Cities of the Jebel Zawiyeh. They were not caravanserais in the conventional sense but rather way stations on the pilgrimage route to Mecca.

A number of spectacular Dead Cities stretch in a rough line northwards from Ma'arat an-Nu'man. They differ from the others in the rich, warm golden stone of their construction. They are also among the lesser known and visited of the Dead Cities, yet are amongst the best and only ten minutes off the main Damascus-Aleppo highway. Just to the north is the village of Dana (not to be confused with the village of the same name in the Jebel Shaikh Barakat) which has some pyramid tombs and the ruins of a 6th century monastery known as Qasr al-Banat. To the northwest is the superb ruined town of Jeradeh (plate 75). It has a number of well preserved villas, a 4th century church, and a series of very impressive towers flanking a street. The tallest tower is still preserved to a height of six storeys, nearly 20 metres high, with a small projecting balcony near the top that was probably a prototype of the machicolation that later achieved such prominence in Arab and Crusader fortifications. This and the other towers of Jeradeh would have been for defence against nomad raids from the desert to the east; with all of them intact the skyline must have resembled some of the medieval towns of Tuscany – it looks impressive enough today.

Further north again is the superb ruined town of Ruwaiha, covering a considerable area – perhaps the most remarkable after Serjilla (plate 76). Its centre is dominated by a large square surrounded by two storeyed Ionic porticoes, the site of an agora. This seems to suggest Greek origins, but the haphazard jumble of streets surrounding it conforms to the normal Eastern pattern. The street to the south, however, is fairly wide and lined with splendid villas, some of them virtually intact (and still lived in). The villas, unlike the design further north, invariably surround a central courtyard, often porticoed on two levels on all four sides. There is a perfectly intact late 4th century tomb in the form of a distyle temple towards the end (plate 77). To the west of the agora is a 4th century church, and the impressive fortified Church of Bizzos to the north. It is one of the largest churches in the region and one of the few fortified churches in Syria (plate 78). Like the similar sized church at Qalb Lozeh, its facade is framed by two towers. In the vicinity are also a number of fine monumental tombs.

The desert edges

The final area of Dead Cities skirts the desert to the east and southeast of Aleppo. They are quite different to those further west: far more wide-spaced, as befits the sparser terrain; often defensive in nature, either against nomadic incursions or the Persian invasions of the 6th century; and there is an increasing use of mudbrick, as the sources of good stone are further away in the hill country around Aleppo. Because of their wider scatter, they do not form as cohesive a group as the others, with Qasr Ibn Wardan and al-Anderin to the south and Resafeh to the east belonging more to other regions (see Chapters 6 and 10). Nevertheless, they belong within the broad framework of the Dead Cities of north Syria.

Most of them stretch in a rough line southeastwards, crossing the old desert route to Palmyra via the Jebel Khass. The first of these is not in fact Byzantine. This is Sfireh, ancient Sipri, the remains of a mid-2nd millennium fortified city where a number of important sculptures and cuneiform texts have been found. From Sfireh, two desert roads branch off, the first following the old caravan route to the east towards via Umm 'Amud to Resafeh, and the second following the old caravan route to Palmyra via Khanazir and Isriyeh. Continuing on the first road to Umm 'Amud, at the edge of the Sabkhat, or salt lake, some distance to the southeast of Sfireh, is the ruined town of Mo'allaq, not far from Umm 'Amud. It has three churches and a number of other ruins. More ruined churches can be seen at Khirbet Jubb al-'Ali and Zabed, further towards the desert to the southeast. The former has particularly fine standing remains; the latter has an unusual tomb on a hill overlooking the site.

Back at Sfireh the second track branches off, bearing more southwards, towards Khanazir. There are a number of minor Byzantine remains on the way, but the first ruined towns are al-Huwar, where there several standing remains, and Bennawi nearby, which has a ruined church. More ruins – mainly churches – can be seen along the route at al-Fisan, Kafr Hut, Suyan, and Serj Farej, until one arrives at Khanazir, ancient Kunasara, on the edge of the desert. It was an important Byzantine town marking a caravan stopping place, and whilst much has been built over recently, several remains can still be seen including the town walls and a large church.

In the desert 56 kilometres to the southeast of Khanazir are the ruins of Isriyeh. Isriyeh, ancient Seriana, was an important desert junction of caravan routes, marking roughly the halfway point between Aleppo and Palmyra as well as the halfway point on the route which bisects it from Selimiyeh to Resafeh. Here can be seen a beautifully intact, white limestone Roman prostyle temple of the 3rd century AD, surrounded by the ruins of the ancient town. Although the outer columns have fallen, the temple still preserves much of its ornamentation, reminiscent of the baroque style of decoration seen at Palmyra, as well as a spiral staircase leading to a sacred high place on its roof.

CHAPTER 10

The Euphrates and the Jazira

The Euphrates is one of the great rivers of the Middle East. With its twin river the Tigris further east, it nurtured the very origins of civilization many thousands of years ago, and has provided the Near East with its lifeblood ever since. The waters of the Euphrates continue to mould the destiny of the Middle East now more than ever, for it is said that whilst present wars in the Middle East are fought over oil, the next will be fought over that even more precious liquid: water. Having provided so much for so long, it is now becoming apparent that there is simply not enough to go around.

The Euphrates is central to this problem. It is shared by three countries: it waters the immense plains of Syria and Iraq, traditional enemies, and rises in the mountains of Turkey, former masters of both. Already, all three countries have constructed mighty dams across the Euphrates in attempts to control it: the Ataturk and Keban Dams in Turkey, the Tabqa Dam in Syria, and the Haditha Dam in Iraq. The construction of the greatest of these, the Ataturk Dam and its many subsidiary dams on the Euphrates tributaries, has already strained relations between Syria and Turkey.

Syria itself is central to the politics of water. Not only for its position on the middle reaches of the Euphrates, but also for its position on the headwaters of the Jordan – a river more passionately fought over than any other. The great rivers of the Middle East, in controlling the destinies of early man, helped to found civilization in the Near East; modern man, in attempting to control these rivers in return, is threatening to bring it to an end.

The part played by the Euphrates in the origins of civilization cannot be underestimated, but it does nonetheless tend to obscure the importance of other rivers in the region. In Syria it has two important tributaries: the Balikh and the Khabur. These water the region known as the Jazira, a region of broad grassland and steppe with adequate rainfall for extensive cultivation that until recently supported a large nomadic population and abundant wildlife. Lying midway between the main cultural 'blocs' of the ancient Near East – Syria-Levant, Anatolia, and Mesopotamia – the Jazira formed a cultural heartland to all three. Thus, remains of some of the earliest cultures in the Near East are to be found in the Jazira, cultures that both borrowed from and contributed to elements of Near Eastern civilization as a whole. Indeed, in turning eastwards, deep into the interior of Syria it seems one has left the great stone monuments of the historical periods of the Levantine coast far behind to face the dusty mounds of a remoter past; the further east one goes the older the civilizations become. The age of sites here seem only to be expressed in lesser or greater terms of 'BC', with some of them of almost incomprehensible antiquity. Here in the Jazira, at the very heart of the ancient Near East, one feels that history began.

The Upper Euphrates

The upper reaches of the Euphrates, between the Turkish border and the great bend where it turns eastwards at Meskine, are dominated by an immense fortress, Qal'at an-Najm, a few miles to the south of the main road between Aleppo and Qamishle. Qal'at an-Najm is one of the most impressive fortresses in Syria, dramatically situated on top of the escarpment overlooking the right bank of the river. It originally guarded a bridge, now gone, built in the Umayyad period that crossed the Euphrates at this point. Most of the castle, however, dates from the 12th and 13th centuries, and it is still marvellously intact today. It is surrounded by a ditch, inside of which is a smooth, steep glacis leading up to the walls of the castle itself – in many ways reminiscent of the citadel of Aleppo. The walls are well preserved, reinforced by square and round towers at regular intervals, and pierced by just the one entrance – again reminiscent of Aleppo. Inside, one can walk through long vaulted galleries, vast pillared rooms, up staircases and out onto battlements and wide open terraces, all still in a remarkable state of preservation, with spectacular views up and down the river.

Qal'at an-Najm was associated with the town of Membij, some 30 kilometres to the west towards Aleppo – indeed, its original name was Qal'at al-Membij. Membij is the site of ancient Mabbog, a town dedicated to the worship of Atargatis, the ancient Syrian goddess of love and water. After the Greek conquest it was known as Hierapolis, and the notoriety of rites associated with the worship of Atargatis spread throughout the Hellenistic and Roman world – and contributed to the popularity of its cult. Hierapolis was heavily fortified against the Persians by Justinian in the 6th century, the remains of which are all that are left to see today.

The area of the upper Euphrates was dominated in the early 1st millennium BC by Neo-Hittite city-states, chief of which was Carchemish. The area is currently being investigated by British archaeologists. Carchemish (modern Jarablus) lies just across the border in Turkish territory, but two of the lesser known city-states, probably coming under Carchemish, can be visited this side of the border: Til Barsip and Hadatu. Til Barsip, modern Tell Ahmar ('Red Mound'), lies on the left bank of the Euphrates, several miles north of the main road. The town is mentioned in Sumerian cuneiform texts as early as the 3rd millennium BC, and remains going back to the 5th millennium have been found. But the most important remains discovered have been from the Neo-Hittite palace of the 8th century BC, and include several impressive lion-gates carved from black basalt. After the Assyrian conquest Til Barsip was renamed Kar Shalmaneser ('Shalmaneser City'), and the palace excavated from this period by the French between 1929 and 1931 contained some particularly beautiful Assyrian wall paintings, now in the Aleppo Museum. Hadatu, modern al-Firazdaq (Arslantash – 'lion-stone' in Turkish), lies further to the northeast on the Jazira plain. This is the site of another Neo-Hittite principality. As its modern name implies, monumental stone reliefs of lions, similar to those from Til Barsip and Carchemish, were found on the surface and later in French excavations in 1928. From the Neo-Assyrian palace of the 8th century BC at Hadatu were also excavated a series of very fine carved ivory reliefs.

Meskine and Lake Asad

Meskine marks the spot where the Euphrates is closest to the Mediterranean. Its position, therefore, has been of considerable strategic and commercial importance. It lies on the site of Emar, an important city-state of the mid-2nd millennium BC, probably a vassal kingdom of Yamhad (Aleppo) further west. Emar had a network of commercial activities all over the Near East, particularly with the Assyrian and Babylonian kingdoms further east. The remains uncovered so far comprise some administrative buildings and temples, one of the latter producing a library of approximately 1500 cuneiform texts.

After the Greek conquest, Meskine was known as Balis or

Barbalissos, still operating as a trade entrepot where goods from Mesopotamia and further east would travel up the Euphrates to be transhipped to the Mediterranean via Aleppo and Antioch. It continued in this role throughout Roman and Byzantine times, but by the middle Islamic period, when its name had reverted to Meskine, its importance had declined considerably. The only remains left of its earlier importance are some fragmentary Byzantine ramparts from Justinian's refortification of the eastern empire, and an unusual octagonal minaret of the 12th century.

Far older remains than Emar have been found in the vicinity of Meskine, but most of them have been covered up by Lake Asad, the immense artificial lake created by the damming of the Euphrates at Tabqa. Whilst this lake has undoubtedly erased many sites of archaeological importance, its construction at the same time prompted one of the most intensive programmes of archaeological investigations in Syria's history, with teams from many countries contributing to the efforts to record and salvage sites in the river valley.

Amongst the earliest of the sites in the Lake Asad basin were Mureybit and Abu Hureyra to the east of Meskine. The former was probably the earlier – indeed at about 11000 BC it was probably one of the very earliest sedentary settlements in the entire Near East. American excavations both there and at Abu Hureyra have revealed important information on the long transition from the hunter-gathering way of life to the settled communities of the Neolithic with, on its way, the domestication of plants and animals and the development of agriculture.

The origins of agriculture documented at Mureybit and Abu Hureyra mark perhaps the first great revolution in history. And discoveries at another site in the Lake Asad basin just north of Meskine have documented the next: the birth of cities. These discoveries, at Habuba Kabira alongside the river and Jebel Aruda on cliffs overlooking it, were amongst the more important in Near Eastern archaeology in the sixties and seventies. Habuba Kabira was a large, well laid-out town consisting of a densely settled area of living quarters, workshops and bazaars, with a large open area of administrative and religious monuments. The whole was defended by strong ramparts of double walls reinforced by square towers. Tell Qannas, dominating the town and the river valley high up on the escarpment, consisted of two temples and several palatial buildings, probably the seat of the rulers. Whether one calls Habuba Kabira a town or a city is hardly important here, for with a date of round about 3500 BC, it is certainly amongst the earliest in the world. But even more important than its size or date relative to other settlements, was its connections. For Habuba Kabira-Tell Qannas was a colony of a far greater city: Uruk (modern Warka,

Biblical Erech), far away in southern Mesopotamia. Whether this was merely a part of an extensive system of trading colonies extending up the Euphrates into southern Turkey from the 'mother city' of Uruk or whether it was a part of the world's first empire – an 'Urukian empire' – is still debated. But the discovery and excavation of Habuba Kabira revealed a mature system of international connections, far more sophisticated and far earlier than had previously been thought.

The area is not without later monuments as well. At Abu Hureyra, in addition to the prehistoric site, there is a circular brick minaret of the 12th century and three decorated brick tombs known as the tombs of the Daughters of Abu Hureyra (who was a companion of the Prophet). Indeed, Abu Hureyra – under its former name of Siffin – figures significantly in early Islamic history, for it was here in 657 that the forces of 'Ali and Mu'awiya met to decide the future of Islam: Mu'awiya, the victor, founded the Umayyad dynasty in Damascus while 'Ali and his supporters were forced to flee to Iraq, where he was eventually martyred.

On the opposite, north, bank are the ruins of the impressive castle of Qal'at al-Jabar, on a cliff overlooking the river. Most of the present structure dates from the time of Nur ed-Din in the 12th century, who captured it from the Crusaders of Edessa who held it briefly. The entrance is through a tunnel cut through the rock, and the interior is still in a good state of preservation, particularly the towers overlooking the cliff.

Resafeh

In the desert some 30 kilometres south of the Euphrates at Raqqa is one of the most extraordinary ruined desert cities in the Middle East – more extraordinary in some ways even than Palmyra, if only because it is far less known. This is the immense walled Byzantine city of Resafeh, ancient Sergiopolis. In about the year 303 AD in the reign of Diocletian an event occurred that brought Resafeh into prominence. A Christian officer in the Roman army, Sergius, was martyred following a particularly brutal series of tortures at the hands of his fellow officers. Martyrdom was not, of course, uncommon in the Roman world even by that late date, but the particularly barbaric nature of St Sergius' martyrdom sent shockwaves through the Christian communities of Syria. A shrine was built over his tomb at Resafeh, which quickly attracted a wide following as a pilgrimage centre. By the time Christianity became officially tolerated, the name was changed to Sergiopolis in his honour. Under the Byzantine emperors, particularly Anastasius (491-518), Sergiopolis was massively embellished, both as a

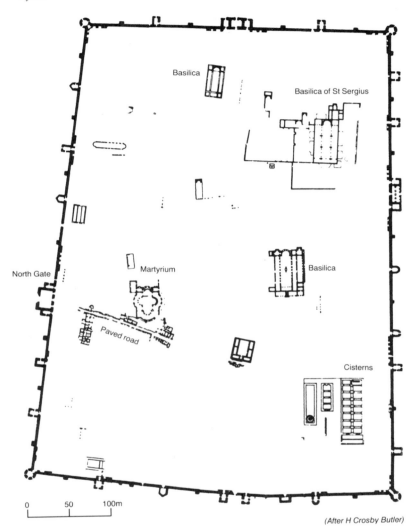

(After H Crosby Butler)

Fig. 27 Resafeh

religious centre and a frontier fortification, and for a while it was renamed Anastasiopolis. It was probably under Anastasius that the Basilica of St Sergius and the vast underground cisterns were built. Its great walls withstood the Persian invasion of Syria in 540 under Chosroes I, but were taken in the next invasion by Chosroes II. The

Umayyad caliphs, particularly Hisham, with their predilection for desert retreats, restored much of its ramparts in the 8th century, but following the collapse of the Umayyad dynasty Resafeh quickly declined and became deserted.

On leaving the Euphrates one crosses a vast level expanse of desert until the utter flatness is interrupted by the walls of Resafeh coming into sight, dominating the horizon like a desert cliff (plate 79). These walls, like the rest of the main monuments in Resafeh, are built of a gypseous stone with white crystalline inclusions; the effect, glistening under the midday sun of the Syrian desert, is an unforgettable spectacle.

The walls enclose a vast rectangle measuring about 400 by 550 metres, pierced by four gateways in the middle of each side (figure 27). The main entrance today is through the north gate, which is also the best preserved (plate 80). This richly decorated triple entrance, framed by Corinthian columns supporting a graceful arcaded pediment, is easily the loveliest city gateway in Syria – and one of the finest intact gateways in the Byzantine world (plate 81). On entering, it is a good idea to climb directly up onto the ramparts, partly to appreciate the superb quality military engineering and the still intact long gallery that ran all the way around the inside, but mainly to obtain a view over the city itself. From this vantage point it resembles a sea of pock-marks and undulating low mounds – most of the domestic structures were built of mud – but with the main monuments emerging like great masonry islands. Chief of these is the great Cathedral of St Sergius, easily dominating all other buildings in Resafeh. It is approached from the north gate by a paved street, parts of which were excavated by German archaeologists in the fifties. It is a regular basilical plan, though the arcades separating the nave from its two aisles originally consisted of just three wide arches each (figure 28, plate 82). This original concept was too ambitious for the weight they had to support: the arcades began to tilt at an alarming angle, and they had to be propped up by the addition of a secondary arcade underneath. These repairs form an interesting juxtaposition.

The Cathedral of St Sergius, built in the early years of the 6th century, probably represents the third resting place of St Sergius' remains. The original sanctuary to St Sergius was a smaller basilica roughly in the middle of the city. The saint's remains were probably housed in a martyrium just to the north of the central apse. This basilica was extensively damaged by earthquake in antiquity – and little is standing today – so that the reliquary was moved to a purpose-built martyrium nearer the north gate. This martyrium is a centrally planned church, consisting of two concentric quatrefoils. It is still standing to a considerable height and its decoration is the most lavish in Resafeh.

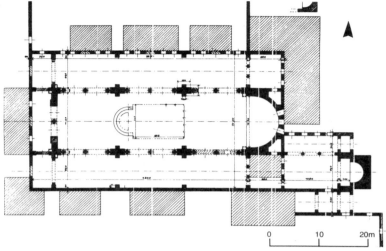

Fig. 28 Basilica of St Sergius at Resafeh

The subsequent construction of the cathedral under the imperial patronage of Anastasius finally caused the saint's remains to be moved there.

The most impressive structures at Resafeh are not above the ground but below it. These are a series of gigantic brick cisterns in the southwest corner of the city, that appear more as immense subterranean cathedrals than anything as mundane as the city water supply. Just outside the city walls to the south, the remains of a square brick palace built by the Caliph Hisham have been excavated by German archaeologists. It is in many ways a smaller version of Hisham's great palace of Qasr al-Hair al-Gharbi out in the desert (Chapter 11). It was savagely pillaged and destroyed in 'Abbasid reprisals against Syria in the 8th century.

Raqqa

The 'Abbasid period in Syria, however, was not all destructive, and one of the greatest of all 'Abbasid monuments still surviving can be seen at Raqqa, on the north bank of the Euphrates. A town was first founded here by the Greeks, called successively Nicephorium, Callinicum and Leontopolis. It remained an important frontier town between the Byzantine and Sasanian empires, but it was not until the 'Abbasid period in the 8th century AD that Raqqa assumed pre-eminence. The 'Abbasid Caliph al-Mansur founded a new city there in 772, calling it ar-Rafiqa, with a circular plan inspired directly by the plan of Baghdad itself. It became a favourite summer resort of Harun al-Rashid, who for a time turned it into his summer capital, as much to escape the heat of Baghdad as to use it as a base for incursions into Byzantine territory. He had a luxurious palace built there, the Qasr as-Salam ('Palace of Peace'), and his son and successor al-Mu'tasim built a second palace. It slowly declined after the 10th century, and was already in ruins by the Mongol conquest.

Al-Mansur's round city of Baghdad itself has now completely vanished, but at Raqqa we can get an impression what this must have been like, for impressive remains are still standing. The plan is in fact in the shape of a horseshoe, with the southern, straight side determined by the old course of the Euphrates which used to pass at this point (the present banks are about a kilometre further south). Its high mud ramparts and ditch still survive in many places. It was pierced by a number of gateways, but the only one surviving is the Baghdad gate in the southeastern corner (plate 83). This gateway, probably dating from the construction of the walls in 772, is one of the more important monuments in the development of early Islamic architecture. It is built entirely of brick, but the bricks are so arranged as to form decorative geometric patterns in high relief over the facade. Such brick decoration is a forerunner of the great heights that the style was later to reach in Persian architecture in the 11th-12th centuries. Indeed, the line of decorative brick arches across the top of the gateway is inspired directly by Persian Sasanian architecture. Islamic architecture it seems, like the 'Abbasid dynasty itself, was already beginning to come under Persian influence.

The centre of Raqqa is dominated by the immense enclosure of the great mosque. This again seems inspired by the layout of al-Mansur's round city of Baghdad, but it also fits easily into the older Syrian urban traditions of city centres dominated by the great temple enclosures. Only parts of the enclosure wall, measuring 93 by 111 metres, and the arcade of the sanctuary wall are still standing. There is also a round minaret, standing in a corner of the courtyard (an unusual position), and a small domed mausoleum in the middle, but these probably date from the 12th century, some 400 years after the construction of the mosque.

Syrian and French archaeologists have uncovered parts of an 'Abbasid palace, probably the one built by Mu'tasim, to the north of the mosque. Known as the Qasr al-Banat ('Palace of the Maidens'), it includes remains of large reception halls opening from a central courtyard with exquisite brick and stucco decoration. During Raqqa's heyday in the 9th and 10th centuries the city spread out far beyond its walls, and extensive areas of mounding today hide the remains of this settlement. Turkish excavations in 1906 and French excavations in 1944 revealed several large structures in these areas, including the remains of the palace of Harun al-Rashid himself. The area is currently being investigated by German archaeologists.

Some 8 kilometres west of Raqqa are the ruins of Heraqla, the site of a pleasure palace built by Harun al-Rashid named after his victory over the Byzantines at Heraklion in Turkey. It consists of a large fortified enclosure, with some remains of a reception hall and other buildings inside.

The Balikh

Raqqa stands at the junction of the Balikh River with the Euphrates. The area of the Balikh is extremely rich in ancient sites of all periods, most of them now being little more than mounds. There are far too many to enumerate even some of them here, but mention must be made of two that have been the scene of important archaeological investigations over the past years: Tell Khuera and Tell Hammam et-Turkman. Tell Hammam et-Turkmen, the scene of Dutch excavations, lies about halfway up and just to the west of the Balikh. It is an immense site where nearly all the periods of the Jazira's history over the past five thousand years are represented. Of particular importance was the discovery of a large settlement of the Ubaid period of the 5th millennium, covering an area unusually large for this period. Tell Khuera is a large mound lying to the east of the Balikh near the Turkish border. It has important remains from the 3rd millennium BC, where a number of Sumerian statues have been excavated by a German expedition.

These and other sites on the Balikh only really have things to see when the archaeologists are actually present excavating on the mounds. But the area is worth visiting if only to appreciate the immense, limitless horizons of the Jazira steppeland. This seemingly endless plain is punctuated only by the occasional mound hiding secrets many thousands of years old, attesting to the importance of the area in antiquity, and the strange beehive-shaped domes of the modern villages. These 'beehive villages' are a curious feature of this part of Syria; the scarcity of timber has meant that houses can only be roofed by beehive-shaped domes of mud (plate 84).

Halebiye and Zalebiye

We have already seen some of the great Euphrates castles at Qal'at al-Najm and Qal'at al-Jabar, but at the fortress town of Halebiye

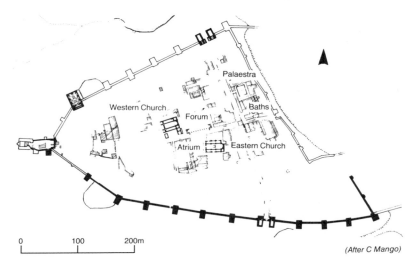

Fig. 29 Halebiye

(ancient Zenobia) we see the greatest of them all – indeed, one of the greatest of all Byzantine fortifications outside the walls of Constantinople itself (figure 29). The site is an old one, for it guards an important ford across the Euphrates, and it became a Palmyrene post in the 3rd century AD guarding the routes up along the Euphrates and across the desert. The Romans took it over after their destruction of Palmyra, but in the subsequent Byzantine period it assumed major importance as one of the empire's main frontier defences against the Sasanian Persians. Accordingly, the emperor Justinian in the 6th century provided it with defences on a massive scale. Despite such precautions, the Persians stormed it twice: under Chosroes I in 540 and again under Chosroes II in 610. The town never recovered, and apart from some minor repairs in the Arab period, it was slowly abandoned.

Today its ramparts, with its regular square towers of the same white calcareous stone that Resafa is built, are one of the most impressive sights in all Syria. They enclose a simply vast area in the shape of a triangle, and are pierced by five gateways, three of them facing the river, emphasizing the importance of the Euphrates as a route in those days. The main entrance today is through the south gate, which leads onto the main north-south street of the town. The interior is very ruinous, though the remains of some porticos – architectural descendants of the great colonnaded streets of the Roman period – still line the street, and there are two ruined churches to the south. Other remains have been identified as a possible forum or market place, a praetorium from the time of Justinian with brick vaulted rooms still surviving up to three storeys high, a bath house, and the very ruined keep.

Parts of the town spread outside the walls as well. In particular, just to the north is the necropolis area, where one can see tower tombs and underground hypogea in the Palmyrene tradition. An outlying Byzantine fort, probably guarding the approaches to Halebiye from the north, is some 10 kilometres further north at Tell Qsubi.

On the opposite bank to Halebiye, some three kilometres further downstream, are the ruins of Zalebiye. This is another mainly Byzantine fortification, defending the approaches of Halebiye from downstream. It consists of a large rectangular enclosure reinforced with square towers after the same style of Halebiye. The main gateway, still well preserved, is on the east side.

Deir ez-Zor and environs

Deir ez-Zor is a modern town, now the capital of the vast eastern plains of Syria and the centre of development projects both on the Euphrates and in the Khabur region to the north. It is a convenient base for excursions downstream to Dura Europos and Mari as well as to the many archaeological sites of the Khabur headwaters in northeastern Syria; there is also a good road that takes one directly back to Damascus across the desert via Palmyra.

Although a modern town, it is an area rich in some of the most important antique remains in Syria, particularly southeastwards along the Euphrates. The first of these remains, at the village of Ashara on the right bank, is the 3rd and 2nd millennium site of Terqa, capital of the kingdom of Khana, where the Americans have been excavating since the 1970s. Terqa was founded as a full-blown city about 3000 BC, curiously without any earlier settlement. It was provided at this time with formidable defences consisting of mudbrick walls some 20 metres thick extending for over a kilometre and a half. These walls stood it in good stead for the next millennium and a half of its history, undergoing a constant programme of repairs and restoration. Over this time, the kingdom of Khana controlled much of the region of the Euphrates in Syria, at times as a rival to the greater kingdom of Mari downstream, at other times as its vassal. Indeed, there is some evidence that Terqa might have been the religious capital of Mari, as it was an important cult centre for the worship of the god Dagan. It declined after about 1500 BC, largely as a result of wider changes that were happening all over the Middle East at the time, associated in part with the rise of the Aramaeans.

The excavations have uncovered numerous buildings within the walled city, including parts of the Temple of Dagan and various domestic buildings. Numerous cuneiform tablets and clay seal impressions and cylinder seals have been found, but perhaps the most interesting find was one of the humblest. This was a jar in a middle-class house containing some carbonized cloves – a small enough find in itself, but evidence of trade with Indonesia nearly 4000 years ago!

Dura Europos

The greatest of the 3rd millennium Middle Euphrates kingdoms, however, was Mari, further downstream just before the Iraqi border. But before getting to Mari one passes a major site of another era altogether: the Greek and Roman caravan city of Dura Europos, overlooking the right bank of the Euphrates near the village of Salihiye. It was founded as a Macedonian military colony in about 300 BC by soldiers in the army of Seleucus I to guard the Euphrates route from Mesopotamia, roughly midway between the two Seleucid capitals of Antioch in the west and Seleucia on the Tigris below Baghdad. It was named after Seleucus' native town of Europos in Macedonia (*dur* is an ancient Semitic prefix meaning 'fort' or 'city'). With the loss of the Seleucid eastern provinces to the Parthians in the late 2nd century BC, Dura Europos came under Parthian domination, but it was allowed to remain as an autonomous city state acting as a commercial go-between for both empires, occupying much the same position as Palmyra. This role increased when the Romans replaced the Seleucids in Syria, when Dura was able to tranship goods coming up the Euphrates from Mesopotamia and the Gulf, across to the increasingly important commercial centre of Palmyra in the desert, and on to the Mediterranean coast. Rome only occupied it during the Severan period, when it became an important forward position on their eastern frontier. But for most of its history it maintained its semi-independence under a loose Parthian overlordship, becoming increasingly orientalized in the process as the links with Macedonia became more and more tenuous. In the 3rd century AD, however, two events combined to bring about a collapse of its fortunes: the destruction of Palmyra by the Romans in the west, and the overthrow of the Parthians by the Sasanians in the east. It quickly declined, so that by the 4th century it was practically deserted.

Dura Europos occupies an easily defensible position on a plateau overlooking the Euphrates, protected by the river escarpment on one side and deep gorges on two others (figure 30). The fourth side, facing the open desert, is defended by a massive wall. It was laid out by the

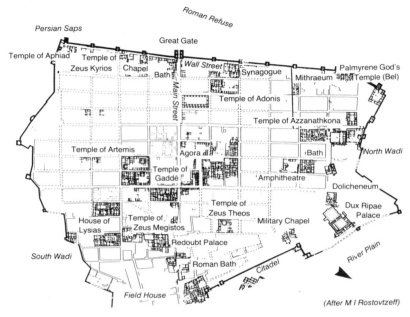

Fig. 30 Dura Europos

Macedonian settlers with all the regular trappings of a Greek city: a street plan following a strict grid pattern dominated in the centre by an open agora or market place, surrounded by commercial buildings on one side and temples to Artemis, Apollo and Zeus to the south. Apart from the actual layout of the city and some fragments of a Doric colonnade in the Temple of Artemis, practically nothing remains of Hellenistic Dura, and most of the monuments date from the Partho-Roman period of the first centuries AD.

The main building material of Dura Europos was mud, in the Mesopotamian tradition, rather than the stone of the great Graeco-Roman cities further west in Syria. Hence, it does not have the immense quantity of remains standing above ground that those cities had; most monuments were hidden under mounds of collapsed debris. But Dura was the scene of large scale excavations by a joint French and American expedition in the 1920s and 1930s. It is from these that most of the monuments we see today were exposed, and whilst its standing remains might not equal those of Palmyra or Bosra, the protective covering afforded by the mud collapse has meant that more has been preserved than in the stone-built cities. Indeed, such was the degree of preservation in many cases that Dura has been described as the 'Pompeii of the East'.

With its position on the borders of both the Roman and Parthian empires, a crossroads between East and West, it comes as no surprise that the inhabitants of Dura Europos practised an immense diversity of religions, and monuments of the Palmyrene, Persian, Semitic, Jewish, Christian and ancient Greek religions have been found. The first of these to be encountered is the Temple of the Palmyrene Gods (in fact a temple to Palmyrene Bel), built into an angle of the city walls soon after entering the city, which underwent several modifications over the first three centuries AD. It was the chance discovery of some superbly preserved frescos in this temple by British soldiers defending their position in the ruins from attacking tribesmen in 1921 that led to the identification and subsequent excavation of Dura Europos. These frescos can now be seen in the museums of Damascus and Yale. Just outside the temple is a Mithraeum. Although Mithraism was an Iranian religion – and frescos inside it depicted Zoroaster and other figures from the religion – it seems that this temple was erected by Roman soldiers, Mithraism being one of the Roman army's most popular cults.

The most important religious buildings were discovered by the archaeologists just inside the Palmyra Gate in the west. These were a Jewish synagogue and, just a few blocks away, a Christian 'church' – or more correctly a meeting house. Both buildings resemble the conventional, private courtyard houses of the day rather than great public monuments, as befitted small religious minorities, and from the street would have been indistinguishable from the ordinary houses of the neighbourhood. The synagogue is particularly impressive for the astonishing series of frescos which decorated its walls depicting scenes from the Old Testament – the oldest Old Testament cycle surviving. It owes its remarkable state of preservation from its situation directly underneath the city walls: apart from being protected by the greater bulk of the ramparts behind, in 256 AD the walls were widened and strengthened by filling in all houses – including the synagogue – adjacent to the walls with sand, the house walls forming casemates. Since excavation, the synagogue and its frescos have been carefully lifted and today forms one of the prime exhibits of the Damascus Museum. The church, like the synagogue, contained wall paintings depicting scenes from the miracles of Christ, and also owed its preservation to the widening of the ramparts behind it, though not as well as the synagogue. It is accurately dated by inscription 231/2 AD, probably scratched into the fresh plaster of one of the rooms by a workman, thus making it the oldest dated church in the world. In addition to Christian symbols depicted on the walls, the building contained a bishop's 'throne' and a stone basin presumably used as a font.

If the buildings of the Jewish and Christian minorities of Dura had to be hidden away in the backstreets, monuments of the Greek religion were appropriately enough situated in the centre of the city by the agora. These were the temples of Artemis, Apollo and Zeus, but the religion of Dura very soon acquired a Semitic overlay: Artemis was equated with Nanaia, an ancient Mesopotamian deity, and temples to two other goddesses were built alongside; Atargatis, a deity popular elsewhere in Syria, and Azzanathkona, a purely local deity found only at Dura (though she too was occasionally equated with Artemis). The temple of Artemis-Nanaia, after its reconstruction in the 1st century AD, resembled Mesopotamian temple styles rather than the peripteral Doric temple that was first laid out by the Greeks. This and the temples of Atargatis and Azzanathkona, also built in the first half of the 1st century, followed the Eastern design of a sanctuary set within a large enclosure.

Other religious remains can be seen elsewhere in the city, particularly to the Palmyrene gods of Bel, Yarhibol and Aglibol, as well as to more obscure Arab gods such as Arsu, Ashera and Sa'ad, and to gods from the Roman occupation such as Jupiter, testifying to the rich diversity of the culture of Dura. But equally important were the great civic monuments as well. Chief of these was the agora in the centre of the city, a large open square originally laid out along classic Greek lines by the first Macedonian engineers. As the city slowly became more orientalized, so too did its architecture, and the agora gradually became transformed into a maze of covered bazaars and street-side shops. The houses too, of which a large area has been cleared to the southeast, resemble the traditional Eastern courtyard houses. The Romans left their mark with the construction of a large praetorium complex taking up nearly a quarter of the city within the walls. As well as a splendid governor's palace, the Dux Ripae, consisting of two colonnaded courtyard buildings, there were barracks, a small theatre, several baths and a parade ground. These were the last major buildings to be erected before the city's destruction by the Persians, and unlike all the other monuments at Dura, are entirely Western in style, with even the Roman foot being used as the standard measurement rather than the local cubit. Overlooking the Euphrates at the north edge of the city are the remains of the citadel, originally laid out by the Greeks. Some impressive towers and stretches of wall still survive, though little remains inside. Outside the walls stretched a vast necropolis area consisting of underground chambers and occasional tomb towers in the Palmyrene style.

Mari

Most of the great Mesopotamian city-states where civilization began lie on the lower Tigris-Euphrates plains in southern Iraq. One of them, however, lay far out on a limb, well upstream on the Euphrates on the route to Anatolia and the Mediterranean. This was the kingdom of Mari, modern Tell Hariri in Syria, which provided the Sumerians with one of their essential links to the west. Through Mari, Sumerian civilization was able to spread westwards until its forms dominated most aspects of ancient Near Eastern culture

This outpost of Sumerian civilization was probably founded in the late 4th millennium, but it was in the Early Dynastic period – the period when the great city-states of Sumer first flourished – that a regular city with strong ramparts was laid out at Mari. Mari figures highly in Sumerian literature as one of the main ruling dynasties, and the commercial advantages of its position enabled it to wield considerable regional power, and its armies even reached deep into southern Mesopotamia. Sargon of Akkad, however, put an end to the independence of all the Sumerian city-states in about 2300 BC. Following the collapse of the Akkadian empire, Mari entered the era of its greatest prosperity, under a new Semitic dynasty of Amorite rulers in the early 2nd millennium, profiting immensely from control of the trade routes. The Amorite rulers were overthrown in about 1800 BC by Shamshi-Adad, king of the newly emerging power of Assyria in northern Mesopotamia, but after his death the Amorite rulers of Mari re-emerged under its greatest king, Zimri-Lim. Under Zimri-Lim Mari experienced a building boom and his great palace and temples were embellished on a scale and with a lavishness that had hardly been seen in the Near East at the time. Zimri-Lim's rise, however, coincided with the rise of another Amorite king in Mesopotamia, Hammurabi of Bablylon. For a while the two fellow Amorite royal houses were allied, but the emergence of Babylon as pre-eminent over all others led to the inevitable great power rivalry, and the two kings clashed in about 1760 BC. Hammurabi destroyed Zimri-Lim's vast palace at Mari, the ramparts were razed and the temples were sacked. Henceforth, Babylon's place as the centre of Mesopotamian civilization was assured; Mari never recovered but quickly disappeared from history, though there was sporadic minor occupation in the Middle Assyrian, Seleucid, Parthian and Sasanian periods.

French excavations have been carried out at Mari more or less without interruption since 1933, and all of the monuments on the site have been laboriously uncovered by the archaeologists. The mud ramparts date from the period of the city's foundation in the 3rd millennium. Next to the western line of these walls are the remains of

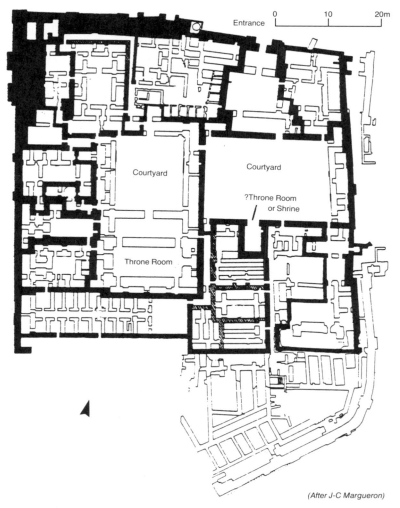

Fig. 31 The palace of Mari

a temple of Ishtar, also from the same period. It consists of series of rooms surrounding an asphalted courtyard, on which were found a basin, an offering table and an altar associated with the rituals. The surrounding rooms were presumably for the priests and attendants, apart from the two to the north, which were both sanctuaries dedicated to the worship of Ishtar. The most notable finds were a series of remarkable Sumerian style statues, now in the Damascus and Aleppo museums.

By far the greatest number of buildings excavated belong to the period of Zimri Lim in the 2nd millennium. Dominating all of these was the royal palace (though it replaced an earlier 3rd millennium palace on the same site). This immense, sprawling building (figure 31) achieved fame all over the Near East – even the king of Ugarit, himself lord of a not inconsiderable palace of his own, longed to visit the one at Mari. And well might it be famous, comprising a maze of over 300 rooms, courts and passages centred on two major courtyards that together spread over some two and a half hectares. By 'palace', however, one does not mean just a royal residence in the European sense: the palace f Mari was the secretariat and civil service of the kingdom as well; the residential quarters took up only about an eighth of the area.

Much of the palace was richly embellished with wall paintings, particularly the royal apartments, but by far the richest finds were the cuneiform texts. These texts, numbering an astonishing 20,000 or so clay tablets, are one of the richest sources we have for the history and geography of the ancient Near East, for Mari's 'commercial empire' stretched from Bahrain and Iran in the east to Cyprus and the Mediterranean in the west. From the extraordinary wealth of documentary material that these tablets provide – many of them still not read – epigraphists have been able to reconstruct not only much of the historical geography of the Near East of the early 2nd millennium, but also details of almost every other aspect of the period they illustrate: the tribes, kings and peoples who inhabited its lands, the materials and goods which they traded, and the everyday life of the people. Most of all they provide a picture of the palace itself, not of a hushed luxury retreat for a remote potentate, but of an exciting, bustling scene of commercial, religious, literary and state activities that took place almost as an extension of the bazaars outside.

Not far from the palace the temple of Dagan has been excavated, comprising some stone remains around a courtyard together with some amorphous remains tentatively identified as one of Syria's few ziggurats (the only other one being at Tell Leilan).

The Khabur and northeastern Syria

The Jazira should perhaps be defined by the rivers that water it, the Balikh and Khabur, rather than the Tigris and Euphrates which only define its eastern and western boundaries. Of these, the Khabur is the larger, comprising a river system that drains much of the northern parts of the Jazira. On and near its banks – or those of its tributaries – can be found one of the richest concentrations of archaeological sites in Syria: ranging from small one-period village sites to large urban areas belonging to virtually every period.

There are far too many to be enumerated here, and much of what can be seen at even the biggest ones only make sense to the archaeologist – and occasionally not even they can make much sense of some of them! Nevertheless, it is still worth mentioning, however briefly, some of the more important sites, and if a visit can be managed when archaeological teams are actually working there, it can prove a most rewarding excursion.

Most of the sites are situated in the headwaters of the Khabur in the far northeast: the so-called 'Khabur triangle'. But there is an important one not far up the Khabur on the east bank, Tell Shaikh Hamad, the ancient Assyrian provincial capital of Dur Katlimu. It is a very large site consisting of a citadel mound and extensive lower mounds representing the ancient urban areas, and has been undergoing investigations by German archaeologists since the seventies. Although material has been found extending back to the 4th millennium, most of the remains belong to the Middle and Late Assyrian periods.

Near the southern tip of the 'triangle' – sometimes referred to as the 'gateway to the Khabur Plains' – is one of the largest sites of the Khabur, Tell Brak, the scene of British excavations in the thirties and again since the seventies. With dates stretching back some seven and a half thousand years it is also one of the richest. Perhaps the most significant discoveries have come from the late 4th millennium 'Eye Temple', and the mid-2nd millennium Mitannian palatial residence.

The continued excavation of the Mitannian residence at Tell Brak might well divulge some of the secrets of this mysterious empire based in the Khabur area which conquered much of the Near East in the 2nd millennium. Indeed, the greatest 'Mitannian mystery' of all continues to tax archaeologists: the whereabouts of the Mitannian royal capital of Washshukanni. For a long while much speculation has centred upon the large site of Tell Fakhariya at the northwestern corner of the Khabur triangle, but American trial soundings there in the forties were inconclusive.

If the whereabouts of one royal capital still remain elusive, the location of another equally elusive 'lost capital', Shamshi-Adad's capital of Shubat Enlil in the Old Assyrian period, was spectacularly discovered in the seventies by American archaeologists at Tell Leilan at the opposite corner of the triangle, in the far northeast. Two elaborate temples were excavated, with cuneiform tablets littering their floors confirming the location of Shubat-Enlil at Tell Leilan.

British excavations were also carried out in the thirties at Chagar

Bazar, north of Tell Brak, where the highly distinctive stripe-painted pottery that characterizes the early 2nd millennium in the Jazira was first studied in detail. If this pottery characterized one period of the civilization of the Jazira, German excavations at the beginning of the century at Tell Halaf at the headwaters of the Khabur near Ras al-'Ain characterized another. This was the distinctive and extremely beautiful painted 'Halaf pottery' belonging to the astonishingly remote date of the 6th millennium BC. This pottery has been discovered on sites all over northern Syria and northern Iraq, attesting to the spread of a very homogeneous culture across an immense area over a thousand years before the rise of the great civilizations of southern Mesopotamia. Indeed, in the vast grasslands of the Jazira steppe around the Khabur one is in the very heart of the ancient Near East, in the earliest years of civilization. In the late afternoon sun surrounded by the silent, limitless horizons of the Jazira, history itself feels equally limitless. The great mounds all around, remnants of great civilizations that once resounded through history, might now be as silent as the plains. But equally, they are telling one of the most exciting stories in the world.

CHAPTER 11

Palmyra and the Desert

Historical background

If T E Lawrence could describe Krak des Chevaliers as 'perhaps . . . the most wholly admirable castle in the world', Palmyra is perhaps the most wholly admirable ruin (plate 85). It is certainly Asia's most spectacular caravan city, but it is so much more as well: it has a romantic history dominated by a beautiful desert queen who humbled Rome itself, it boasts an outstanding art and architecture, and its desert setting is one of the most spectacular of any city in the world. It is this last aspect, the desert, that is perhaps Palmyra's greatest fascination, for nothing could present a greater contrast to the flourishing, immensely wealthy city that Palmyra evidently was to the stark, lifeless emptiness of the wilderness that surrounds it (plate 93). Damascus, that other great caravan city of Syria, had the lush oasis as its hinterland, and Antioch, at the end of the caravan route, had the hundreds of Dead Cities behind it; but for Palmyra's hinterland there is nothing. Beyond the gates of Palmyra there was only the wild beauty of the wilderness. Today, the monuments themselves take on the golden light of the desert colours, and the long lines of columns that march across the ruin fields conjure images of the lines of camels that brought the wealth of Asia across the desert to Palmyra (plate 92).

But in another sense, Palmyra's hinterland spanned most of western Asia, for Palmyra's history is a history of trade. Palmyra also possessed the desert's most precious commodity: water (plate 86). Trade and water: together, they were responsible for Palmyra's greatness. Desert caravans had to come through Palmyra or perish, so whoever controlled Palmyra and its springs, controlled the routes.

These springs attracted the attention of nomads and more settled communities since earliest times. Japanese archaeologists have discovered evidence of Palaeolithic Man in caves to the east of Palmyra, whilst Neolithic material has been found near 'Ain Eqfa, the sulphur springs of Palmyra itself. By the end of the 3rd millennium BC, there was already a permanent settlement established on the site of the Temple of Bel, and the first written references to it (under its Semitic name of Tadmor) occur in Assyrian and Mari records of the early 2nd millennium. The famous reference to 'Tadmor in the wilderness' in the Bible as a city built by Solomon is now seen as a mistake, but such associations with Solomon, of legendary wealth, and the wilderness are nonetheless apt.

But Palmyra, or Tadmor as it was known, remained little more than the centre of a desert chiefdom and watering hole for groups of nomads and occasional caravans off the normal beat, until in 106 AD an event occurred that was to change its fortunes dramatically. Trajan annexed the kingdom of Petra, which had hitherto controlled the trade of western Asia. With the collapse of Petra trade routes moved further north, a move demanded as much by the increasing rise of Antioch as the main centre of Roman power in the east as by the collapse of Petra itself. Parallel to these events was the rise of Parthia in the east. Between the two, Rome and Parthia, lay Palmyra, acting both as middleman and buffer state. On one side lay all the wealth of Asia, and on the other the seemingly insatiable demands for this wealth by Rome. All roads may have led to Rome, but many led via Palmyra.

The Palmyrenes were quick to both realize and exploit this fact. They organized a network of caravan routes spanning much of western Asia and the Mediterranean that channelled the merchandise through Palmyra. Already by 137 AD a stele discovered at Palmyra records slaves and salt, dried foods and dyed purple cloth, perfumes and prostitutes as coming through, while evidence from excavations have added silk, jade, muslin, spices, ebony, incense, ivory, precious stones and glass to the ever expanding list. And gold. Such was the demand in Rome for luxury goods from the East that the Roman empire was becoming seriously depleted of gold to pay for it. This gold was channelled like the other goods through Palmyra, and one can be sure that much of it went no further.

The entire city revolved around trade. A caravan would be financed and organized by a single merchant, by a consortium of merchants, or by the city itself, depending on the size. The city treasurer was one of the highest offices in the state, taxes were clearly – and fairly – regulated and collected, the revenues being used either to invest in further trade ventures or – more usually – to embellish the city. Indeed,

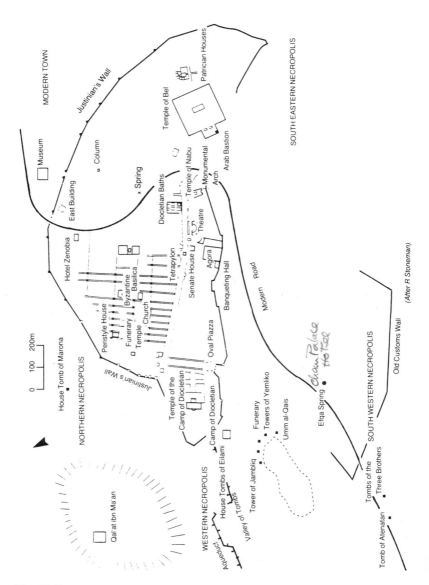

Fig. 32 Palmyra

the latter was given particularly high priority by both state and industry: by the 2nd century AD many of the monuments were privately endowed by merchants with a lavishness and ostentation – some might say vulgarity – rarely seen elsewhere. As befitted an architecture of private enterprise, the emphasis was more on show and display rather than strict forms of classical aesthetics. This was designed to reflect the credit of the merchants paying for it all, who were allowed in turn to erect statues glorifying themselves on the columns lining the city's main boulevards. Such was the private endowment of the arts that even the rebuilding of the greatest of all the city's monuments, the temple of Bel itself, was entirely financed in 139 AD by a leading merchant, Male Agrippa. It was this same private entrepreneur who paid out of his own pocket for the state visit to Palmyra by the Emperor Hadrian ten years earlier.

Although Roman influence became increasingly important, especially after the beginning of the 2nd century, Palmyra was able to maintain its semi-independence from Rome, with the Roman presence in the city represented only by a garrison stationed there – much like a British 'residency' in the princely states of India. In this way, Palmyra was the exact counterpart of Dura Europos, its sister caravan city on the Euphrates, which was under nominal Parthian protection. Both cities were able to form close economic links so as to exploit the commercial possibilities of their respective overlords. But with the collapse of the Parthians and their replacement in Persia by the new Sasanian dynasty, this happy state of affairs all started to go disastrously wrong. The upset in the balance of power, new power vacuums and changed policies of the Sasanians culminated with the eventual sacking of Palmyra under Aurelian in 273 and direct rule by Rome, with the establishment of a massive fortified camp in Palmyra itself under Diocletian in 300. The Palmyrenes, happy for so long making money for themselves, had little heart left after the sack of their beautiful city to go on making money for their new masters, so with the loss of independence came the loss of trade. Although the city itself hung on for a while longer – the temple of Bel was converted to a church, there was a Bishop of Palmyra in the 5th century and the city defences were even repaired by Justinian in the 6th – it was just a faint shadow of its former self, eventually crumbling back into the desert that formed it.

But the influence of Palmyra and its art was not quite over, and the history of this remarkable city was to have a curious footnote, for in 18th century England there was a sort of Palmyrene artistic renaissance. In 1749 and 1750 two English travellers, Wood and Dawkins, visited Palmyra. In 1753 they published a book on their visit, *The Ruins of Palmyra*. It was a book as lavish as the ruins it depicts, full of magnificently detailed engravings of the ruins, the architecture and – most important – the architectural decoration. This book had an immense impact on the neo-classical movement in England: 'Palmyra ceilings' and 'Palmyra cornices' – copies of Palmyrene prototypes – became immensely popular in the stately homes of Britain, particularly with the Adams. Blair Castle, Dumfries House, Osterly Park Manor, Drayton House, and many others all have interior detail inspired directly by the architecture of this distant desert city.

Temple of Bel

The temple of Bel is Palmyra's greatest monument, reflecting this wealth more than any other, and so forms a suitable starting point to explore the ruins. Its immense enclosure dwarfs all other buildings in Palmyra, dominating the city plan like a city within a city, belonging within the ancient tradition of great temple enclosures (figure 33, plate 86). As a place of worship it probably has a very ancient history: investigations by Swiss archaeologists revealed remains of the first Hellenistic settlement at Palmyra here, as well as Bronze Age remains before that. There was probably a temple dedicated to Bel on this spot, therefore, from at least the Hellenistic period, but the present structure, according to a dedicatory inscription, dates – at least in foundation – from 45 AD. It underwent many rebuildings and alterations since then, however. Its rebuilding by Male Agrippa in the 2nd century and subsequent conversion to a church in the 5th century we have already noted. In the 12th century it was fortified and converted to a citadel by the Arabs. In the 20th century the maze of village houses that had grown up in its ruins were cleared and a certain amount of restoration and excavation was carried out by French archaeologists in the thirties and forties, leaving it much as we see today.

The temenos covers an area about 200 metres square (figure 33). It was originally entered through an opulent propylaeum consisting of a massive triple entrance flanked by ornate 'Syrian niches', but much of this is obscured by its 13th century conversion into a fortress. Entry was also gained via a rather curious tunnel and ramp to the left of the propylaeum; this may have been used for sacrificial animals, as it leads out near the outside altar.

Indeed, this altar is in some ways more the focal point of the immense enclosure than the sanctuary itself. The sanctuary was merely the residence and throne room of the god, for private audience. But out here in the open air was where public sacrifices would be made to his honour, where the public could participate in mass worship. Hence, the

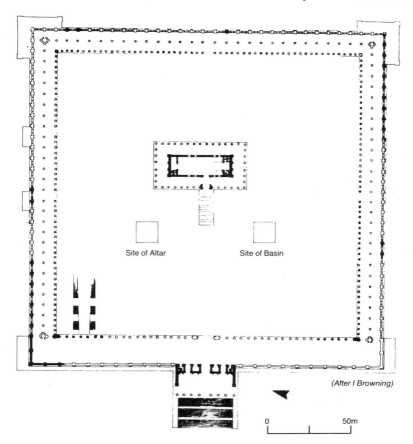

Site of Altar   Site of Basin

(After I Browning)

0   50m

Fig. 33 The Temple of Bel at Palmyra

immense enclosure required to hold such a congregation. And the enclosure itself certainly acted as a splendid setting for the spectacles enacted in it. It was surrounded on all sides by magnificent double porticos of giant Corinthian colonnades, the columns fluted and carrying the ubiquitous Palmyrene statue brackets halfway up (plate 87).

The temple proper, the sanctuary standing in the middle of the enclosure, has a superficial resemblance to conventional classical Greek models: a peripteral temple on a stepped podium (plate 88). But like so much of eastern Roman architecture, the resemblance is only skin-deep, and underneath it has more in common with ancient

185

Mesopotamian and Semitic temple prototypes than with classical forms. The most obvious anomaly is the entrance, on the lateral side rather than at one end. Furthermore, this disproportionately tall, elaborate entrance interrupts the colonnade of the peristasis, which has been seen as a possible Ptolemaic Egyptian feature. Another obvious non-classical feature are the 'Assyrian' style crow-step merlons that have been restored on top of the cornice (though these may be mistakenly restored). The architectural orders too have been mixed: the columns of the peristyle outside were of the Corinthian order (the capitals appear blank today, but were supposedly originally clad in gilded bronze), but the engaged columns of the sanctuary wall are Ionic. Inside, the layout is entirely different to classical forms, and here the reason for the entrance being on the long side becomes apparent. For both ends of the sanctuary are elaborately decorated adytons or shrines approached by short flights of steps – thrones of the gods in the true sense. The north adyton is the more elaborate and probably the more important, housing the Palmyrene 'trinity' of Bel, Yarhibol and Aglibol, while the south one may have housed a portable image of Bel to be taken out for religious processions.

And flanking the interior adytons are perhaps the most curious, 'unclassical' features of the temple: spiral staircases leading to the roof. For the classical style triangular pediments of the exterior hid a flat terrace: a sacred 'high place' that, from ancient Mesopotamian ziggurats to its ultimate derivation in Islamic minarets, is almost a universal feature of Semitic religious architecture.

The peristyle surrounding the outside of the temple was roofed with massive stone slabs, two of which have been reconstructed on the ground outside the entrance. They are worth examining for the astonishing detail of the decoration that covers them. One depicts the gods Aglibol and Malikbel surrounded by images of fertility: pomegranates, grapes, pine cones, a kid goat. The other has a procession that consists of a camel, priests and veiled women.

The main colonnaded street and associated monuments

While the temple temenos dominates the city plan of Palmyra, the great colonnaded street – the Cardo Maximus – leading to the temple bisects it (figure 34). The colonnaded streets are also Palmyra's most famous feature and the long lines of columns marching across the landscape provide unforgettable vistas rarely matched elsewhere in architecture. It probably had its origins as Palmyra's main market street, being monumentalized in the 2nd century AD by the addition of the

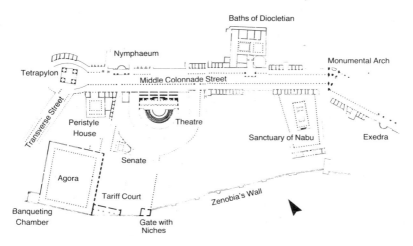

(After I Browning)

Fig. 34 The central area of Palmyra

colonnades. With the great temple of Bel marking its eastern end, it has been suggested that this lavish monumentalization meant that it was a sacred processional way rather than a conventional thoroughfare. Behind such lavishness, however, were not wayside shrines but modest shops, with the name and trade of the proprietor often inscribed over the door, as if to remind us that this most splendid and monumental of all streets of antiquity was in fact nothing more than a grand oriental bazaar. Palmyrenes after all worshipped commerce as much as they did Bel, and for the merchants of Palmyra to embellish their bazaars as much as their temples was entirely in character.

The colonnade from the temple of Bel to the monumental arch has all but disappeared, apart from four columns marking an exedra of uncertain function. The extant colonnade begins at the monumental arch (plates 89, 90). This arch follows the conventional triple-arch pattern of Roman triumphal arches, but there is no evidence that it represented any triumph. Its unusual V-shaped plan probably just masks the transition of a 30° turn in the street at this point, at the same time emphasizing and providing a focal point for the colonnades beyond.

Beyond, the uninterrupted flow of columns with their projecting brackets is an unforgettable spectacle. This line draws one's eye on to another monumental arch, the tetrapylon, and emphasizes the porticos to monumental buildings behind and the arches opening to other

187

streets leading off (plate 91). The tetrapylon, consisting of four kiosks or pavilions each built of monolithic pink granite columns brought all the way from Aswan in Upper Egypt (though only one column is original; the other fifteen are modern replicas) marks the intersection of two colonnaded streets. It also marks another bend in the Cardo, leading to the longest single stretch of colonnades (plate 92), interrupted only by another large exedra – possibly a nymphaeum (a monumental fountain dedicated to the nymphs) – terminating in a funerary temple at the western end (plate 93). The funerary temple is in fact a tomb in the form of a prostyle temple, with a crypt underneath. This stretch of the Cardo is in many ways the more picturesque, for it has not been cleared and architectural fragments are piled one on top of the other between the colonnades creating the very archetypal image of the romantic ruin (plate 94).

The colonnaded street performed many functions: a main thoroughfare, a possible processional way, and a grand bazaar as we have seen. But perhaps most of all it functioned as a monumental facade to the buildings behind it. The first building we come to is the temple of Nabu, on the left immediately after the monumental arch. This is essentially a smaller version of the great temple of Bel, consisting of the sanctuary on a podium and an open-air altar surrounded by a porticoed enclosure. It has some unusual features, however. The most obvious is its oblique angle to the street colonnade. Furthermore, the main entrance faces the south, and not the Cardo as one would expect. Both these features suggest that there was an earlier temple here whose shape had to be adapted to accommodate the awkward angle when the street colonnade was built in the 2nd century AD. The other feature of interest is the deity itself: Nabu. Although his cult was linked to Apollo, the worship of Nabu was very unusual amongst the western Semites: Nabu was the son of Marduk, the patron god of Babylon, and the occurrence of his cult here emphasizes the Palmyrene links with the east – or perhaps the existence of a significant Mesopotamian community at Palmyra.

On the right side of the Cardo just after the temple of Nabu, a portico of monolithic porphyry columns marks the entrance to the baths of Diocletian. The basic layout surrounding a central pool is clearly visible, following standard Western patterns, but there is not a great deal standing. Opposite, an arch in the colonnade marks the opening of a secondary colonnaded street – or Decumanus – leading off the Cardo. This street bends around the theatre creating a magnificent curved colonnade, and leads to the so-called 'Caravan Gate' in the south wall of the city. Adjacent to this gate is a large rectangular enclosure that – appropriately enough – has been identified as a caravanserai or customs court. This certainly seems to be the business end of the city, for next to the customs court another large enclosure marks the agora or market place, with an assembly hall opening off its western corner. The agora is surrounded on all four sides by a colonnaded portico supporting the by now ubiquitous statue brackets. Here, inscriptions tell us whose statues originally stood on them: the east side it seems was reserved for senators.

The reference to senators implies some imitation of Roman institutions, and a small peristyle building tucked behind the theatre just to the north of the agora has been identified as the senate house. The Roman connotations, however, are probably illusory, and are probably just a Latinized reference to the traditional Arab institution of a gathering of tribal elders or chiefs, still common in traditional Arab communities today.

The theatre follows the conventional Roman, as opposed to Greek, pattern (semi-circular in plan, rather than horseshoe). The elaborate scenae frons, however, with alternating recessed and projecting decorative elements incorporating three doorways onto the stage, belongs more to the eastern 'baroque' style of Roman architecture. Its auditorium is now much reduced, with only nine rows of seats, but originally would have been higher with some thirty rows. More interesting in some ways than the theatre itself is the row of stalls outside the theatre to the west. No doubt these would have pedalled the ancient equivalents of popcorn, sweets, drinks and cinema magazines to the theatre-going public; these stalls bring the past much more to life than the auditorium itself does.

One arrives back on the Cardo opposite another portico projecting onto the street just before the tetrapylon. Behind this portico is a very ruined exedra, the remains of a nymphaeum.

The Temple of Ba'al-Shamin and nearby monuments

A transverse colonnaded street – the Decumanus – intersects the Cardo at the tetrapylon. It leads to the north to the temple of Ba'al-Shamin, the god of fertility and storms. It is the only fully excavated temple in Palmyra, excavated by Swiss archaeologists in the fifties (plate 95). The temple has a complex architectural history that sets it apart from the Bel and Nabu temples – or perhaps that is merely because it has been subject to far closer archaeological scrutiny than the others. The sanctuary has two courtyards, to the north and south. The north temenos is the earlier: it was certainly in existence by 17 AD and progressively extended, modified and restored over the next two and a half centuries, exemplified by the mixed Corinthian and 'Egyptian

Corinthian' orders of the colonnades. The sanctuary in its present form dates from 130 AD, and the south temenos was probably added soon after.

The sanctuary is one of the best preserved in the eastern Roman world. It owes this to its conversion to a church in the Byzantine period and subsequent careful restoration of the interior back to its original state in the 20th century. It also exemplifies more than most the eastern style of Roman temple interiors, for it has a particularly elaborate adyton and is lit by windows in each of the four walls – a very unusual feature in classical architecture.

The Decumanus leads on to the north gate in the northern ramparts. These walls were probably Diocletian's fortification of the city, though it was subsequently re-fortified by Justinian. Adjacent to the north gate are the remains of a possible barracks.

Just to the west of the Ba'al-Shamin temple are the remains of a fairly conventional Byzantine basilica, one of several in Palmyra. The surrounding area was essentially residential, with houses built mainly of mud-brick virtually identical to domestic architecture in the region until the advent of concrete blocks. These have all collapsed over the centuries, leaving the grid plan of the streets clearly visible, but a number of columns still standing represent the peristyles of more wealthy houses.

The West Decumanus and Diocletian's Camp

The western colonnaded street, or West Decumanus, that intersects the Cardo just in front of the funerary temple, is in some ways more monumental than the Cardo itself. It is much wider – some 10 metres – and opens out at its southern end into a colonnaded oval enclosure or 'piazza'. This oval piazza is virtually unique in eastern Roman town planning; the only other occurrence – on an even grander scale – is at Jerash, and seems to anticipate by some 1500 years the magnificent oval colonnaded piazza built by Bernini at the Vatican. As at Jerash, the oval piazza probably marks the main entrance to the city from the south and west and it is presumably for this reason that the West Decumanus is wider and grander than the Cardo.

Flanking most of the western length of the West Decumanus is the large complex known as the Camp of Diocletian, taking up almost as large an area as the temple of Bel complex. The comparison is no accidental one, for before the Romans erected their garrison here following their sack of Palmyra in the late 3rd century, the site was probably a temple temenos dedicated to the 'Nameless God'. Indeed, it is significant that within the camp itself are the remains of a temple of

Allat, probably marking an earlier sacred spot before the camp was built. 'Allat' in Arabic is the feminine form of 'Allah', who was later to be recognized as the one and only, omnipotent 'nameless' God by Islam. Allat however, the feminine form, was equated both with the ancient Mesopotamian Ishtar and with the Roman Venus. It is said of the Arabic language that 'most words mean itself, something similar, its exact opposite, something completely irrelevant and something to do with a camel' all at once, and much the same can be said of Allat, who was the goddess of both love and reproduction as well as destruction! Perhaps it is simpler merely to leave it as the 'Nameless God'.

The Camp of Diocletian was like a city within a city – as well it had to be, the Romans coming as they did as conquerors. Like a city in miniature it was laid out in the form of an immense square intersected by two colonnaded streets – the Via Principalis and the Via Praetoria – with the intersection marked by a tetrapylon. In this way the camp bears a close similarity to Diocletian's contemporary great palace at Spolato (Split in Croatia) though there is some suggestion that it may have been a palace – perhaps Zenobia's – before Diocletian. It is unlikely, however, that the Palmyrenes would have erected a palace in a religious precinct.

The camp has been the scene of extensive investigations by Polish archaeologists since the fifties. The western half of the camp is dominated by an open courtyard in front of a splendid monumental flight of steps leading up to a high podium on which are military offices and the Temple of the Standards, an apsidal building. Such a temple was a standard feature of Roman military encampments.

The Valley of Tombs

The hill behind the Camp of Diocletian affords a splendid view over the whole of the city of Palmyra. But behind is a view equally impressive albeit in complete contrast: the vast necropolis of strange tower tombs that housed the dead, stretching out into the desert hills beyond the living city like some guardian spirit houses from a C S Lewis fantasy (plate 96).

Indeed, it is a veritable landscape of death, the towers of the dead merely reinforcing the death implicit in the harsh desolation of the desert surroundings. In entering this strange dead world, however, one leaves behind something else apart from the world of the living in the city itself. For one also leaves behind the Graeco-Roman world. The Graeco-Roman veneer of Palmyra, never more than skin deep at the best of times, is stripped away altogether in this architecture of the dead, revealing something far deeper and older, belonging to an ancient Semitic world far more alien than the brash new cultures of Greece and Rome imposed on the Near East. In man's final journey it seems, he returns to his roots.

It comes as no surprise, therefore, to learn that some of the tower tombs are amongst the oldest monuments at Palmyra. There are two main categories of tomb at Palmyra: above ground and below ground. The former can additionally be subdivided into three: house tombs, temple tombs and tower tombs, and it is these latter that are the most distinctive.

They also form the earliest type, so that by the mid-2nd century AD, with increasing Romanisation, they had generally gone out of fashion, being replaced by underground tombs – hypogea – which were generally more consistent with Roman practice. The earlier popularity of such a strange custom as burying one's dead in towers is presumably related to the ancient Semitic practice of sacred high places. A tower tomb would invariably be built just for a specific family, albeit for extended families – the largest could hold up to 400 bodies. Typically, it would be several storeys in height, each storey consisting of tiers of loculi – body slots – ranged around the room, each loculus being sealed by a stone slab usually depicting a portrait of the occupant. The interiors would usually be lavishly – spectacularly in some cases – decorated in carved relief, and often painted as well, demonstrating in death as much as in life the wealth of a particular merchant family.

The best tomb towers can be seen in a line along the foot of a hill called Umm al-Bilqis flanking the north of the valley. They are all tombs of notable Palmyrene families, identified by inscriptions. The tallest, a four-storey tower with an exceptionally fine interior, is known as the tomb of Iamlichu, from an inscription dated 83 AD which reads: 'Iamlichu, son of Mokimu Akalish, son of Maliku, son of Belakab, son of Mike, son of Maththa, Councillor of Tadmor'. At the end of the valley is one of the best preserved, the tomb of Elahbel dated 103 AD, housing the prominent Maani family.

Of the other categories of funerary architecture, we have already seem a temple tomb marking the western end of the Cardo. There is a particularly fine house tomb, today known as the Qasr al-Abyadh ('White Palace') beyond the end of the valley, and an almost perfectly intact one, the tomb of Marona, standing fairly isolated just to the north of the city walls. The latter was built by Julius Arlius Marona in 236 AD and, as befits its late date, is more consistent with Roman funerary practice.

The other main category is the underground hypogeum, and the whole area of the Valley of Tombs is pockmarked with the remains of hundreds of them, many of them collapsed. They are generally later in date than the tower tombs, and are usually either cross-shaped or

T-shaped, entered from one end by a staircase descending into the ground. One of the finest in the Valley of Tombs was the Hypogeum of the Yarhai, just near the tomb of Elahbel, which has been reconstructed in the Damascus Museum. The most impressive of all, however, can be seen in the southwestern necropolis.

The southwestern area

Although some tomb towers are standing in this area, the southwestern necropolis is made up almost entirely of hypogea, attesting to its later date as a burial ground. The most impressive is the Hypogeum of the Three Brothers, dating from the middle of the 2nd century. On descending a staircase into the ground, the tomb is entered through a beautifully carved stone door with inscriptions of the three brothers, Male, Saadai and Naamain. Inside are sixty-five recesses, each containing six loculi – a burial capacity totalling an astonishing three hundred and sixty bodies! It is constructed from brick barrel vaults, which are plastered over and painted with an exquisite series of frescos. These depict various Greek mythological scenes that combine Hellenistic and Parthian styles. In the right arm of the tomb are three particularly fine sarcophogi with reclining figures on top of them.

Indeed, it is death that preserved the best pictures of life in ancient Palmyra. An immense wealth of the distinctive art of Palmyra has come down to us preserved in the funerary architecture: frescos, portrait reliefs, and sculptures of entire families. We not only know the names of the people who built and lived in Palmyra, but what they looked like as well, for the portraits are very individual and lifelike. They provide an astonishing picture, of faces that would be familiar in any modern Syrian city today, for they have the tight curls and Semitic features of the modern Syrian. Most of all they depict a lifestyle that was as happy and as urbane as anywhere in the world – it is certainly not a desert art depicting a provincial backwater away from the mainstreams of culture.

The remarkable state of preservation of Palmyrene art is due to the stable conditions of the underground tombs, with frescos in some cases surviving as fresh as the day they were painted. The southwestern necropolis has many such hypogea, some of them every bit as splendid as the Hypogeum of the Three Brothers, but it is perhaps best to appreciate their art in the more conducive surroundings of the museum at Palmyra (in the modern town of Tadmor) or in the Damascus Museum, where the best have been placed for safe keeping.

Also in this area is the sulphur spring of 'Ain Eqfa, emerging from a cave that extends for many hundreds of metres into the hill behind. Its waters are at a constant 33°C, and its health giving properties were presumably an attraction since earliest times, as many architectural fragments around it attest. Between the springs and the temple of Bel stands a lone column, an honorific monument of uncertain function.

The Arab castle

Dominating the site like a great sentinel is the Castle of Fakhr ud-Din ibn Ma'ani. It stands on the highest hill overlooking the site, and the ditch that has been cut around the top of the hill for added protection gives an impression of the castle erupting out of a volcano crater. The climb is well worth the effort, for the view from on top is the best in Palmyra, but the castle itself is in far too dangerous a condition to enter.

Fakhr ud-Din ibn Ma'ani was a Druze emir who established his rule over much of Lebanon and Syria in the first half of the 17th century in opposition to the Ottomans. The castle was probably first built, however, by the Mamluks in the 13th century. Although Palmyra itself had long gone, the location still marked an important crossing point of the desert traffic, and its permanent source of fresh water made it one of the most strategic centres of the desert.

The desert

Qasr al-Hair ash-Sharqi

Perhaps the most surprising remains in the desert date from the time of the Umayyad caliphs in the first century or so of Islam. In these early days the caliphs still felt that their roots lay in the deserts of their Arabian ancestry, and would retire from the fleshpots of Damascus into a number of 'country' retreats built deep within the deserts of Syria and Jordan. Since as often as not they took their fleshpots with them, they were more likely escaping from the opprobrium of their fellow Muslims rather than seeking to rediscover real or imagined roots in a mythical desert past, but whatever they were, their remains are amongst the most striking to be found in the deserts.

Chief of these were two Umayyad desert palaces, Qasr al-Hair ash-Sharqi ('eastern') and Qasr al-Hair al-Gharbi ('western'), located in the desert east and west of Palmyra respectively. The former lies roughly halfway between Palmyra and Deir ez-Zor, and this probably determined its origins as a fortified station on the old trade routes to the east. Certainly Palmyrene remains have been found here during the course of American excavations in the sixties and seventies, but by far the bulk of the standing remains are Umayyad, built by the Caliph

Hisham in the 8th century.

To call it a 'palace' is perhaps a misnomer. It is more an immense desert settlement, of which the palatial residence formed but a part. Immense it certainly is, consisting of a vast outer enclosure surrounded by extremely fine stone walls surviving in parts up to 12 metres high. This outer enclosure contains traces of old gardens and some houses. Inside are two fortified enclosures fairly close together. The smaller one is the better preserved. It is some 75 metres square with a particularly fine facade, and was probably a caravanserai. The larger, nearly twice as big, is badly ruined inside, which comprised a palace consisting of six identical residences, an administrative building, a mosque and some oil presses. Qasr al-Hair ash-Sharqi remained a considerable desert centre long after the collapse of the Umayyad dynasty, declining probably only with the Mongol devastations of the 13th century.

Qasr al-Hair al-Gharbi
Whilst probably a pleasure palace, it is notable that Qasr al-Hair al-Gharbi too lies on a caravan route, approximately midway between Palmyra and Damascus, so like its namesake further east probably performed an important economic function as well. Qasr al-Hair al-Gharbi was also built by the Caliph Hisham, but the site was already well established long before the Umayyads. An 18 kilometre long canal and the 600 metre long Harbaqa dam, some 16 kilometres west of the palace, were built by the Palmyrenes in the 1st century AD, attesting to the importance of desert reclamation schemes in the area in antiquity. There are also some Ghassanid remains of the 6th century incorporated into the palace, but the main building there now is the palace built by the Caliph Hisham in the 8th century.

This palace is far more unambiguously a royal pleasure palace than Qasr al-Hair ash-Sharqi. It is in the form of a large square courtyard building, about 70 metres each side, that follows much the same plan as the Roman desert fortifications. There, however, the resemblance stops, for the walls – particularly the entrance – were covered in an immensely exuberant array of rich brick and stucco decorations depicting abstract geometric patterns, rows of blind arches and figures in high relief. The extremely ornate entrance to the palace has been dismantled and reconstructed as the main entrance to the Damascus Museum. Pleasure gardens surrounded the palace, and there are remains of a small bath house just to the north, containing more decorations of marble, stucco and wall paintings. There are also remains of a mosque and a caravanserai, dating from the Umayyad period.

Beyond and all around is the great Syrian desert. It is not a flat desert of dunes of popular imagination, but is punctuated by ranges of mountains rising to spectacular heights in many places. No desert is ever entirely deserted. The Syrian desert in particular has been traversed since earliest antiquity, not only by the nomads who hunted game and herded their flocks in its wastes, but by armies, peoples and ideas. Nowhere demonstrates this more than the spectacular ruins of Palmyra in the heart of the desert. But the desert has a surprising quantity of other remains as well: the deserted cities of Resafeh and al-Anderin and the hundreds of lesser remains that skirt the outermost areas of the Dead Cities and the Hauran. But with the possible exception of Resafeh, these were located on the still fertile fringes; those situated deep within the desert exist in splendid isolation with no such fertile belt forming their hinterland.

The desert is an appropriate place to finish a tour of Syria. It is the most enduring image of the Middle East: the desert has dominated the life, the civilization and the minds of its people and inspired its religious leaders since remotest antiquity. No story of Middle Eastern civilization – so much a part of world civilization as a whole – can be told without continual reference to the deserts. It is the Middle East's most continuous theme: in the settled areas, new construction is rapidly changing the face of the Middle East beyond recognition, with the ubiquitous concrete block architecture imposing a drab sameness from the shores of the Mediterranean to the Arabian Sea. Only the desert remains the same. For the visitor, long after images of the great ruin fields, the caravan cities and the castles of Syria have faded, the images of the desert remain to haunt one's memories. The vast horizons, the fields of frozen lava flows, the utterly bare mountain ranges that glow with colours that only a desert can produce, are amongst the most beautiful to be seen anywhere.

But it has all the doom-laden beauty of a Puccini opera. For the desert, so long a source of invigoration that constantly fertilised the civilizations on its rim, is at the same time an ever present threat to the life that has been so tenaciously won on its fringes. Like the ancient Semitic god Allat, the desert represents both reproduction and fertility as well as destruction and death. The desert does indeed provide an apt symbol for the Middle East.

APPENDIX

Practical Tips

I t is not intended here to provide details of hotels, prices, timetables, tour operators, entry requirements, exchange rates, and so forth, as these date so easily. The following information is intended rather to help plan a visit to Syria and make it a more rewarding one.

Manners and customs

A visit to Syria can be both a pleasurable and rewarding experience. It is vitally important, however, to bear certain points in mind that might entail a modification of your usual outlook, as many norms of public behaviour that might be perfectly acceptable elsewhere may not be so in Syria. Much of the following is aimed at first-time visitors to the Middle East, though each country has peculiarities all its own.

One of the greatest attractions of a visit to Syria is finding out about a culture and way of life different from one's own. Syria is a predominantly Muslim country. Try and respect the Muslim code of behaviour in public places; not only is it important to be on one's 'best behaviour' as a foreign visitor, but it also makes life much easier for oneself. In Muslim countries, particularly in rural areas, dress is very conservative. Whilst many younger Syrians in Aleppo and Damascus might dress quite flamboyantly, it is generally wiser for visitors to err on the conservative side, if only not to attract untoward attention. Inevitably, the onus usually falls on women, who are advised to wear fairly modest clothes: Syrian women rarely wear trousers or jeans, but for Western women a loose top over trousers is probably the most convenient and perfectly acceptable. Women are usually requested to wear a head-scarf when entering a mosque. Shorts, short skirts, sleeveless tops and revealing clothing generally – for both sexes – might well give unnecessary offence.

Syria is one of the most photogenic countries in the region, so bring plenty of film! But be particularly careful when taking photographs. Military subjects, public buildings, women and people praying might cause embarrassment or even disruption. When photographing ethnic scenes, it is always wiser to ask first, particularly if women are in the scene.

Food

One of the greatest pleasures of travel is eating. In Syria the gastronome will be delighted with all the range that an entirely different cuisine can present. Whether one calls this cuisine Lebanese, Syrian, or just Middle Eastern is irrelevant; the main point is that it is delicious.

Syria is particularly well situated to receive several culinary influences. The main ones are the elaborate cuisines of the Mediterranean to the west and Turkey to the north, tempered by the simpler forms of Arabian cooking to the south. The Mandate has also bequeathed a tradition of French cuisine to Syria, so altogether, its food is amongst the finest in the Middle East.

The only limitations on the food are those imposed by Muslim dietary laws, which prohibit meat from animals incorrectly slaughtered (*haram*), blood, and pig flesh in any form. Strictly speaking, shell-fish and alcohol are forbidden too, but these – especially the former – are adhered to only with varying strictness. Lamb and chicken are the preferred meats; fish is popular on the coast, but beef and poultry other than chicken is relatively rare. Spices are essential ingredients, but never to the same extent as in Indian cuisine; the taste of the basic ingredients always predominates over the spices. Pulses are also popular, and Syrian cuisine surpasses itself in the art of making a wide variety of delicious dishes from this humble ingredient, such as *hummus* from chickpeas. Cracked wheat or *burghul* is another common ingredient, used as a substitute for rice as well as to make specific dishes such as *qubba*, a type of meat-ball, and *tabbouleh*, a type of salad. Sesame is another essential; the seeds are used as a garnishing to breads and pastries, the oil used for cooking, and the paste, or *tahina*, used in various dips, as well as in *halwa*, the basic ingredient for many sweets.

Eating is a great social occasion in Syria. It is an essential aspect of the Arab tradition of hospitality, and is always used as an occasion for getting together. The dinner table is the place where families and friends gather at the least excuse, and considerable importance is attached to the quality and variety of the food available. Some etiquette is strictly observed, such as always using one's right hand to eat, but otherwise etiquette is kept to a refreshing minimum – eating with one's hands and licking the fingers are perfectly acceptable (indeed, often obligatory) – and the relaxed, social atmosphere makes for a far more enjoyable meal and greater appreciation of the food – which after all is the main object. The main meal of the day is lunch, usually eaten late (after 2 pm) and often followed by a rest or siesta. Evening meals are comparatively minor affairs, though breakfasts can be surprisingly elaborate, consisting of eggs, *hummus*, yoghurt, white cheese, olives, and fresh bread. These breakfasts, however, are usually taken about mid-morning; there is an earlier 'first breakfast' consisting of just bread and tea after waking up. Apart from the meals, there are the endless tea- and coffee-breaks, and the Syrian tea-house is one of the country's basic lifelines: a place to sit down, have refreshments and a snack, to talk, smoke the water-pipe, play chess or backgammon, or simply to relax and watch the world go by. No visit to Syria is complete without absorbing the atmosphere of this essential institution.

By far the 'queen of dishes' of Syrian cuisine is the *mezza*. *Mezza* means 'table', and that is exactly what it is: a whole table covered with different small dishes of the 'starter', or hors d'oeuvre, savory kind, usually accompanied by drinks. The variety of different dishes that can be used in a *mezza* is as endless as the cook's imagination: dips of every conceivable type, pastries, deep-fried vegetables, nuts, salads, kebabs, stuffed vine leaves and other stuffed vegetables, olives, white cheese, and miniature forms of main dishes of every description. A *mezze* can be a precursor to a main meal, or it can form an entire meal in itself – I once sat down to a *mezze* consisting of twenty-seven different dishes, ranging from salad to grilled quail!

Main dishes – if one has any room after the *mezza*! – is often of the rice and meat variety, though with endless variations of stews, sauces and cooked, grilled and baked meats. Side dishes range from elaborations of the *mezza* theme to every conceivable type of vegetable stuffed with every imaginable type of filling. Contrary to popular belief, alcohol is available in Syria – indeed, it is cheaper than most European countries – and many local wines are on sale. With a *mezze*, the more usual accompaniment is the local *arak*, an aniseed-flavoured spirit like Pernod. No visit to Syria would be complete without at least trying this beverage. Local beer is also available, as are various local brandies – imported spirits tend to be expensive.

The sweets derive from Turkish traditions, and are usually pastries such as *baklawa*, *kadhayif* and *kanafi*. They are quite sweet and heavy for Western tastes, but the pistachios and almonds used in their stuffing and rose-water and orange-water used in garnishing are flavours never found in Western cuisines. A rather newer sweet tradition that has grown up in Syria is hand-made chocolates, and, for the connoisseur, there are numerous delights to be found in Damascus' chocolate shops.

Most of the above dishes come from the Turko-Levantine culinary tradition, which dominates Syrian food. Little has been said so far about the Arabian tradition, and perhaps this is the best note on which to end. The Beduin tradition is represented by simpler forms, comprising dates, milk products and lamb, and the Beduin *mansaf*, consisting of a whole roast lamb covered in a yoghurt-based sauce served on a bed of rice, is still the main celebratory feast of Syria today.

Handicrafts

In a Middle East where traditional arts and crafts have all but died out, Syria comes as a pleasant surprise. Indeed, such is the continuing high quality of handicrafts in Syria that Damascus still amply fulfills its reputation as one of the greatest bazaars of the East.

The main area in Damascus for handicrafts is not the Hamidiyyah souq (leading to the Umayyad Mosque) where most tourists go, but in the streets in and around the Bab Sharqi and Bab Touma in the eastern parts of the Old City. Here can not only be found the full range of traditional Damascene handicrafts at reasonable prices, but also factories where they are made. A tour round the silk factory just outside the Bab Sharqi, for example, where some of Queen Elizabeth's coronation robes were specially woven to order, is an education in itself. In fact it would be difficult to leave Damascus without obtaining that most quintessential of all Damascene handicrafts: the exquisite brocaded silks, which has given the English language the word 'damask'. To this day, Damascus silks still maintain the quality that made the city famous throughout the world as a silk-weaving centre (Damascus in the middle ages was even exporting silk to China).

Silks are not the only product to buy; there is so much more that a visit to Damascus can end up very expensive! Chief amongst the traditional Damascene handicrafts is the inlay work: wooden furniture and objects inlaid with veneers of different coloured woods and mother-of-pearl to form endless varieties of abstract patterns. In the National Museum in Damascus – as well as some private houses in the old city – entire rooms can be seen treated in this way, and one can still buy elaborate pieces of furniture ranging from coffee tables to whole wardobes covered in Damascene inlay work. Since such pieces of furniture can cost small fortunes, most travellers are content with a more humble backgammon board or pen-box. Other traditional handicrafts are metalwork (which gave English another word, 'damascened', referring to the technique of inlaying silver into metal), jewellery, and various other forms of fabrics apart from silks, such as hand-printed cloths and embroideries.

A wide range of carpets are also available in the souqs of Damascus and Aleppo, and whilst one can buy Syrian rugs here, the best varieties come from outside Syria (particularly Iran, as a result of the close ties between the two countries), with Damascus and Aleppo acting as entrepots for the carpet industry rather than manufacturing centres.

A more modern – albeit surprising – Syrian 'handicraft' is the car, for the Syrians are masters at keeping old cars going. Syria is a car-spotter's paradise. Old cars of every make and nationality are still going strong, from the highly chromed and finned gas-guzzling giants of the American fifties and sixties to the more elegant curves of the French thirties. There are even astonishing hybrids that will defy the most expert car-spotter's definition: a Volkswagen Beetle with the engine in the front, for example, or a jeep that starts off at the front as a Toyota Landcruiser but by the back has merged imperceptibly into a Landrover.

The bazaars of Syria are also goldmines for those who collect traditional forms of costume, as the ethnic makeup provides a very wide range. These range from the traditional Arab men's costume of *dishdasha, 'abba* (cloak) and *farwa* (overcoat), with the headdress of *kafiyyah* (headcloth) and *'iqal* (headband – originally a tethering rope for a camel), to the Turkish baggy trousers and Kurdish 'boiler suits' and cummerbunds. Women's costume holds even greater variety, from the richly embroidered dresses of the Arabs with their pronounced regional variations to the immensely flamboyant and colourful garb of the Kurdish women to the east.

But best of all, the bazaars of Syria can be enjoyed simply for themselves: one need do little more than just wander about. A ramble through a great Eastern bazaar, observing the colour, the smells, the variety and the people; taking in both the mundane and the exotic; soaking up the atmosphere and the strangeness, is an experience that cannot be matched in Europe. There are, in fact, few greater pleasures anywhere in the world.

Timings

The following are very approximate times, based on personal experience only, given to aid travellers in planning their own itinerary. All are based on private, rather than public, transport. They are generally rounded upwards to the nearest quarter-hour, and incorporate time spent stopping for refreshments, taking photographs, wrong turns, etc. (so distances can be covered faster if necessary).

Chapter 4

Damascus-Saidnaya: ¾ hr

Saidnaya-Yabrud: 1 ¼ hr

Damascus-Ma'alula: ¾ hr

Damascus-Dmeir: 1 hr

Chapter 5

Damascus-Dera'a: 1 ½ hrs

Damascus-Suwaida: 2 ¼ hrs

Dera'a-Bosra: ½ hr

Dera'a-Ezra'a: ¼ hr

Bosra-Suwaida: 1 hr

Suwaida-Shahba: ½ hr

Shahba-Shaqqa: ¼ hr

Suwaida-'Atil: ¼ hr

'Atil-Slim: ¼ hr

Suwaida-Qanawat: ¼ hr

Suwaida-Kafr: ¼ hr

Suwaida-Ezra'a: 1 hr

Ezra'a-Inkhil: ½ hr

Inkhil-Sanamain: ¼ hr

Chapter 6

Damascus-Homs: 2 ½ hrs

Homs-Palmyra: 2 hrs

Homs-Qatna: ½ hr

Homs-Tell Nebi Mend: ¾ hr

Homs-Krak des

Homs-Hama: ¾ hr

   Chevaliers: 1 ¼ hrs

Homs-Tartus: 2 hrs

Damascus-Hama: 3 ¼ hrs

Hama-Qasr Ibn Wardan: 1 hr

Hama-Shaizar: ½ hr

Hama-Apamea: 1 hr

Hama-Misyaf: ¾ hr

Hama-Tartus (via Misyaf): 2 ½ hrs

Chapter 7

Damascus-Tartus: 4 hrs

Homs-Tartus: 2 hrs

Tartus-Amrit: ¼ hr

Tartus-Safita: ½ hr

Tartus-Hosn-i Sulaiman: 1 ¾ hr

Tartus-Marqab: ¾ hr

Tartus-Qadmus: 1 ¾ hrs

Tartus-Misyaf: 2 ½ hrs

Tartus-Jebleh: 1 hr

Tartus-Latakia: 1 ½ hr

Aleppo-Latakia: 5 hrs

Latakia-Ugarit: ¼ hr

Latakia-Saladin Castle: 1 ¼ hrs

Saladin Castle-Jisr al-Shughur: 1 ½ hrs

Chapter 8

Aleppo-Damascus: 6 hrs

Aleppo-Latakia: 5 hrs

Aleppo-Jisr al-Shughur: 1 ¾ hrs

Jisr al-Shughur-Apamea: ¾ hr

Aleppo-Azzaz: 2 hrs

Aleppo-Ebla: 1 hr

Aleppo-Cyrrhus: 3 hrs

Chapter 9

Aleppo-Ma'arat an-Nu'man: 1 hr

Ma'arat an-Nu'man-Shinsharah: ½ hr

Ma'arat an-Nu'man-Jeradah: ½ hr

Ma'arat an-Nu'man-Ruwaiha: ½ hr

Aleppo-Urum al-Joz: 1¼ hrs

Urum al-Joz – al-Bara: ½ hr

al-Bara-Serjilla: ¼ hr

Aleppo-Qal'at Sema'an: ½ hr

Aleppo-Qalb Lozeh: 4 hrs

Chapter 11

Damascus-Palmyra: 3¼ hrs

Homs-Palmyra: 2 hrs

TIME CHART

Approx. Dates	Period	Principle events
8000-4000 BC	Neolithic and Chalcolithic	First settlements; development of agriculture
4000-3000 BC	Early Bronze	First cities; Mesopotamian colonies
3000-2000 BC	Early Bronze	Development of writing; Kingdom of Ebla; Akkadian Empire; Amorite invasions
2000-1600 BC	Old Syrian	Amorite dynasties; Kingdom of Mari; Old Assyrian Empire; Egyptian influence
1600-1200 BC	Middle Syrian	Mitannian Empire; Hittite Empire; New Kingdom Egypt; height of Ugarit; first alphabet; Battle of Qadesh; invasion of Sea Peoples
1200-300 BC	Late Syrian	Arrival of Aramaeans; Neo-Hittite and Aramaean city-states; New Assyrian Empire; Phoenician city-states; Neo-Babylonian Empire; Persian Empire; Alexander the Great
300 BC-300 AD	Graeco-Roman	Seleucid Empire; Foundation of Antioch; Decapolis; Nabatean kingdom; Roman conquest; Parthian wars; rise of Palmyra
300-600 AD	Byzantine	Christian architecture; the Dead Cities; Sasanian invasions; Aramaic revival; Ghassanid kingdom
600-800 AD	Early Islamic	Arab conquest; Umayyad Dynasty with capital at Damascus; 'Abbasid Dynasty with capital moved to Baghdad
800-1500 AD	Middle Islamic	Hamdanid Dynasty of Aleppo; Saljuq and Atabeg dynasties; Crusades; Ayyubid Dynasty; Assassins; Mongol invasions; Mamluks
1500+ AD	Modern	Ottoman Dynasty; European interests; Arab Revolt; French Mandate; independence 1946

SUGGESTED READING

General

Beaumont, Peter, Blake, Gerald H., and Wagstaff, J. Malcolm, *The Middle East. A Geographical Study*, London, 1988.

Burns, Ross, *Monuments of Syria*, London, 1993.

Fedden, Robin, *Syria and Lebanon*, London, 1965.

Hitti, Philip K., *History of Syria*, London, 1957.

Jenner, Michael, *Syria in View*, London, 1986.

Roden, Claudia, *A Book of Middle Eastern Food*, London, 1968.

Thubron, Colin, *Mirror to Damascus*, London, 1967.

Weiss, Harvey (ed.), *Ebla to Damascus. Art and Archaeology of Ancient Syria*, Washington, 1985.

Guides

Blue Guide to the Middle East, Paris, 1966.

Finlay, Hugh, *Jordan and Syria. A Travel Survival Kit*, South Yarra (Australia), 1987.

Syria

Hureau, Jean, *Syria Today*, Paris, 1984.

Saouaf, Soubhi, *Six Tours in the Vicinity of Aleppo*, Aleppo, 1957.

Pre-Classical

Bermant, Chaim, and Weitzman, Michael, *Ebla. An Archaeological Enigma*, London, 1979.

Burney, Charles, *From Village to Empire. An Introduction To Near Eastern Archaeology*, Oxford, 1977.

Frankfort, Henri, *The Art and Architecture of the Ancient Orient*, Harmondsworth, 1970.

Matthiae, Paolo, *Ebla. An Empire Rediscovered*, London, 1980.

Roaf, Michael, *Cultural Atlas of Mesopotamia and the Ancient Near East*, Oxford, 1990.

Graeco-Roman

Ball, Warwick, *Rome in the East*, forthcoming

Browning, Iain, *Palmyra*, London, 1979.

Butler, Howard Crosby, *Publications of the Princeton University Expeditions to Syria in 1904, 1905, and 1909*, 2 vols, Leiden, 1906-1920.

College, Malcolm R, *The Art of Palmyra*, London, 1976.

Hopkins, Clark, *The Discovery of Dura Europos*, Yale, 1979.

Lyttelton, Margaret, *Baroque Architecture in Classical Antiquity*, London, 1974.

Rostovtzeff, M, *Caravan Cities*, Oxford, 1932.

Stoneman, Richard, *Palmyra and its Empire*, Ann Arbor, 1992

Ward-Perkins, J B, *Roman Imperial Architecture*, Harmondsworth, 1981.

Byzantine

Butler, Howard Crosby, *Early Churches in Syria, Fourth to Seventh Centuries*, Amsterdam, 1969.

Krautheimer, R, *Early Christian and Byzantine Architecture*, Harmondsworth, 1986.

Tchalenko, G, *Villages antiques de la Syrie du nord*, 3 vols, Paris, 1953.

Islamic

Creswell, K A C, *Early Muslim Architecture*, Oxford, 1969.

Ettinghausen, Richard, and Grabar, Oleg, *The Art and Architecture of Islam 650-1250*, Harmondsworth, 1987.

Guillaume, Alfred, *Islam*, Harmondsworth, 1967.

Crusader

Muller-Wiener, Wolfgang, *Castles of the Crusaders*, London, 1966.

Runciman, Steven, *A History of the Crusades*, 3 vols, Harmondsworth, 1971.

GLOSSARY OF ARCHITECTURAL TERMS

Adyton   A large niche, usually forming a temple sanctuary.

Agora   Greek market place.

Apse   A large round niche in a basilica at the end of a nave. Usually forms the focal point of a churches, where it faces east.

Arceate   Column and arch style (as opposed to *trabeate*).

Ashlar   Regular masonry of squared stones.

Barbican   An outer tower of a castle, not directly connected to the main fortifications.

Basilica   Originally a Roman meeting hall, later the most common plan of Byzantine churches, consisting of a nave flanked by two aisles with an apse at one or both ends.

Cardo   The main north-south transverse street or streets of a classical town plan.

Cella   The central chamber of a temple sanctuary.

Clerestory   Row of windows above the arcades that divide the nave from the aisles in a basilica.

Cyclopean Masonry consisting of massive stone blocks, usually irregular but precisely fitted together.

Decumanus The main east-west street or streets of a classical town plan.

Donjon The keep or main tower of a castle.

Entablature The decorated superstructure carried by a colonnade.

Exedra Semi-circular recess.

Fosse A defensive ditch surrounding a fortification.

Glacis A steep, artificial slope below a fortification wall to prevent a direct approach by an attacker.

Hammam A public baths in Islamic countries.

Hypogeum An underground burial vault.

In antis Where the side walls of a prostyle temple project to flank the columns forming the front.

Iwan In Persian and Islamic architecture a monumental vaulted portal or opening.

Khan A caravanserai.

Loculus A shaft or slot for a body in a tomb.

Machicolation In fortification, projecting galleries at or near the tops of walls.

Madrasa An Islamic religious school.

Martyrium A church or shrine, usually following a central (circular) plan, erected over a place of martyrdom.

Merlons Decorative crenallations around the top of a building.

Mihrab Prayer niche in a mosque facing Mecca.

Minaret The tower on a mosque from which the call to prayer is given.

Syria

Minbar   A pulpit to the right of the *mihrab* in a mosque.

Narthex   Vestibule of a church.

Nave   The central hall of a basilica.

Necropolis   An area of tombs and burials.

Orthostat   Upright stone slab, usually decorative, forming the lower part of a wall.

Palaestra   A porticoed exercise or sports ground in classical architecture.

Peripteral   A temple with rows of columns around all four walls (as opposed to *prostyle*).

Peristasis   The ring of columns around a peripteral temple.

Propylaeum   A monumental entrance to a complex.

Prostyle   A temple with a row of columns just at the front (as opposed to *peripteral*).

Qibla   The end wall of a mosque that faces Mecca.

Quatrefoil   A building plan in the shape of four semi-circles forming a cross.

Scenae frons   The backdrop of a theatre stage.

Tell   A mound or hill, usually artificial, marking an archaeological site.

Temenos   A sacred enclosure.

Tetrapylon   Four-way arch.

Tetrastyle   A temple facade carried by four columns.

Trabeate   Column and lintel style (as opposed to *arceate*).

Index

'Abbasids 25 infra, 26, 166
Abraham 67, 130
Abu 'l 'Abbas 25
Abu Hurayra 9
Abu Hureyr 162
Abu Qubais 99
Abu Sufian 154
Abuba Kabira 162
Achaemenians 15, 53
Achiqbash house 135
Adeliya Madrasa 63
Ahireh 85
'Ain Dara 136
'Ain Eqfa 181
'Ain Jalut 29
'Aintab (see Gaziantep) 33, 127
Ajailat 82
Akkadians 6, 12, 125
'Alaiqa 117
'Alawis 7
Aleppo 2, 4, 125 infra
 citadel 130
 Great Mosque 133 infra
 walls 130 infra
Alexander the Great 16, 93
Alexander Severus 18, 73
Alexandretta 32, 127
'Ali 25, 163
Allat 191
Alp Arslan 27
Alphabet 13
Amorites 13, 125
Amrit 15, 37, 113 infra, 115
Anastasius 163
Anatolia 4
Al-Andarin 106
Antioch 17, 116, 126
Antiochus IV 98
Anz 79
Apamea 44, 100, 102 infra, 103
Apollinarianism 22
Apollinarius 21
'Arab al-Mulk 118
Arab Revolt 32
Arabia 2, 6
Arabian cooking 198

Arabic 6
Arabs 5
Araimeh 112
Aram 53
Aramaeans 13, 14, 53
Aramaic 6, 14
Aretas III 72
Arianism 21
Arius 21
Armenians 8, 50
Army Museum 65
Arneh 68
Arpad 136
Arvad 15
Arwad 109, 110, 112 infra
Ashur 14
Ashurnasirpal II 14
Assassins 7, 27
Assyrians 6, 14, 15, 53, 178
Assyrians (old East Syrian Church) 7
Atabegs 27
'Atil 82
Aurelian 20, 183
Ayyubids 28, 55
Azem Palace (Damascus) 48, 59 infra
Azems 32
Azzaz 136

Baal 18
Ba'al-Shamin 81, 189
Bab al-Faradis 61
Bab al-Faraj 61
Bab al-Hawa 150
Bab Jabiya 63
Bab Kisan 61
Bab as-Saghir 62
Bab as-Salam 61
Bab Sharqi 200
Bab Sharqi 61
Bab Touma 60, 200
Babisqa 150
Babylon 175, 188
Babylonians 15, 53, 126
Baetocecea 115
Baghdad 6, 52, 25, 167
Bahira 74

Syria

Baldwin 28
Balfour Declaration 33
Balikh 4, 160, 168 infra
Bamouqqa 150, 151
Banaqfur 152
Bani Isra'il 118
Bani Qahtan 118
Baniyas 88, 115
Banqusa 150
Baptists 7
Baqirha 151
Al-Bara 153
Bel 184
Benabil 152
Bennawi 157
Beroea 126
Berzeh 67
Black Desert 69
Bohemond 100
Bohemond II 117
Bosra 40, 54, 72 infra, 78
Boudeh 154
Bouqras 9
Al-Braijjeh 150
Brekeh 85
British 3, 32, 33
Bronze Age 71, 184
Buddhism 22
Bur Deiruni 150
Buraq 85
Burj Baqirha 151
Burj al-Bazzaq 114
Burj Haidar 149
Burj Mudakhkar 150
Burj as-Sabi 116
Burqush 68
Busan 72, 82
Bustwar 117
Byzantines 20 infra, 23
  architecture 41 infra, 46, 142 infra
Byzantium 18

Cairo 6
Caliphate 27
Canaanites 13, 109, 119
Caracalla 18, 91
Caravan routes 2, 16, 52
Caravanserais 47, 64
Carchemish 14, 126, 161
Carrhae 17
Central Asia 14
Chagar Bazar 178
Chalcis 137
Chalcolithic 52, 71
Chaldeans 7
Chastel Blanc 113
Chastel Rouge 112
Chosroes I 164, 169
Chosroes I Anushirvan 23, 102, 127
Chosroes II 23, 164, 169
Christianity 2, 7, 16, 20 infra, 22
Circassians 8, 30
Colonnades 36
Constantine 18
Constantinople 20, 28

Copts 7
Crassus 17
Crusades 27 infra, 30
  architecture 48 infra
Cyrrhus 136 infra
Cyrus 15

Dagan 121, 177
Dallal house 135
Dalloza 153
Damascus 2, 4, 14, 52 infra, 66
Dana 145, 156
Darius III 15
Dawwar 152
Dead Cities 43, 71, 141 infra
Decapolis 54
Deir al-Khaf 79
Deir Sema'an 144
Deir Seta 152
Deir Sema'an 149
Deir Sobat 154
Dermemish 149
Diocletian 183
Diospolis 119
Diyarbakir 33
Diyatheh 72
Dmeir 68
Druze 7, 194
Dur Katlimu 178
Dura Europos 42, 65, 171 infra
Dushares 79

Early Bronze Age 11
Eating 198
Ebla 11, 137 infra
Eblaites 12, 138
Edessa 17, 127
Egypt 2
Egyptians 13
Elagabalus 18, 91
Emar 161
Emesa 17, 90
England 29, 127
English 32
Euphrates 4, 90, 159, 160, 166, 168 infra
Eusebius 21
Ezra'a 85

Fafertin 149
Fakhr ud-Din Ibn Ma'ani 194
Fasufian 149
Fatimids 27, 126
Feisal 32
Al-Firazdaq (Arslantash) 161
Al-Firdaus 134
First Crusade 27
First World War 32, 127
Al-Fisan 157
Food 198 infra
Fourth Crusade 28
France 29, 127
Franks 27
Frederick Barbarossa 29
French 3, 32
French Mandate 7, 65, 135

212

Galienus 19, 115
Gaziantep (see 'Aintab) 33
Geography 3, 5
Germany 29, 32
Ghab 4, 90
Ghassanids 6, 22, 73, 195
Golan 88 infra
Graeco-Roman 16, 20, 22, 37 infra, 41
Greek Orthodox 7
Gulf 17
Guy de Lusignan 29
Guzana 126

Habuba Kabira 11
Hadad 125
Hadatu 161
Haddad 56
Hadrian 54, 183
Halawiya 44, 133
Halbun 67
Halebiye 23, 45, 106, 168 infra
Hama 4, 97 infra, 99
Hamdanids 26, 126
Hamidiyyah 200
Hammam Nur ed-Din 64
Hammam et-Turkman 11
Hammams 47, 64
Hammurabi 175
Handicrafts 200 infra
Harbaqa 195
Harim 152
Harran 17
Harun al-Rashid 167
Hass 155
Hatay 33
Hauran 5, 69 infra, 87
Hawarin 93
Hayat 85
Hebariyeh 71
Hejaz Railway 32
Hejaz Railway Station 65
Hellenism 17, 25, 71, 184
Hellenized East 6
Heraclianus 19
Heraclius 23
Heraqla 168
Herod the Great 81, 119
Hisham 165
Hit 85
Hittin 29
Hittites 14, 90, 126
Holland 127
Homs 4, 90 infra, 91
Hosn as-Sulaiman 115 infra
Hospital of Nur ed-Din 64
Hospitallers 50, 95
Hotel Baron 135
Hulagu 127
Hurrians 14
Al-Huwar 157

Ibrahim ibn Adham 118
Imtan 78
Inat 78
India 2, 14, 24

Indo-Europeans 14
Iraq 4, 25
Iron Age 12
Ishtar 136, 176
Islam 3, 6, 7 infra, 22, 23 infra, 24
  architecture 46 infra, 48
Isma'ilis 7, 99, 104
Isriyeh 158

Janissaries 31
Jazira 4, 5, 159, 168, 177 infra
Jebel al-'Ala 149 infra
Jebel Arab 69
Jebel Aruda 162
Jebel Barisha 149 infra
Jebel Druze 69
Jebel Riha 152
Jebel Sais 88
Jebel Sema'an 144 infra, 149
Jebel esh-Shaikh 68
Jebel Shaikh Barakat 144 infra, 145, 149
Jebel Zawiyeh 152 infra
Jebleh 118
Jeradeh 156
Jerash 71
Jericho 10
Jerusalem 28, 51
Jews 8, 17
Jmarrin 72
John Cantacuzenus 116
John Chrysostom 21
John II Comnenus 100
John the Baptist 57, 133
Jordan 2, 6, 31
Jordan River 3, 88, 90
Joscelin 127
Jubb al-'Ali 157
Jubbul 136
Judas Maccabeus 17
Julia Domna 18
Jusiya al-Jadid 93
Jusiya al-Kharab 93
Justinian 23, 169, 183

Ka'ba 115
Kafr 82
Kafr Darian 151
Kafr Hut 157
Kafr Qal'a 152
Kafr Ruma 155
Kahf 117
Keep 49
Kfar Nabu 149
Khabur 4, 160, 177 infra
Khalid ibn al-Walid 91
Khan Asad Pasha 64
Khan al-Gumruk 64, 132
Khan al-Harir 64
Khan as-Sabun 132
Khan Sulaiman Pasha 64
Khan al-Wazir 131
Khana 170
Khanazir 157
Kharab Shams 149
Khawabi 112, 113

Syria

Khirbet al-Ambashi 88
Khirbet al-Baidha 88
Khirbet Hass 155
Khirbet Jama 82
Khirbet Shaikh 'Ali 150
Khirbet Tizin 150
Kimar 149
King's Highway 73
King-Crane Commission 33
Kitchens of Sultan Sulaiman 66
Kokanaya 152
Krak des Chevaliers 50, 93 infra, 97
Ksaijbeh 150
Kurds 7, 28, 60

Labweh 71
Lake Asad 162
Lake Qattina 93
Laodicea 119
Laqbeh 99
Latakia 119 infra
Late Bronze Age 12
Lawrence, T E 33, 135
Lebanon 2, 4, 15, 31
Leijja 85 infra, 87

Ma'alula 7, 66
Ma'arat an-Nu'man 155, 156
Al-Ma'bid 114
Al-Maghazil 114
Mahelbeh 123
Majdal ash-Shar 72, 79
Malah 78
Mamluks 29, 30 infra, 31
Mandate 198
Manichaeism 22
Maniqeh 118
Al-Mansur 167
Mar Sarkis 67
Mari 11, 170, 175 infra
Maristan Arghun 133
Marj as-Saffar 29
Maronites 7
Marqab 51, 108, 115 infra, 116
Mashquq 78
Mausoleum of Oghurlu 66
Maximianopolis 85
Me'ez 152
Mecca 6, 40, 54, 115
Medes 15
Mediterranean 2, 3
Meghara 153
Membij 160
Menin 67
Meskine 160, 161
Mesopotamia 2, 4, 11, 35
Middle Assyrian Empire 14
Middle Bronze Age 12
Minet al-Baidha 121
Mishrifeh 91
Mismiyeh 85
Misyaf 99 infra
Mitannians 14, 178
Mithraeum 173
Mithraism 18, 173

Mithras 18
Miyamas 82
Mo'allaq 157
Monasticism 21
Mongols 15, 29
Monophysitism 22
Mosul 126
Mt Hermon 4, 68
Mozaffari Mosque 66
Mu'awiya 163
Mudiq 99, 100 infra, 102
Muhammad 7, 73
Munqids 100
Muqaddamiyya 134
Mureybit 9, 162
Mushabbak 144
Mushannaf 82
Al-Mu'tasim 167
Mutawallis II 14
Mycenaeans 36, 121

Nabateans 6, 17, 54
Nabi Khouri 136
Nabu 188
Namara 87, 88
Naram Sin 125
National Museum 65
Natufian period 10
Neo-Hittites 14, 97
Neolithic 10, 52, 120, 181
Nestorians 7, 21, 22
Nestorius 21
New Assyrian Empire 14
Nicephorus Phocas 110
Nimrud Castle 88
Nineveh 15
Nisibis 21
Normans 27
Nur ed-Din 110
Nurids 49, 55
Nuriya Madrasa 63
Nusairis 3, 7

Odaynath 19
Old Assyrian Empire 14, 178
Old Man of the Mountain 117
Old Testament 53
Orontes 3, 4, 18, 90
Ottomans 26, 30 infra, 33

Palace 48
Palaeolithic 181
Paleologi 126
Palestine 2, 13, 21, 31
Palmyra 6, 18 infra, 19, 20, 22, 41, 65, 180
  infra
Paltos 118
Parthians 17, 112, 171
Peoples of the Sea 120
Persia 2, 15
Persians 17, 53, 167, 126
Petra 17, 40, 181
Philip the Arab 16
Philip Augustus 29

Philippopolis 82
Phoenicians 12, 15
Pompey 17, 102
Posidium 123

Qadesh 11, 14, 90
Qadmus 117
Qal'at al-Hosn 93
Qal'at al-Jabar 163
Qal'at an-Najm 160
Qal'at Qalota 149
Qal'at ar-Rus 118
Qal'at Salahuddin (Sahyun) 45, 108, 123 infra
Qal'at Sema'an 144
Qal'at ash-Sham 104
Qal'at as-Subaibeh 88
Qalawun 100, 113, 129
Qalb Lozeh 151
Qanawat 40, 79 infra, 82
Qasr al-Antar 106
Qasr al-Banat 150, 156, 167
Qasr al-Hair al-Gharbi 65, 195 infra
Qasr al-Hair ash-Sharqi 194 infra
Qasr Iblisu 150
Qasr Ibn Wardan 23, 104 infra, 106
Qasr Nimrud 67
Qasyun Hill 55
Qatna 11, 37, 90
Qatura 144
Qaymari Hospital 66
Qinnesrin 137
Qirq Bizah 151
Qunaitra 88
Qusaibeh 117

Rabbel II 77
Rabi'a 155
Rakhleh 68
Ramad 52
Rameses II 14, 92
Ramitha 119
Raqqa 166 infra
Ra's Shamra (Ugarit) 10, 120
Ra's al-Basit 123
Ra's Ibn Hani 119
Raymond de St Gilles 110, 118
Raymond II 95
Refadah 144
Reginald of Chatillon 28, 127
Resafeh 44, 45, 157, 163 infra
Richard the Lionheart 29
Ridwan 27
Rift valley 4
Rijm al-'Is 71
Roger of Antioch 116
Romans 16, 17, 171
  architecture 38 infra, 41, 142 infra
Rome 15
Routes 48
Ruwaiha 156

Sabaean 114
Safa 87 infra, 88
Safaitic 87

Safita 49, 95, 112
Sahr 85
Sahyun, see Qal'at Salahuddin
Saif ad-Daula 26, 126
St Ananias 61
St George 85
St Paul 54
St Sergius 163
St Simeon Stylites 44, 143, 145 infra
Saladin 27, 28, 59 infra, 60
Salamiya 104
Saleh 82
Salihiye 52, 66 infra, 171
Salkhad 78
Sanamain 86
Sarfud 151
Sargon of Akkad 12, 15, 98
Sarmada 150
Sasanians 19, 23, 167, 171
Sayegh house 135
Second World War 33
Seia 81
Seidnaya 67
Seleucids 17, 53, 126, 171
Seleucus I Nicator 17, 102, 119
Selim I 31
Seljuks 26, 55
Semites 6, 12
Semitic 22
Septimus Severus 18, 54
Sergiopolis 163
Serj Farej 157
Serjibla 150
Serjilla 154
Sfireh 157
Shahba 18, 40, 82 infra, 84
Shaikh Sulaiman 149
Shaizar 99, 100 infra
Shalmaneser I 14
Shalmaneser III 14
Shamshi-Adad 175, 178
Shaqqa 85
Shi'ism 7, 25, 27
Shinsharah 155
Shubat Enlil 37, 178
Si' 81
Siffin 163
Silk 98, 181, 200
Silk Road 1
Sitt ar-Rum 144
Slim 82
Soghanak 149
South Arabian 37, 114
Street Called Straight 62
Suleimaniye 65
Sultaniyya 134
Sumerian 11
Sunni 7
Sur 85
Suwaida 69
Suwailim 82
Suwara 85
Suyan 157
Sykes-Picot Agreement 33
Synagogue 173

Syrian Catholics (mistakenly known as the Melkites) 7
Syrian Desert 4
Syrian Orthodox (old West Syrian Church, known as Monophysites or Jacobites) 7

Tabqa Dam 159
Tadmor 181
Tafha 85
Tamerlane 30, 127
Tancred 93, 118
Taqleh 149
Tartus 51, 109 infra, 112
Tatmarash 136
Telanissos 149
Tell 'Adeh 145
Tell Ahmar 161
Tell Aqibrin 150
Tell Brak 11, 178
Tell Debbeh 71
Tell Fakhariya 178
Tell Halaf 10, 126, 179
Tell Hammam et-Turkman 168
Tell Hariri 175
Tell Jubeh 71
Tell Khuera 168
Tell Leilan 11, 37, 177, 178
Tell Mardikh 11, 137
Tell Nebi Mend 92
Tell Qannas 162
Tell Qsubi 170
Tell Rifa'at 136
Tell Shaikh Hamad 178
Tell Zheir 71
Templars 110
Terqa 170
Third Crusade 29
Tiglath-Pileser III 14, 136
Til Barsip 126, 161
Timurids 26
Tinib 136
Tombs 48
Tortosa 51, 95, 109
Tower tombs 192
Trade 21, 22
Trade routes 2, 17, 19, 38, 52
Trajan 72, 181
Transjordan 33
Tripoli 31, 112
Tukulti-Ninurta I 14
Turkey 2
Turks 26, 30, 33
Turmanin 144
Tutah 134
Tuthmosis I 13

Ugarit 9, 11, 119, 120 infra, 123
'Umar ibn al-Khattab 78
Umayyad Mosque, Damascus 55 infra, 59
Umayyads 24, 25
Umm 'Amud 157
Umm Debab 85
Umm al-Jemal 72
Umm al-Qutain 79

Umm al-Rumman 79
United States 33
Urfa 17, 33
Uruk 11, 162
Urum al-Joz 153
Al-Utrush 134

Valerian 115
Venice 127
Via Trajana 73

Wadi Sham 87
Wahab-Allath 19
Al-Walid 57
Washshukanni 178
Wildlife 5
Writing 2

Yabrud 67
Yahmur 108, 112
Yamhad (Aleppo) 13, 125
Yarmouk 23
Yazid 93
Yemen 72

Zabed 157
Zahiriya Madrasa 64
Zalaf 87
Zalebiye 170
Zeno 147
Zenobia 19
Ziggurats 37, 177
Zimri-Lim 175
Zor'a 85
Zoroastrianism 22